Mr. Justice

John Marshall	WILLIAM WINSLOW CROSSKEY
Roger B. Taney	CARL BRENT SWISHER
Joseph P. Bradley	CHARLES FAIRMAN
John Marshall Harlan	ALAN F. WESTIN
Oliver Wendell Holmes	FRANCIS BIDDLE
Charles Evans Hughes	MERLO J. PUSEY
Louis D. Brandeis	PAUL A. FREUND
George Sutherland	J. FRANCIS PASCHAL
Harlan F. Stone	ALLISON DUNHAM
Benjamin N. Cardozo	ANDREW KAUFMAN
Frank Murphy	JOHN P. ROCHE
Wiley Rutledge	JOHN PAUL STEVENS

Mr. Justice

Edited by

ALLISON DUNHAM & PHILIP B. KURLAND
Revised and Enlarged

Phoenix Books

THE UNIVERSITY OF CHICAGO PRESS
CHICAGO AND LONDON

This book is also available in a clothbound edition from
THE UNIVERSITY OF CHICAGO PRESS

Library of Congress Catalog Card Number: 64-15821

THE UNIVERSITY OF CHICAGO PRESS, CHICAGO & LONDON
The University of Toronto Press, Toronto 5, Canada

© *1956, 1964 by The University of Chicago. Published 1956*
Revised and Enlarged Edition 1964
First Phoenix Edition 1964
Second Impression 1965
Printed in the United States of America

To Nan and Mary Jane

Preface

The first edition of this volume of biographical essays started, as many books on public law are wont to do, with a quotation from Felix Frankfurter. In 1937, he asserted that

American legal history has done very little to rescue the Court from the limbo of impersonality. . . . Until we have penetrating studies of the influence of [the Justices who had a major share in shaping the doctrine of American constitutional law], we shall not have an adequate history of the Supreme Court, and, therefore, of the United States.

This is not an affirmation of the Emerson dictum that "there is properly no history; only biography." But it does proffer sufficient expert testimony to the need to delineate the individual contributions of the Justices if we are to attempt fully to understand the Supreme Court, an institution that has come to play a greater and greater role in the government of the United States. The history of the Supreme Court can be written without the biographical studies of which the Justice spoke. Indeed, it is being written by a group of most eminent legal scholars under the leadership of Professor Paul A. Freund. True, they have more biographical studies than were available at the time that Frankfurter made his complaint. The contributors to this volume have, in large measure, been responsible for the improvement that has come about. They have authored ten of the "penetrating studies" that the Justice demanded. And it is not without interest that four of the contributors to this volume are also engaged in the preparation of volumes of the history sponsored by the Holmes bequest committee. But the deficit remains. Much by way of Supreme Court biography has yet to be done.

vii

We are not so bold as to suggest that the papers included here will fill the gap. Our objectives are less ambitious. We would, with the republication of this volume, seek to accomplish two things. First, we believe that the authors of these essays have been able, in the words of Professor Alexander Bickel, to afford "insight into the man, and through him insight into the process he engaged in—that intriguing and . . . singular American phenomenon, the practice of statecraft on the bench." Second, we hope that these essays will be able to reach an audience not yet ready or willing to undertake the study of the multi-volumed history of the Court or the many volumes of very able biography that we have sought to epitomize here. The Court, now more than ever, is in need of being understood by those outside the professions concerned directly with a study of its work. We like to continue to think that this volume will make a contribution, however small, toward that understanding.

Philip B. Kurland
Allison Dunham

Contents

List of Illustrations

Mr. Justice

Courtesy of Harris & Ewing

MR. CHIEF JUSTICE MARSHALL

Mr. Chief Justice Marshall

WILLIAM WINSLOW CROSSKEY

John Marshall was born on September 24, 1755, in what is now Fauquier County, Virginia. He died in Philadelphia, while holding the office of Chief Justice of the United States, a few weeks less than eighty years later. Thus when Americans in 1955 marked the two-hundredth anniversary of his birth, one hundred and twenty years had elapsed since he completed the judicial labors for which he is so greatly celebrated. Three other Americans preceded Marshall in the office that he held, and ten have succeeded him in that long interval since his death. Some very distinguished and able men have been Chief Justices; but, by universal consent, Marshall is recognized to stand pre-eminent—indeed, unrivaled—among them. The appelation, "the great Chief Justice," is still, as it long has been, a completely unambiguous reference to John Marshall.

I mean not to dissent from this universal view of Marshall's greatness; yet I do think that the true nature of his judicial career, particularly as it related to constitutional interpretation, has long been generally misunderstood. According to the usual view, Marshall is conceived to have dominated his associates on the Supreme Court so completely that he was able to make the constitutional decisions of that tribunal express his own ideas and nothing else. His ideas, it is further commonly assumed, were those of his political party, the Federalists. Consequently, the common view is that John Marshall was able to use, and did use, his domination of the Court to read the old

3

Federalist constitutional views into the Court's decisions and thus to lay the foundations upon which our constitutional law ever since has rested, or—as some might wish to insist—the foundations upon which it rested until the notorious "Roosevelt Court fight" of a generation ago.

For the general prevalence of this view of John Marshall's work in constitutional law, his biographer, Albert J. Beveridge, is undoubtedly in considerable measure responsible.[1] But such a view of Marshall's work antedated Beveridge's biography. Justice Holmes, for one, took such a view of the subject fifteen years before the first of Beveridge's volumes appeared. The occasion was the centennial, in 1901, of Marshall's inauguration as Chief Justice of the Supreme Court of the United States, and Holmes, as Chief Justice of Massachusetts, was answering a motion that the Supreme Judicial Court of that state adjourn in commemoration of the event. Holmes was not so gracious on this occasion as he usually was. He felt honest doubt about Marshall's greatness and rather inappropriately expressed it. He doubted, he said, "whether, after [Alexander] Hamilton and the Constitution itself, Marshall's work proved more than a strong intellect, a good style, personal ascendancy in his court, courage, justice and the convictions of his party." Holmes conceded, however, that it had been a "fortunate" thing that the appointment of a Chief Justice in 1801 had fallen to John Adams rather than to Thomas Jefferson, "and so g[i]ve[n] it," as he explained, "to a Federalist and loose constructionist to start the working of the Constitution. . . . "[2] These remarks of Holmes plainly evince the same view of Marshall's work that I have already mentioned as the view commonly taken: Marshall dominated the Court; he used his dominance to read Federalist party doctrines into the Constitution; and thus the basis of our constitutional law was laid. Along with these ideas, we have in the case of Holmes the further notion, which is also a common one, that the old Federalist constitutional views were based upon a "loose" construction of the Constitution.

Let me begin with this last idea. Is it true that the old Federalist constitutional views depended upon a loose construction of the Constitution? It most certainly is not. The Federalist views depended, first of all, upon a strict adherence to certain rules of documentary interpretation that were then quite generally accepted as proper. They depended, further, upon giving meaning to every single provision that the Constitution contained and, also, upon giving significance to every difference in phraseology to be found in its various provisions. The Federalist views depended, in other words, upon a literal reading of the Constitution in all its parts; and in the few cases, if there were any such, where the Federalists thought that more than one meaning was possible, the ambiguity was to be resolved, they believed, by a strict adherence to the then accepted rule of choosing the meaning that best comported with the objects, or purposes, of the Constitution as stated in the Preamble. In any ordinary use of words, the Federalist views depended, then, upon a rigorous, not a loose, construction of the document.[3]

The views of the Federalists' opponents, the Jeffersonians, were the views that really depended upon a loose construction. The Jeffersonian views called for disregarding certain parts of the Constitution completely. These parts—the parts that then were known as "the general phrases" of the document—were to be made absolutely meaningless. Other parts were to be twisted from their original meaning in a manner unfavorable to the national powers, and limitations undeniably not contained in the document were to be read into it.[4]

If these are the facts about the Federalist and Jeffersonian views of the Constitution, how has the notion come to be accepted, in what is known as history, that the old Federalist views depended upon a loose construction of the document?

In part, this is a result of the paucity and imperfection of the records of the Federalist period. The Senate of the United States during its first five years sat behind closed doors; no record of its debates for this period exists. In addition, there was no official reporting of the debates in either house of Congress during the early years. There was, it is true, some private reporting, part of which was afterward republished in, and as, *The Annals of Congress,* in the 1830's; but these private reports from the formative period of American government are both imperfect and incomplete.[5]

As for the courts of justice of the period—particularly the Supreme Court—the cases before them did not bring up constitutional issues that went to the essence of the old Federalist views of the subject; and this remained true, in the main, during the first six or seven years of John Marshall's Chief Justiceship, when there was still a Federalist majority on the Court. The result of all these factors, taken together, was an imperfect and meager recording of the Federalist views; they became forgotten. And because the Jeffersonians, with their usual perversity, accused the Federalists of advocating a loose construction—the offense of which they themselves were guilty —and because, furthermore, the Jeffersonians won out politically, their charge has stuck by reason of simple ignorance today as to what the old Federalist views were.

The situation I have just described has manifestly been favorable, likewise, to the rise of the misconception of John Marshall's work to which I have already alluded. But in the case of Marshall, there have been other factors at work, too. For one thing, Marshall persuaded the Court to follow the practice of delivering court opinions, instead of individual opinions, in the cases decided; and in most of the cases, Marshall wrote and delivered the Court's opinions himself, especially in those involving constitutional issues. Consequently, it is usually assumed today that everything in these opinions represents Marshall's own views and hence Federalist views.

Yet, if we remember that nearly all of Marshall's constitutional opinions were delivered for a Court with a hand-picked Jeffersonian majority upon it, it is certainly undeniable that such a view of the Marshall opinions is one inherently improbable.

Such a view of the matter is, moreover, at variance with what Marshall himself described as the practice of his Court. Its practice, he indicated in 1819, was what the "course of every tribunal must necessarily be." ". . . the opinion which is to be delivered as the opinion of the court is," he said, "previously submitted to the consideration of all the judges; and if any part of the reasoning be disapproved, it must be so modified as to receive the approbation of all, before it can be delivered as the opinion of all."[6] I do not myself see how the facts could possibly have been otherwise than as Marshall stated them; or how it can be supposed, for a moment, that he did not, in many instances, have to compromise, or give up, his own and the Federalist views of the Constitution.

There are still other factors that have contributed to the misconception of Marshall's work. One was his settled practice of not dissenting when he disagreed with the views of the Court. We have his own word for this. In *Bank of United States* v. *Dandridge,* in 1827, he said it had long been his "custom when [he] ha[d] the misfortune to differ from th[e] Court, [to] acquiesce silently in its opinion."[7] Justice Joseph Story, who usually agreed with Marshall's constitutional views, followed the same practice.[8] And the associate of both, Justice William Johnson, said, in 1822, "in some" instances, Marshall actually wrote and delivered the Court's opinion even "when [it was] contrary to his own Judgement and Vote." The Associate Justices were lazy, Johnson said; Marshall was willing to perform the labor of writing the opinions, and the Associates were content to let him do it.[9]

Now, surely, in the light of this last-mentioned practice, it is perilous in the extreme to ascribe to John Marshall and hence to the old Federalists, who produced the Constitution, everything that his opinions contain. One is likewise unwarranted in making such ascriptions merely on the basis of Marshall's silent acquiescence in various of the views of his Court. Why Marshall followed the practices I have just outlined, he never explained. But the fact is that the period of his Chief Justiceship was a period of constitutional decay. Time after time, Marshall was forced into compromise or outright defeat upon what can easily be shown were his own views or else the old Federalist views of the Constitution, which, it is natural to suppose, he shared. It probably seemed to Marshall thoroughly unwise to underline such facts as these before the country and thus perhaps to encourage further attacks upon the Constitution, to the defense of which his life after 1801 was so largely devoted.

I have said that the period of John Marshall's Chief Justiceship was a period of constitutional decay. This was especially true, as respects the Supreme Court during the twenty-three year period after 1812, when most of the famous Marshall constitutional decisions were rendered; for in 1812 the Jeffersonians at last obtained a dependable majority on the Court.[10] With the single exception of Joseph Story,[11] all the Justices appointed up to that time during Marshall's tenure, and nearly all of those appointed thereafter during his years on the Court, were hand-picked to vote against him on his own and the old Federalist views of the Constitution. To suppose, then, as is ordinarily done, that Marshall was able to get these men to agree with his own and the Federalist views in case after case is certainly to suppose the improbable; and it is easy to demonstrate, by a consideration of particular cases, that Marshall had no such astounding success with the Court.

It is pertinent to begin with the old Federalist doctrine that the Common Law of England and the acts of Parliament in amendment of the Common Law, to the extent that these were in their nature applicable to American conditions, were "Laws of the United States" as well as laws of the separate states of the country. This doctrine is so discredited today that I have actually been accused by various modern legal scholars of being myself guilty of a lack of scholarship in believing that anybody ever believed such a thing. But the shoe is on the other foot. There is not a doubt that this was once a commonly held view.[12]

One may ask what was the constitutional and political importance of this old forgotten proposition. For one thing, it was important in interpreting one of the mandatory categories of the national judicial power in the third article of the Constitution, the category, that is, of "all Cases, in Law and Equity, arising under . . . the Laws of the United States." For if the Common Law was one of "the Laws of the United States," the national judicial power would extend, it was thought, by virtue of this provision, to every case presenting any Common Law question as a question of national law.[13] Because, however, of the fact that the original Judiciary Act of 1789 had conferred upon the lower national courts, within this category, a criminal jurisdiction only, the question of the status of the Common Law as one of "the Laws of the United States" arose, in the early days of the government, chiefly in criminal cases.[14]

Concretely, what was at stake in these cases? Take one of them that arose in 1798. One Worrall had tried to bribe an official of the national government. Congress had never passed a statute forbidding such conduct or making it a crime. The question was: Could Worrall be punished?[15] Again, there were various places in the United States—such as the sites of "Forts, Magazines, Arsenals, dock-Yards, and other needful Buildings" —that were under the exclusive jurisdiction of the United States by the terms of the Constitution. Congress had never passed a statute forbidding, and making criminal in these places, such acts as murder, robbery, rape, and the like. The question, then, was whether these and other unforbidden offenses could be committed in such places with impunity.[16] The Federalists' answer was a sensible and resounding "No." It was sufficient, they held, that these various acts were crimes at Common Law; for the Common Law, they held, was one of "the Laws of the United States."[17] The Jeffersonians denied this and contended that the foregoing and other offenses could be committed without penalty, as against the United States, in the absence of Acts of Congress of the kind I have already described.[18]

Why did the Jeffersonians take this seemingly foolish position? To understand their reasons, it is necessary to take into consideration another belief of the late eighteenth century, of which little is heard today. This was the belief, which the Jeffersonians apparently shared with the Federalists, that the legislature of every government, including Congress, had power to make rules of decision for its own courts of justice in all cases that its courts had power to decide. If the Common Law was one of "the Laws of the United States," and if, by consequence, the judicial power of the United States extended to all cases under the Common Law as national law, then because the Common Law itself extended to all subjects, the rule-making power would belong to Congress, would extend to all subjects, too. In other words, Congress would have, on this ground entirely separate from all others, the practical equivalent of a general national legislative authority. Now, Jeffersonianism was a political revolt, chiefly Southern in inspiration, against the sort of generally empowered national government for which the Constitution was intended to provide. The proposition that led to the consequence I have just stated had therefore to be denied; and it was denied; and its denial became one of the cardinal tenets of Jeffersonianism.[19]

A case involving the Common Law criminal jurisdiction of the national courts was presented to the Supreme Court for decision shortly after the initial appearance of a Jeffersonian majority on that tribunal in 1812. This was the case of *United States* v. *Hudson and Goodwin*,[20] which the Jeffersonians had nursed along for six long years, until they finally obtained their majority on the Court.[21] Upon at last getting the case before the Court, the Attorney-General, however, refused to argue it on behalf of the United States: it was simply too absurd for words. Therefore, the Jeffersonian majority stepped forward and did what they were supposed to do: they ruled against the Common Law criminal jurisdiction of the national courts and, hence, against the view that the Common Law was one of "the Laws of the United States."

From all that appears in the report of this case by William Cranch, the decision of the Court was unanimous. But, in actual fact, it was not unanimous. For this, we have the word of Joseph Story, one of the participating Justices. The determination had been made, Story said, by a bare majority of the Court of seven. This statement he made in a case on circuit in Massachusetts in the year immediately following.[22] He also said, at another time, that he had it on the "highest authority" —by which he apparently meant Chief Justice Marshall—that in 1804 when the first Jeffersonian had been appointed to the Court, all the Justices previously on the Court were committed to the support of the Common Law jurisdiction, except Samuel Chase,[23] who was not, I may add, a Federalist, as is usually supposed, but an anti-Federalist who happened not to like Thomas Jefferson. Justice Story's own opposition to the Court's determination of the Common Law point in 1812 appears from his circuit court opinion of 1813, and there were two of the Justices of the Supreme Court of 1812 who had been on the Court in 1804. These were John Marshall and Bushrod Washington. Thus these two, with Joseph Story, made up the minority of three in the case of 1812. In this initial instance, then, Jeffersonianism was triumphant; the ideas of John Marshall, and of the Federalist party from which he came, were completely repudiated.[24]

It is desirable to consider another of the old Federalist doctrines: the doctrine that, over and above and beyond its spe-

cifically enumerated powers, Congress possessed a general
lawmaking authority for all the objects of the government that
the Preamble of the Constitution states. Authority in the government, as distinct from its different departments and officers, was deemed by the Federalists to result from this plain
statement of the government's purposes, or objects. The detail
in the document related, in the main, to the division of this
resulting governmental power between the different departments and officers. And the Federalists pointed out that the
last of Congress' enumerated powers in the Legislative Article
is not only a power "to make all Laws" which shall be "necessary and proper" to carry into execution Congress' own specifically enumerated powers but a power, likewise, "to make all
Laws" which shall be "necessary and proper" to carry into
execution "all other Powers vested by the Constitution in the
Government of the United States" or in any of its departments
or officers. Mere inspection of the Constitution discloses that
there are, in the document, no enumerated powers *of the government,* as distinct from the enumerated powers of its different departments and officers. The "other Powers of the Government" branch of this final power of Congress is therefore
meaningless, unless it is a reference to "Powers of the Government" that are not enumerated, such as those that resulted,
under eighteenth-century views, from the preambular statement of the government's general objects. This, the Federalists
maintained, was what the clause had been intended to mean;
and they also maintained—or, at any rate, some of them did—
that the Common Defence and General Welfare Clause earlier
in the same section had been intended as a separate and substantive grant of power to Congress to act for these two great
purposes.[25]

When the first Bank of the United States under the Constitution was formed in 1791, the doctrines supportive of the general national lawmaking authority of Congress were apparently the main reliance within Congress itself in support of the

constitutionality of the proposed bank. Edmund Randolph, as Attorney-General, in one of the opinions he gave to President Washington, spoke of these views as "the doctrines of the friends of the bill."[26] In these circumstances it is not surprising that the same doctrines were presented to the Supreme Court, in support of the second bank under the Constitution when in 1819 the bank's constitutionality was questioned in the case of *McCulloch* v. *Maryland*.[27] The doctrines were presented by one of the great advocates of the time, William Pinkney, of Maryland. After hearing Pinkney's argument, Justice Joseph Story declared that "all the cobwebs of sophistry and metaphysics about State rights and State sovereignty [had been] brushed away [by Pinkney] with" what Story described as "a mighty besom." "Never [in] my whole life," said Story, have I "heard a greater speech; it was worth a journey from Salem [to Washington] to hear it."[28]

What did Pinkney say? It is not known exactly, but it is known that he spoke for three days.[29] Thus what we have in Wheaton's Reports is only a meager outline. The part relating to the old Federalist doctrine of general power begins by pointing out that "all the objects of the government are national objects" and by insisting that "the means [for accomplishing these objects] are, and must be, [such as are] fitted to accomplish them." "The objects," said Pinkney, "are enumerated in the constitution," whereupon he read the Preamble. "For the attainment of these vast objects," he then went on, "the government is armed with powers and faculties corresponding in magnitude." He next ran over the various congressional powers enumerated in the Legislative Article, presenting the Common Defence and General Welfare Clause as a separate substantive grant; the commerce power, apparently, as comprehensive; and the "necessary and proper" clause with emphasis upon the fact that it extended to "all the powers of the Government." Then he concluded by castigating those who "doubted [that] a government invested with such immense powers ha[d] authority to erect a corporation within the sphere of its general objects, and in order to accomplish some of those objects!"[30] As may be perceived, the reliance in this part of Pinkney's argument was primarily upon the objects stated in the Preamble.

What did Chief Justice Marshall have to say about these old Federalist ideas in the Court's opinion? He said nothing about them; he ignored them completely, though there are one or two passages which suggest that he may originally have noticed them favorably before the opinion was seen by his judicial brethren.[31] Instead of noticing the old Federalist ideas that Pinkney had urged, Marshall declared, early in the opinion, "this government is acknowledged by all, to be one of enumerated powers." "The principle, that it can exercise only the powers granted to it, would seem too apparent," he said, "to have required to be enforced by all those arguments which its enlightened friends, while it was depending before the people, [had] found it necessary to urge." "[T]hat principle," he flatly declared, "is now universally admitted."[32] At least as the principle is understood today, William Pinkney did not admit it, and there were a good many other men who did not admit it at the time when Marshall wrote.[33] Yet all the Chief Justice could do for the old ideas Pinkney had urged was to add, in the opinion, that "the question respecting the extent of the powers actually granted" was, of course, "perpetually arising, and w[ould] probably continue to arise, as long as our system sh[ould] exist."[34] This, perhaps, could be taken as saving the question of the true interpretation of the Common Defence and General Welfare Clause and, also, of the "Powers of Government" branch of the "necessary and proper" clause, because each of these is, after all, among the enumerated, that is, the "actually granted," powers of Congress.

I have said that in 1791 the doctrine of general authority for all the purposes that the Preamble states was the main reliance, in Congress itself, in support of the constitutionality of the first Bank of the United States. This doctrine was not, however, the sole reliance of the friends of the bank bill in Congress. In addition, they relied upon the enumerated fiscal powers, especially in the light of the "necessary and proper" clause, as being themselves sufficient to warrant the proposed enactment. And there was reliance also upon Congress' power to regulate commerce as likewise sufficient in itself to warrant the intended act of incorporation.[35] In the opinion that Alexander Hamilton gave to President Washington a little later, the commerce power and the fiscal powers were also relied upon to support the act. Unlike the men in Congress, Hamilton did not discuss the general authority of the government.[36]

It has often been said that John Marshall's opinion in *McCulloch* v. *Maryland* is little more than a repetition of the opinion that Hamilton gave to President Washington in 1791. There are undoubtedly resemblances between these two opinions, as, indeed, there could hardly fail to be. But there are differences also; and the differences indicate, I think, that John Marshall, in 1819, was already having trouble getting some of his brethren to agree to another of the old Federalist views of the Constitution, the view that the commerce power of Congress is comprehensive.[37]

The mere fact that there was reliance upon the commerce power by Hamilton and by the men in Congress in support of the constitutionality of the bank is, in itself, a sure indication of how these old Federalists understood this particular congressional power. For to be relevant to the subject and ground the conclusion that these men drew, the power had to be understood as complete. Had it instead been taken as subject to an interstate limitation, the conclusion they drew would not have followed; for the bank, it must be remembered, was being incorporated to carry on its business, not only in foreign and interstate commerce, but in intrastate commerce as well.[38]

Examination of Hamilton's opinion will show that he developed his argument based on the commerce power, and relied upon it as sufficient to support his conclusion, quite as much as he did his argument based on Congress' fiscal powers. Chief Justice Marshall followed Hamilton, in *McCulloch* v. *Maryland* to the extent of citing Congress' "power to regulate commerce" as among the powers that were relevant to the case;[39] but the Chief Justice went no further. In the actual discussion in the opinion, the reliance is wholly upon Congress' fiscal powers; and today, after more than a century's acceptance of the interstate theory of the commerce power, the very fact that Marshall cited this power as relevant in *McCulloch* v. *Maryland* is generally forgotten. The accepted doctrine is that Congress' power to incorporate national banks depends upon its fiscal powers alone.

To have grounded the conclusion in *McCulloch* v. *Maryland*, not only upon the fiscal powers of Congress, but, alternatively, upon its commerce power, would have been to make the case a far, far broader precedent in favor of congressional power than the case, as it was decided, actually was. For to have put the case upon this alternative ground would have been to recognize that Congress' power to regulate commerce was complete: that Congress could regulate all domestic as well as all foreign commerce. The situation in the *McCulloch* case was this: the Bank of the United States there involved was not the old Federalist bank incorporated in 1791; it was a newer bank created by a Jeffersonian Congress and approved by the second Jeffersonian President, James Madison, in 1816. The men of the Jeffersonian majority on Marshall's Court were apparently willing to uphold this act of their own party, but, equally apparently, they wished to do this on the narrowest possible ground. Thus the decision was put on the fiscal powers only, and the relevance of the commerce power was not developed in the case. Again, a doctrine that the old Federalists had considered relevant to Congress' incorporating a bank was excluded from the *McCulloch* case rather than read into this famous Marshall opinion.

The Chief Justice's citation of the commerce power suggests, nevertheless, that its relevancy may have been developed and relied upon in some earlier version of the opinion. Whether this actually happened or not, the citation certainly seems to indicate that Marshall himself, like Hamilton and other Federalists in 1791, considered the commerce power to be relevant; and, for reasons I have already assigned, this means that he must have regarded it as a complete power over the subject: a power to regulate all domestic as well as all foreign commerce. This surmise is borne out by what Marshall had to say two years later about this power, in *Cohens* v. *Virginia.* It was in the famous passage that begins: "[T]he United States form for many, and for most important purposes, a single nation." "In war," Marshall continued, "we are one people. In making peace, we are one people." Finally, he declared, "In all commercial regulations, we are one and the same people." "[F]or all these purposes, [America's] government," he said, "is complete; to all these objects, it is competent."[40]

I do not see how it is possible to read these statements from the *Cohens* case as other than a plain recognition by Chief Justice Marshall that the power of Congress to regulate commerce was a complete power—that it extended to all domestic as well as all foreign commerce. The language Marshall used is totally irreconcilable with the view that he thought the power one to regulate foreign and interstate commerce only. How Marshall was able to get these statements approved by his judicial brethren in the *Cohens* case, I do not know; but the statements are there, and their meaning seems plain. Thus we may take it that John Marshall, in 1821, took the same view of the national commerce power that Alexander Hamilton and other Federalists had taken in the early 1790's.

This view, I might add, was also the view taken by the majority of the men in Congress in the 1820's.[41] It seems, however, not to have been the view of the Jeffersonian majority on Marshall's Court. For when the famous New York steamboat monopoly case of *Gibbons* v. *Ogden*[42] was decided in 1824, Marshall receded from the position he had taken three years earlier in *Cohens* v. *Virginia*. In the *Gibbons* case, Marshall no longer maintained that the United States formed a single nation as to "all commercial regulations." Instead, though referring to the language of the Constitution as "comprehensive," he declared that the power it gave might "very properly be restricted to that commerce which concerns more States than one." Again, Marshall failed to read into one of the Court's decisions what it is clear was his own and an old Federalist view of the Constitution.

But although that fact is certain, it is a mistake to suppose, as is frequently done, that in the Gibbons case Marshall interpreted the commerce power in the meager dimensions in which that power existed during the major part of subsequent American history. In other words, it is a mistake to suppose that Marshall in the *Gibbons* case interpreted Congress' internal power over commerce as a power to regulate interstate commerce only. The Chief Justice said that the power was being restricted to "that commerce which concerns more States than one"; and his opinion makes abundantly clear what he meant by these words. He meant by them all commerce of a domestic kind that was of interest, or importance, to more than a single state; and he meant this whether the particular commerce was interstate or not. Marshall said, moreover, that with respect to all such commerce, Congress' power was "plenary"—"as absolut[e]," he declared, "as [a commerce power] would be in a single government." And whenever Congress acted under this great power, any conflicting state law must yield whether the law in question was one for the regulation of a state's own purely domestic commerce or one for the regulation of its system of internal police.[43]

That *Gibbons* v. *Ogden* was not contemporaneously understood as adopting the interstate theory of the commerce power is shown, moreover, by what happened in the following year, in the state of New York. The interstate theory was not then entirely unknown. It had been devised, somewhat earlier, by lawyers for the New York steamboat monopoly and had been applied by the highest court of the state, in 1812, to uphold the monopoly as between citizens of the state, in respect to traffic between the New York cities of New York and Albany. This was in the case of *Livingston* v. *Van Ingen*,[44] a case which, because the defendants were bought off by the successful plaintiffs, was not appealed to the Supreme Court of the United States. *Gibbons* v. *Ogden,* though not adopting the interstate theory, had actually involved steamboat movements between New York and New Jersey. The decision, then, left technically open the question whether the New York monopoly law was still good with respect to movements such as had been involved in the *Van Ingen* case, that is, with respect to movements wholly within the state. A case was accordingly begun in the New York courts, a few weeks after the *Gibbons* decision, to settle this question. Under the title of *North River Steamboat Company* v. *Livingston*,[45] the case was carried to the highest court of the state in 1825. The New York court thereupon overruled the interstate doctrine of its earlier decision and, on the authority of the *Gibbons* case, brought the New York steamboat monopoly completely to an end, both in intra-state and interstate commerce.

It is needless to say that the New York court would never have taken such action had it understood the Supreme Court's decision of the preceding year as one adopting the interstate theory of the commerce power.[46] But if the interstate theory did not originate in *Gibbons* v. *Ogden*, it may be asked how, and when, the theory did originate. The answer is that the theory was read into John Marshall's decision in the *Gibbons* case by his Jacksonian successor, Roger Brooke Taney. Marshall's doctrine of plenary national supremacy, which he had announced so clearly in the *Gibbons* case, was overturned within two years of his death by the Jacksonian Court. This occurred in *New York* v. *Miln*,[47] in 1837, when it was indicated by the Court that the whole field of internal police was free of the national supremacy. Ten years later Chief Justice Taney blew this unwarranted concept up to include the regulation of all intrastate commerce. He did this in his oft-quoted definition of the states' police powers, in the License cases of 1847.

The "police power of a State," said Chief Justice Taney, is "the power of sovereignty, the power to govern men and things within the limits of [a state's] dominions." Then, in specific reference to the subject of commerce, he added that "every State [might] regulate its own internal traffic, according to its own judgment," and "free," he declared, "from any controlling power on the part of the general government." He was "not aware," he added, "that these principles ha[d] ever been questioned."[48] One might suppose from this statement that Chief Justice Taney had never read *Gibbons* v. *Ogden;* but his own memories went back to the founding of the government, and we may feel quite sure he knew exactly what he was about. His statements, at any rate, constitute, I believe, the earliest evidence of adherence to the interstate theory of the commerce power to be found in the Supreme Court's reports. The theory was not actually applied against Congress until 1869.[49]

One other matter to be considered is the intended place of the Supreme Court in the country's juridical system, particularly what happened to the Court's intended position in that system during Marshall's tenure of office. The original inten-

unfavorably to the claim of the plaintiff in the *Huidekoper* case before that action had even been started. Marshall and his Court, nevertheless, decided the same point in favor of the plaintiff. It is important to understand that Marshall and his associates could not possibly have been ignorant of the purpose of the *Huidekoper* litigation, for the use of ejectment actions to settle land titles in the manner I have described was a common practice among lawyers of the period.[54] Marshall and the others must, then, have thought that they had power to settle the title in the case before them by settling the meaning of the Pennsylvania statute upon which the title depended. Any other view would make their disregard of the Pennsylvania precedents frivolous to an extreme degree.[55]

The Court of 1805 still had, to be sure, a majority of Federalists upon it. Thus there is still the question of what happened to this old Federalist doctrine of the Court's general juridical supremacy after the Supreme Court fell under Jeffersonian domination in 1812. The answer is that the doctrine at first fared surprisingly well. Thus in 1813, in another case carried to the Supreme Court to settle the Fairfax title, the Court—minus Chief Justice Marshall of course—decided all the points involved in the title, whether of common law, state law, or national law, in exactly the way John Marshall had hoped the Court would do in the case of 1796.[56] This later case, moreover, was appealed to the Supreme Court from the state courts, not the national courts, of Virginia; and when the Virginia state court in 1815 attacked the Supreme Court's decision as unconstitutional, that body, upon a second appeal to it in 1816, vindicated its earlier action and consequently its claim to the general juridical dominion over the nation.

This was in the famous case of *Martin* v. *Hunter's Lessee,* Justice Story speaking for the Court.[57] That case, I am aware, is today usually taken as a claim of judicial supremacy merely as to so-called "federal questions," that is, as to questions of the meaning of the Constitution, statutes, and treaties of the

United States. The case, in fact, was much more than this, as, I am confident, any lawyer will agree who will take the trouble to read the case in context with the earlier phases of the Fairfax litigation; that is, in context with the two opinions in the Virginia court and the earlier Supreme Court decision, of 1813, which the *Martin* opinion was written to vindicate.[58] The case, in view of the land title it was intended to settle and the earlier decision it was meant to vindicate, was *necessarily* a claim of judicial supremacy over the Virginia court as to questions of all kinds of law whatsoever.

The principles of the *Martin* case were a second time affirmed in *Cohens* v. *Virginia* in 1821.[59] The Virginia court, however, never acknowledged these principles, though it did contrive to avoid a clash with the Supreme Court on any of the involved points of law; and the Marshalls kept their lands. A somewhat similar policy was followed with respect to the *Huidekoper* decision by the Supreme Court of Pennsylvania. Then, in the middle 1820's the Supreme Court of the United States began to weaken; and in a series of decisions culminating in *Wheaton* v. *Peters* in 1834,[60] the Supreme Court abdicated its supremacy over the state courts with respect to all questions of state law and common law. At the time, indeed, it seemed as if the Court were abdicating its right, even, of independent decision with respect to all such questions. Thus John Marshall at the very close of his career was obliged to witness once more an extensive denial by his Court of principles in which, as it has been pointed out, he firmly believed and which, furthermore, he must have known were the views of the Federalist founders of the government.

It would be possible to add to the foregoing instances; but enough has been said, I hope, to convince the reader that the usual view of John Marshall's career is hardly tenable. John Marshall did not carry on a continual frontal assault, uniformly successful, upon the subversive principles of Jeffersonianism. Instead, he fought a long and stubborn rearguard action to defend the Constitution against those principles. And it was, on the whole, a losing fight. Time after time during his long career, Marshall was forced into compromise or defeat; and the result was a pretty complete transformation of the Constitution by the date of his death.

No one, it may be added, was more aware of what was going on than John Marshall. As his biographer has shown from the letters of his closing years, Marshall died almost in despair of the future of the Union. He was convinced that the South—his own state of Virginia in particular—had determined to convert the Union into a loose confederation.[61] And that he was not far wrong is shown by the action I have already noted of the southerners who dominated the Taney Court that came into power upon Marshall's death in 1835. The Taney Court's initial action, in substituting the principle of the inviolability of the states' police powers for Marshall's principle of plenary national supremacy, was greeted by one of the nationalists of the time as "a return to the principles of the Articles of Confederation."[62] Such, there can be no doubt, it truly was, especially after the concept of state police power was blown up to include the regulation of all intrastate commerce, as it was in the *License Cases* of 1847.[63]

These two principles—the interstate theory of Congress' power over commerce and the inviolability of the police powers of the states—were certainly basic to American constitutional law until very recent times; and these principles derived, not from the decisions of John Marshall, but from unjustified glosses upon his decisions by Roger Brooke Taney and the Jacksonian Court that came into power upon Marshall's death. So far, moreover, as constitutional law actually has been based on Marshall's decisions, it has involved much more of Jeffersonianism than of federalism, much more of the views of Marshall's associates on the Court than of Marshall's own ideas. And the fragments of federalism that did survive in the Marshall decisions represented, in the main, no more than what Marshall's associates felt compelled to agree to, in order to reach results that they desired to reach on other grounds. In saying these things, I do not mean to imply that John Marshall had no victories at all, for this would not be true; but I do mean to say that on the great fundamental theses of federalism—the theses that went to the very character of the government, the theses that I have here reviewed—John Marshall was defeated, either by his own Court or by the Taney Court that succeeded him.

Does this conclusion impugn Marshall's claim to greatness? I can only say that, so far as I am concerned, I do not think it does. A man may be great in tragedy as well as triumph, in defeat as well as victory. And since there was, it seems to me, much more of tragedy and defeat than of triumph and victory in John Marshall's career as defender of the Constitution, the traditional estimate of the nature of his career ought, I think, to be revised to show him as he truly was. His greatness, clearly, was not that of triumphant victory. It was a greatness that consisted in devoting half a lifetime to a cause in which he profoundly believed; in faithful service to that cause in the face of overwhelming odds; in unflagging courage in the face of those odds and in the face of constantly recurring defeats. There can be no doubt, moreover, that John Marshall, in spite of the circumstances in which he worked, accomplished a very great deal in the way of minimizing damage; that it was, indeed, a "fortunate" thing, as Oliver Wendell Holmes observed, in 1901, that it fell to Marshall, and not to an appointee of Thomas Jefferson, to serve in the critical early years of the nineteenth century as Chief Justice of the United States. The circumstance, I think, probably saved the Union.

Although I take a very different view of Marshall's work than is usually taken, he still remains to me "the great Chief Justice." There is not one of his predecessors, not one of those who succeeded him, that I should think, for a moment, of nominating in his place.

WILLIAM WINSLOW CROSSKEY *is professor emeritus of law at the Law School of the University of Chicago. He served as law clerk to Chief Justice Taft and then practiced in New York before joining the Chicago faculty. He is the author of* Politics and the Constitution in the History of the United States, *1953.*

NOTES

1. Cf., for example, Beveridge, *The Life of John Marshall* (1919), IV, 59–61.

2. Holmes, *Collected Legal Papers* (1920), pp. 266, 268–69. For a more recent expression of this view of Marshall's work, see Cahn, "John Marshall—Our 'Greatest Dissenter,' " *New York Times Magazine,* August 21, 1955, p. 14.

3. The old Federalist views of the Constitution are developed fully in Crosskey, *Politics and the Constitution in the History of the United States* (1953), *passim,* hereinafter cited as *P. and C.* as *P. and C.*

4. *Ibid.*

5. *The Annals of Congress* covering the early years of the government was a reprint of Thomas Lloyd's contemporaneously published *Congressional Register,* a private report of debates in the House of Representatives. The most casual inspection of Lloyd's *Register* discloses that it was not a complete report of these debates but a report of picked and chosen parts, and of picked and chosen speeches. The reporting is uneven. Some of it is very well done and obviously complete, as, for example, the debates on June 8, 1789, when James Madison proposed the initial amendments to the Constitution. Other debates—for example, those on the same amendments, on August 19, 1789—are omitted entirely. And still other parts of the reporting—for example, that on the same subject, two days earlier—are, on the basis of other and better surviving evidence, demonstrably inaccurate. In the instance mentioned, this other and better evidence consists of the official journals of the House and the Senate. Cf. *P. and C.,* pp. 702–3. See also note 35 *infra.*

6. The quoted material is from an anonymous newspaper essay which Marshall wrote and had published in the *Philadelphia Union* in 1819. See Beveridge, *op. cit.,* IV, 318–22.

7. 12 Wheat. 64, 90 (1827). The *Dandridge* case itself and *Ogden* v. *Saunders,* 12 Wheat. 213 (1827), appear to be the only cases in which Marshall departed from his practice of silent acquiescence.

8. See Story's own statement to this effect in *Cary* v. *Curtis,* 3 How. 236, 252 (1845).

9. Morgan, *Mr. Justice William Johnson and the Constitution,* 57 Harv. L. Rev. 328, 333 (1944).

10. There was an anti-Federalist majority on the Court after 1807; but this was true only if the anti-Jeffersonian anti-Federalist, Samuel Chase, was counted. That the Jeffersonians did not trust Chase is shown by their attempt to remove him from office by impeachment in 1805. Cf. also Jefferson's attitude when the death of Justice William Cushing in 1810 opened the way for another Jeffersonian appointment. "Old Cushing is dead," he wrote to Albert Gallatin. "At length, then, we have a chance of getting a Republican majority in the Supreme Judiciary." *The Works of Thomas Jefferson* (Federal ed., 1904–5), XI, 153.

11. Jefferson was opposed to President Madison's appointment of Joseph Story: he said Story was "unquestionably a tory." See Beveridge, *op. cit.,* IV, 106–10, especially 109.

12. The angriest of my accusers has been Professor Julius Goebel of the Columbia Law School faculty. See his *Ex Parte Clio,* 54 Col. L. Rev. 450 (1954).

13. State criminal prosecutions at common law would not have been included. The Common Law applied in such cases, not as the national law, but as state law; and the "Cases . . . in which a State shall be a Party," of Article III, included, by reason of the earlier enumeration in that article, only certain "Controversies," or civil suits. Cf. Judge Peters' opinion in *United States* v. *Worrall,* 2 Dall. 384 (1798).

14. As I have pointed out elsewhere, this view of the Common Law also underlay the rules of decision which, under section 34 of the first Judiciary Act, were followed in the national courts in equity and admiralty cases. See *P. and C.,* pp. 865–902. The only reported case in which this phase of the subject is taken up is Justice Story's circuit court case of *United States* v. *Coolidge,* 1 Gall. 488 (1813).

15. *United States* v. *Worrall,* 2 Dall. 384.

16. See the letter of District Judge Richard Peters, cited in *P. and C.,* p. 782.

17. See, for example, the answer of the Federalist Massachusetts legislature of 1799 to the Virginia Resolutions of the year before. *Elliot's Debates* (2d [24 cm.] ed., 1836), IV, 533, 536. The Federalist view on this subject is recorded in many other places. See, for example, the opinion of Judge Peters in the *Worrall* case, cited in note 13 *supra.* See also Henfield's case, discussed in *P. and C.,* chap. xx, sec. 3.

18. See James Madison's report to the Virginia House of Dele-

gates of 1799 on the Virginia Resolutions of the year before. *Elliot, op. cit.,* IV, 546, 561 ff.

19. James Madison, St. George Tucker, and Thomas Jefferson all pointed out in their writings the consequence stated in the text and insisted upon it as the chief reason for rejecting the doctrine under discussion. Their statements are cited at length in *P. and C.,* pp. 560–61, 699, 763–64. See also *ibid.,* 630–33, 669–74.

20. 7 Cranch 32.

21. The background of the *Hudson and Goodwin* case is fully developed in *P. and C.,* pp. 766–84.

22. *United States* v. *Coolidge,* 1 Gall. 488, 495 (1813).

23. W. W. Story, *Life and Letters of Joseph Story* (1851), I, 299.

24. There are also a letter of Marshall's from 1800, in the Library of Congress, and certain pronouncements of his in Aaron Burr's trial, in 1807, which corroborate the inference drawn from Justice Story's statements. See *P. and C.,* p. 1356, note 45.

25. See the materials cited in *P. and C.,* pp. 193–288, 241–42. The views against which the opponents of the Federalists argued are often a good indication of what the Federalist views were in cases where the Federalist views are imperfectly recorded. Cf. Thomas Jefferson's and Edmund Randolph's opinions on the bank. *P. and C.,* pp. 196–97, 206–16, 248–49.

To the foregoing may be added an interesting statement made by James Madison when he introduced in Congress the initial amendments to the Constitution on June 8, 1789. Madison was meeting the objection, which had been made by some of the writers in the ratification campaign, "that in the Federal Government [a bill of rights was] unnecessary, because the powers [were] enumerated, and it follow[ed] that all that [were] not granted by the constitution [were] retained." This argument, Madison admitted, was "not entirely without foundation"; yet it was "not," he said, "conclusive to the extent which ha[d] been supposed." "It [was] true, *the powers of the General Government* [were] circumscribed, they were directed *to particular objects.*" But "within those limits," there was, he insisted, the same possibility of abuses such as a bill of rights would forbid, as there was in the case of the states, "because, in the constitution of the United States there was," he said, "a clause granting to Congress the power to make all laws which sh[ould] be necessary and proper for carrying into execution *all the powers* vested *in the Government of the United States,* or in any department or office thereof." "This enables them," he explained, meaning Congress, "*to fulfil every purpose for which the Government was established*" (italics added). And if there can be any doubt as to what Madison meant by the word "purpose," that doubt is allayed by his reference in the next succeeding paragraph to the "securing" of the people's "liberties" "to themselves and [their] posterity" as an "express purpose" for which the "new system" of government was "ordained and established" (*Annals of Congress*, I, 438–39).

In other words, Madison was measuring "the powers *of the government*" by the "objects" stated in the Preamble; and he was measuring "the powers *of Congress*," in their totality, by the fact that that body was expressly empowered to make "all" necessary and proper laws to carry into execution "*all* the powers vested *in the Government*." Hence he concluded that Congress was empowered to "fulfil every purpose for which the Government was established"; or, in other words, every "purpose" or "object" that the Preamble states.

The foregoing passages corroborate inferences I have elsewhere drawn, on the basis of evidence of other kinds, as to the nature of Madison's real views on the scope of the national powers, in 1789. See *P. and C.*, pp. 406–8, 688–90. The passages I now cite I somehow overlooked on these earlier occasions.

26. See *P. and C.*, pp. 193–205, 211.

27. 4 Wheat. 316.

28. Story, *op. cit.*, I, 324–25; cited in Beveridge, *op. cit.*, IV, 287.

29. *Ibid.*

30. 4 Wheat. at 381–82.

31. See the second paragraph on p. 406 of the opinion and the first paragraph beginning on p. 421 thereof.

32. 4 Wheat. 405.

33. Cf. the debates in Congress cited in *P. and C.*, pp. 234–35, 240–42.

34. 4 Wheat. at 405.

35. Cf. *P. and C.*, pp. 196–205. The only extant report of the debates in the House of Representatives (*Annals of Congress*, II, 1894–1960) is very incomplete and imperfect. The inference of great incompleteness arises in part from the disparity between the total volume of the recorded debates and the time known to have been consumed in them. Besides this, the recorded speeches, as well as the opinions later rendered to President Washington by Edmund Randolph and Thomas Jefferson, contain references to arguments not found in the recorded speeches. There are references, even, to whole speeches that are not recorded. And, finally, there is a want of fullness and logical coherence, in developing various doctrines in the recorded speeches, which indicates fragmentary and garbled reporting. A brief example will make clear what is meant. James Jackson, of Georgia, denying the adequacy of the commerce power, is reported to have said: "The power to regulate trade is

said to involve this [incorporating power] as a necessary means; but the powers consequent on this express power are specified, such as regulating light houses, ships, harbors, &c." (*Annals of Congress*, II, 1917). There are, of course, no "specified" powers over "light houses, ships, [or] harbors" in the Constitution. What Jackson said, or meant, is thus completely obscure.

36. *Works of Alexander Hamilton* (Federal ed., 1904), II, 445–93; cf. *P. and C.*, pp. 216–28.

37. On this general subject, see *P. and C.*, pp. 17–292.

38. I am aware that there are in Hamilton's opinion on the bank some passages which, isolatedly considered, might be taken by a modern reader as evidence that he understood the commerce power as subject to an interstate limitation; but, as I have elsewhere shown these passages arose out of certain peculiarities of eighteenth-century speech (see *P. and C.*, pp. 218–28). Cf. also *The Federalist*, No. VI, and index thereof, where, under the general head of "Dissensions"—or "War"—"between the States," Hamilton listed and discussed Shays' Rebellion, an insurrection entirely internal to Massachusetts, and, likewise, the subject of intrastate tranquillity generally.

39. 4 Wheat. at 406.

40. 6 Wheat. 264, 412–14 (1821).

41. Cf. the debates in Congress cited in *P. and C.*, pp. 240–50.

42. 9 Wheat. 1, 194 (1824).

43. 9 Wheat. at 197 and 209–10. Cf. discussion of this case in *P. and C.*, 250–92.

44. 9 Johns. (N.Y.) 507 (1812); cf. discussion of this case in *P. and C.*, pp. 250–92.

45. I Hopk. (N.Y. Ch.) 151 (1824); 3 Cow. (N.Y.) 711 (1825); cf. discussion in *P. and C.*, 268–80.

46. For further evidence that *Gibbons* v. *Ogden* was not contemporaneously understood as adopting the interstate theory of the national power, see *P. and C.*, pp. 280–87.

47. 11 Pet. 102, 138 (1837).

48. 5 How. 504, 574, 582 (1847).

49. *United States* v. *DeWitt*, 9 Wall. 41.

50. *Barnes* v. *Irvine*, 5 Watts (Pa.) 557, 558 (1836).

51. On this general subject, see *P. and C.*, chaps. xviii–xxi and xxiii–xxvi.

52. On this general subject, see *P. and C.*, chap. xxiv, secs. 3 and 4. The case referred to in the text is dealt with at pp. 789–93.

53. 3 Cranch 1 (1805).

54. Cf. the statement of Chief Justice Oliver Ellsworth in *Sims* v. *Irvine*, 3 Dall. 425 (1799), another ejectment action intended to settle a land title under state law, that "the case ha[d] been brought

here [to the Supreme Court of the United States] to settle the title."

55. For a full consideration of the *Huidekoper* case, see *P. and C.*, chap. xxiii, sec. 4.

56. *Fairfax's Devisee* v. *Hunter's Lessee*, 7 Cranch 603 (1813). See *P. and C.*, chap. xxiv, sec. 3.

57. 1 Wheat. 304 (1816). See *P. and C.*, chap. xxiv, sec. 4.

58. That is, in order: *Hunter* v. *Fairfax's Devisee*, 1 Munf. (Va.) 218 (1810); *Fairfax's Devisee* v. *Hunter's Lessee*, 7 Cranch 603 (1813); *Hunter* v. *Martin*, 4 Munf. (Va.) 1 (1815); and *Martin* v. *Hunter's Lessee*, 1 Wheat. 304 (1816). Cf. *P. and C.*, chap. xxiv, secs. 3 and 4.

59. 6 Wheat. 264 (1821).

60. The important members of the series were: *Jackson* ex dem. *St. John* v. *Chew*, 12 Wheat. 153 (1827); *Green* v. *Neal's Lessee*, 6 Pet. 291 (1832); and *Wheaton* v. *Peters*, 8 Pet. 591 (1834). For a full discussion, see *P. and C.*, chap. xxv.

61. See Beveridge, *op. cit.*, IV, chap. x, especially pp. 575–78.

62. *The North American Review*, XLVI (1838), 126, 154. The commentator was said to be Henry Wheaton.

63. *Loc. cit.*, note 48 *supra*.

MR. CHIEF JUSTICE TANEY

Mr. Chief Justice Taney

By
CARL BRENT SWISHER

Chief Justice Roger B. Taney suffered abuse and condemnation such as has never been poured upon any other member of the Supreme Court. His name, proclaimed Charles Sumner in the United States Senate, was to be "hooted down the pages of history."[1] Post–Civil War historians did much to bear out Sumner's prediction; but history in recent years has brought about a considerable amount of re-examination of the Taney record, to the end that the volume of hooting has been vastly reduced and broad significance has been attached to his efforts and achievements. Indeed, two Chief Justices of the present century, Hughes and Warren, have delivered public addresses according him praise. It is to be presumed that the editors of this volume, in selecting Taney as one of the Justices to be discussed, sought not an opportunity for renewed hooting or for indiscriminate eulogy but rather for objective appraisal of this onetime highly controversial figure.

It is, of course, possible to compare and contrast Taney to other Justices. Brandeis, for example, would have been proud in some, though not in all, respects to have been regarded as Taney's legal heir. Sutherland, in contrast, would have had little in common with Taney. For Taney's placement, however, we shall have to turn to his position in history, to his lodgment between the John Marshall regime and the cataclysm of the Civil War. We shall have to think of the reaction against the older federalism, the influx of Jacksonian democracy, the

35

marking of time in the expansion of federal power pending solution of the North-South conflict, and the impact which that controversy had upon constitutional law and our whole institutional pattern. Taney was at once a product of, and an important determining factor in, the era in which he lived. Only as such can he be correctly appraised.

In attempting to characterize Taney's life we should first stress awareness that no accumulation of biographical and historical facts can yield more than an approximate conception of the career of a man who lived a century ago. If, as is obviously true, the person now at our elbow, even if seen day after day and year after year, is something of a stranger, much more of a stranger is the man who lived in another age, another environment, and another climate of opinion. We cannot hope to enter fully into his mind and to feel as he did the impact of events and ideas. Confidence of statement can be justified only by knowledge that we have done our best in the collection and interpretation of available facts; never by the assumption that we have enough facts, enough of the right facts, to render our case infallible. He who interprets history must give to it the full play of his imagination. He must go far beyond the stage of microscopic study of collected data. He must treat history somewhat as T. S. Eliot has his fictitious psychiatrist in *The Cocktail Party* treat a patient:

> I learn a good deal by merely observing you,
> And letting you talk as long as you please,
> And taking note of what you do not say.[2]

The records of history-in-the-making leave a great deal unsaid for at least two reasons. The first is that within a given historical climate of opinion, as among people in any period who know one another well, a great deal is left unsaid for the reason that it is fully understood by the people on that historical ground. People who have lived closely together for many years can communicate a great deal by a glance, an inflection, a gesture, or—paraphrasing Eliot's language—by what they do not say. The records are deficient for another reason which has more in common with Eliot's idea. People may consciously or unconsciously refrain from telling the full truth with its full implications for the reason that the truth about themselves would be unpalatable. For this reason also we are likely to find history somewhat opaque.

For Taney the written record leaves huge gaps. He drafted only the beginnings of an autobiography, and those beginnings disclose the normal difficulties experienced by men in attempting to present their own lives in perspective. The volume entitled *Memoir of Roger Brooke Taney, LL.D.*, published in 1872 by his friend Samuel Tyler, preserved for us rich but fragmentary materials in an atmosphere that called not so much for critical objectivity as for defense against attacks such as that of Charles Sumner. Taney never prepared a systematic statement of his legal and political philosophy. Against the controversial historical background of his period his biographer must present materials drawn from the fragmentary sources already indicated, from judicial opinions linked to highly particularized disputes of long ago, from his opinions as Attorney General, from published and unpublished letters from many sources, and from incidental items in the biographies and records of his contemporaries. Although adhering to the generalizations phrased in my biography of Taney, which went to press in 1935, and in the statement which follows hereafter, I must admit that the gleanings of facts often merely illustrate rather than conclusively prove the generalizations believed to be valid. With this admission of unsureness I proceed with the story, concerned primarily, not with praise, not with condemnation, but with promoting understanding of an influential Chief Justice in a turbulent period of American history.

When we approach Taney's judicial period, 1836 to 1864, merely in our capacity as students of constitutional law, we emphasize the evolution of the American federal system, the interpretation of the Commerce Clause as it restricts the exercise of state power, the beginnings of developments of the doctrine of state police power, interpretations of state and federal power with respect to slavery, and various other legal problems then somewhat less important. When for that period we concentrate on the Supreme Court as an institution, additional items come to the fore. We note changes in the character of the men appointed to the Court, the vast difference between the leadership of Taney and that of his predecessor, Chief Justice Marshall; the tendency toward multiplicity of opinions; the underlying preoccupation with slavery issues even when not directly involved in cases at hand; the debacle produced by the unfortunate attempt in the *Dred Scott* case to heal by judicial fiat a sectional breach too deep for judicial treatment; and, toward the end of the period, the relative feebleness of the Court as the country turned to force of arms to solve the problems that were judicially unsolvable. When we approach the subject from the point of view of Taney himself, we go beyond the matter of his formal leadership of the Court to the character of the man, to the qualities and equipment and interests that shaped his thinking and conditioned his judicial performance. Since our discussion here is personalized in the man, in the Chief Justice, we shall concentrate on the personality and trace outward to constitutional patterns as the task requires.

We can summarize at the outset by saying that Taney went to the Court with a conviction as to the sanctity of rights of physical and tangible property and the community rights connected therewith; that he distrusted mercantile and banking interests that were strong enough and ruthlessly selfish enough to endanger the interests of stable property and of the community; that he had a deep sense of local patriotism for Maryland, which easily extended to southern states with a similar culture; that although he favored voluntary and responsible loosening of the bonds of slavery, he was firmly opposed to wholesale and largely irresponsible manumission as a result of northern coercion; that he was committed to the position that the Negro was basically inferior to the white man and had no assured constitutional rights; and that although a firm believer in the Union he was also and apparently in greater degree a believer in the rights of the states and of what was to become the minority region of the South. Since it is in the light of these propositions that the important aspects of Taney's judicial career are to be explained, they will be developed here at greater length.

Taney was born in the conservative tradition of the landed aristocracy of the South. His father, Michael Taney, was the fifth of that name to reside in southern Maryland, and the Chief Justice's own eldest son was named for him and was expected to inherit the family plantation. Said Roger Taney in his incomplete autobiographical statement: "My father, Michael Taney, owned a good landed estate, on which he always resided, and slaves. His property was sufficient to enable him to live comfortably, and to educate his children."[3] It was a good life, comfortable and rewarding, and was expected to continue into the future, generation after generation. Michael Taney was a member of the Federalist party; he supported the federal Constitution to insure protection for the basic rights of property as property was known to him. Since for Roger, the second son, there was no plantation to inherit, the father chose for him the conservative and honorable profession of the law. Said Roger, "He looked upon distinction in the profession of the law as a stepping-stone to political power."[4] After admission to the Bar, Roger served a number of terms in the Maryland legislature and worked his way into the leadership of the Federalist party in the state.

Taney's experience with the Federalist party during and after the War of 1812 helped condition his attitude toward mercantile interests and northern interests generally with implications for his future judicial career. The issues of the war split the party. Many Federalist leaders in New England and other northern areas resented the war as an interference with ocean trade and the internal business resulting therefrom and sought its termination. In Maryland the party was sharply divided. Taney, as a representative of interior and landed interests, became the leader of the vigorously loyal branch. In a rough draft of an account written long afterward he stated the situation as follows:

During the war the deepest dissatisfaction was felt by the greater number of the prominent Federalists of the state with the eastern Federalists. For while the enemy was in the midst of us spoiling our cities, and burning our houses and plundering our property, and the citizens of the state without distinction of party were putting forth their whole strength and bleeding in its defense, those with whom the Maryland Federalists had been associated as political friends in the eastern states and whom they had regarded and treated as leaders of the party were holding the Hartford Convention; talking about disunion, conferring with one another in secret conclave; demanding from us, as one of the southern states, a surrender of a portion of the political weight secured to us by the Constitution; making this demand too in the hour of our distress when the enemy was upon us. They were moreover using every exertion in their power to destroy the credit and cripple the resources of the general government, feeble as it then was; and leaving us to defend ourselves as well as we could by our own resources. It will readily be imagined that after this, the Federalists of Maryland would hardly desire to continue the party association and continue the lead in hands who appeared to be not only indifferent to the sufferings of our citizens but ready to take advantage of the peril in which the state was placed to extort from it the surrender of a portion of its legitimate power. We thought it time that the party connection should be dissolved.[5]

This document, drafted more than thirty years after the war came to an end, revealed the perpetually boiling resentment of the Chief Justice against the regional and financial interests which in his judgment had attacked the interests of the state to which he was intensely loyal. "My family on both the father and mother's side have been for so many generations Maryland people," he said in the same document, "that I have always felt

strong Maryland attachments." These attachments are important factors in explanation of Taney's attitudes in some fields
of constitutional interpretation.

The breakdown of the Federalist organization left Taney
without party affiliation. In the 1820's he aligned himself with
Andrew Jackson, who in Tennessee was a landholder and
owner of slaves in the tradition of the Taneys. Political service
brought in 1831 a political reward—appointment as Attorney
General of the United States, a position in which Taney for
the first time moved from Maryland localism to the national
scene. He had not desired the position he maintained with
apparent sincerity. He was a lawyer by profession and proud
of his profession. In the way of political honors he had been
satisfied with the attorney generalship of Maryland, where he
served as one of a long line of distinguished lawyers without
serious disturbance of his private practice. He accepted a call
from Jackson when a cabinet reorganization became necessary, hoping still in large part to earn his livelihood at the bar
in Maryland—his federal office would yield only $4,000 a year—
and to expand his private practice before the Supreme Court
in Washington.

His duties as Attorney General enabled Taney to develop
arguments in defense of the rights of the states and against the
expansion of the power of the moneyed interests of the country. State action with respect to slaves became a critical matter with the Nat Turner rebellion of slaves in Virginia in 1831,
an uprising which sent a thrill of terror through the slave
states and intensified the hostility to free Negroes, who by
their envied position in contrast with slaves might bring about
other attacks on the white masters. In the border states a typical reaction was that of Taney's younger brother, Octavius,
who proposed in the Maryland legislature a resolution in behalf of a program to "facilitate the removal of free persons of
color from our state, and from the United States."[6]

Attorney General Taney was brought into the picture when

the Secretary of State, in response to a protest from the British government, asked him whether a treaty with Great Britain was violated by a South Carolina statute. The statute required that free Negroes employed on ships entering South Carolina ports should be imprisoned while the ships were in port. When the ships departed, the Negroes might go with them if the ship owners paid the cost of imprisonment; otherwise they were to be sold to pay the costs. The question undoubtedly caused uneasiness in Taney's mind, for in personal relations with Negroes he was eminently humane. He freed his own slaves, caring for them thereafter, and he helped at least one worthy Negro to purchase his freedom. Taney delayed answer to the request for an opinion, giving another in the meantime on a Pennsylvania statute of a different kind. Pennsylvania had provided that slaves entering her ports should become free on arrival. Taney upheld the authority of the state, there being no conflict with any treaty, and expressed, incidentally, the opinion that the United States could not "by treaty control the several states in the exercise of this power."[7]

After a long delay the Secretary of State asked a second time for an opinion on the South Carolina statute. Taney gave an opinion of which we have no official draft. It was not published in the official volume of opinions, as was that on the Pennsylvania statute. Under the date of May 28, 1832, we have in Taney's hand, in the papers of his office, a working draft with many passages interlined and with sections written and then crossed out. We have in the files of the Department of State in the hand of a copyist, but with corrections in Taney's hand, a supplement to the opinion that evidently was sent.[8] From the two documents we are able to work out Taney's position. He held that the South Carolina statute did not violate the treaty with Great Britain, since by the treaty the permission to British subjects to enter and reside in this country was expressly made subject to the laws and statutes of the country, in which the South Carolina statute was included.

The opinion as available to us did not stop with this simple holding. It ranged discursively, indicating Taney's preoccupation with all angles of the sectional and racial controversy. He contended that

South Carolina or any other slave holding state has a right to guard itself from the danger to be apprehended from the introduction of free people of color among their slaves—and have not by the Constitution of the United States surrendered the right to pass the laws necessary for that purpose. I think this right is reserved to the states and cannot be abrogated by the United States either by legislation or by treaty. And if by a fair construction of the treaty with England it came in conflict with the law of South Carolina it does not by any means follow that the law must yield to it. The Constitution it is true has declared that a treaty shall be the supreme law. But in order to make it so the stipulation must be within the treaty making power. A treaty would be void which interfered with the powers expressly delegated to Congress. So it would be void if it came into conflict with the rights reserved to the states. And although the non-fulfillment of such a treaty would give just ground of complaint to the other party and the United States would be bound to make reparation for the breach of it, yet it would not be the supreme law here and would not lawfully be carried into execution by the government of the United States. If therefore the treaty were susceptible of the interpretation claimed for it by the British Government, still it could not be enforced if South Carolina had a right to prohibit the introduction of free people of color within her limits.

This and further argument as to the limits of the treaty-making power when encroaching on the rights of the states should have considerable current interest for people involved in the controversy over the scope of the existing treaty power.

At the end of the long first draft Taney admitted that the Supreme Court might not agree with him, and in showing himself unimpressed by what he thought might be the Court's position he went as far as did Abraham Lincoln after the *Dred Scott* decision in suggesting that the country would not be permanently bound by the holdings of the Court at a particular time. He thought it his duty to inform the Secretary of State of the probability that the Supreme Court would find the

South Carolina statute unconstitutional if a case were brought before it. He continued:

It is unnecessary now to say what in that event ought to be done. But whatever may be the force of the decision of the Supreme Court in binding the parties and settling their rights in the particular case before them, I am not prepared to admit that a construction given to the Constitution by the Supreme Court in deciding any one or more cases fixes of itself irrevocably and permanently its construction in that particular and binds the states and the legislative and executive branches of the general government forever afterwards to conform to it and to adopt it in every other case as the true reading of the instrument although all of them may unite in believing it erroneous. If the judgment pronounced by the Court be conclusive it does not follow that the reasoning or principles which it announces in coming to its conclusions are equally binding and obligatory. It will however be time enough for the Executive to determine this point when a case shall arise which compels it to decide. . . . And whatever may be proper to be done if the Court should hereafter declare the law in question to be void, yet until that shall happen I am very clear that it ought to be regarded by the Executive as a valid law passed by competent authority, and consequently a law which according to the treaty every subject of Great Britain is bound to observe.

Throughout the opinion, written four years before Taney's appointment to the Court whose judgment he then distrusted, runs evidence of the defensiveness so characteristic of the South with respect to slavery and other state-rights issues. It was the defensiveness that minority groups normally feel in the presence of disagreeing majorities, a defensiveness tinged with a seeming sense of guilt even as righteousness is indignantly protested. On the score of attitudes toward the judiciary, the document suggests, furthermore, that President Jackson may well have had the hearty support of his Attorney General if in connection with the Cherokee Indian cases[9] he blurted out the statement tradition attributed to him, "John Marshall has made his decision. Now let him enforce it!"

This 1832 opinion has further significance in connection with the *Dred Scott* decision of a quarter of a century later. In it

Taney clearly states what became his *Dred Scott* position with respect to the citizenship rights of Negroes:

> The African race in the United States even when free, are everywhere a degraded class, and exercise no political influence. The privileges they are allowed to enjoy, are accorded to them as a matter of kindness and benevolence rather than of right. They are the only class of persons who can be held as mere property, as slaves. And where they are nominally admitted by law to the privileges of citizenship, they have no effectual power to defend them, and are permitted to be citizens by the sufferance of the white population and hold whatever rights they enjoy at their mercy. They were never regarded as a constituent portion of the sovereignty of any state. But as a separate and degraded people to whom the sovereignty of each state might accord or withhold such privileges as they might deem proper. They were not looked upon as citizens by the contracting parties who formed the Constitution. They were evidently not supposed to be included by the term *citizens*. And have not been intended to be embraced in any of the provisions of that Constitution but those which point to them in terms not to be mistaken.

A student of law from the University of California at Los Angeles asserted on the basis of analysis of words habitually used by Chief Justice Taney and Justice Wayne that Taney, poor in health and pressed for an early draft of an opinion, did not write a major portion of the opinion attributed to him in the *Dred Scott* case but adopted instead one written by Justice Wayne.[10] The contention may be valid. Judges often give one another anonymous help, and the unacknowledged use of the legal arguments of other men when writing opinions is not, as in many other fields, normally regarded as reprehensible plagiarism. But whoever constructed in Taney's *Dred Scott* opinion the major line of argument with respect to jurisdiction, a comparison with the language there used as to the status of Negroes with that used by Taney in 1832 indicates that that doctrinaire portion, whether for better or for worse, was his own. Note the following in comparison with the preceding quotation as Taney

asks and then answers the question whether Negroes are con-
stituent members of this sovereignty:

> We think they are not, and that they are not included, and were
> not intended to be included, under the word "citizens" in the Con-
> stitution, and can, therefore, claim none of the rights and privileges
> which that instrument provides for and secures to citizens of the
> United States. On the contrary, they were at that time considered
> as a subordinate and inferior class of beings, who had been sub-
> jugated by the dominant race, and whether emancipated or not,
> yet remained subject to their authority, and had no rights or
> privileges but such as those who held the power and the govern-
> ment might choose to grant them. . . .
> They had for more than a century before been regarded as be-
> ings of an inferior order, and altogether unfit to associate with the
> white race either in social or political relations; so far inferior,
> that they had no rights which the white man was bound to re-
> spect; and that the negro might justly and lawfully be reduced
> to slavery for his benefit. He was bought and sold, and treated
> as an ordinary article of merchandise and traffic, whenever a profit
> could be made by it. This opinion was at that time fixed and uni-
> versal in the civilized portion of the white race.[11]

The implication of these parallel quotations is that with respect
to the constitutional status of Negroes Taney made up his
mind long before he as a Justice was called upon to pass on
the question, and that he never submitted the question to re-
examination.

Taney's state-rights attitudes and his dislike of private financial power built up with government aid were intensified by
his struggle with the Bank of the United States. That story is
too complicated for retelling here. Suffice it to say that that
bank, chartered by Congress in 1816 to bring order out of the
chaos of postwar finances, was the most powerful banking institution in the country. The bank gradually achieved its purpose, exercised a strong and curbing influence over many state
banks, and in doing so made enemies among state banks and
their supporters. More concerned with its own growing power
than with party politics as such, it involved itself in the presidential election of 1832 in an attempt to force immediately the

renewal of its charter which was to expire in 1836. The fortunes of politics brought the bank into conflict with President Jackson, who on the advice of Taney and others vetoed the bill to recharter the bank and won popular support and election to a second term. Through its control of credit the bank waged a war which shook the finances of the country as Taney, moved to the position of Secretary of the Treasury, sought to weaken the political power of the bank by ceasing to use it as a depository of federal funds.

Although the bank was chartered by Congress, the federal government owned only one-fifth of the stock and appointed only one-fifth of the directors. It was therefore more of a private than a public agency. Stock ownership was largely in northern and urban areas and in foreign countries. For many years Taney had pursued financial and managerial interests in state banks in Maryland and had served as counsel for such banks. He could be expected to be hostile to the Bank of the United States with its vast coercive power operating largely with non-Maryland capital and managed from headquarters in Philadelphia. When in 1832 Congress presented to Jackson a bill to renew the charter, Taney urged him to veto it, and he wrote much of Jackson's veto message.

Taney's opinion urging the veto is interesting here for its legal strategy. Unlike some state-rights extremists he did not challenge the Supreme Court's decision in *McCulloch* v. *Maryland*[12] that Congress had the power to establish a bank to serve as its fiscal agent. But in accepting the decision he interpreted it to deprive friends of the bank of much of the comfort they had derived from it. In his mind the Court had committed itself but little beyond saying that Congress had power to establish a bank to serve as the fiscal agent of the government. Congress had power to establish a public corporation, he affirmed, a kind of corporation subject always to control of the government. But this did not mean that Congress had the power to establish what was in effect a private corporation and give to it powers and immunities as a private agency. It did not mean that the act establishing the Bank of the United States was constitutional in its entirety. The Supreme Court had not passed on that broad subject and had had no power to do so. Determination of whether or not particular powers and privileges and immunities were needed by the government's fiscal agent was a matter for Congress and not for the courts. It involved questions on which the courts were not equipped to pass. From this point Taney proceeded to the argument that much of the organization of the Bank of the United States was unconstitutional and that the President, in the exercise of his legislative power, ought to veto the bill to recharter the bank.[13]

We know that Taney won his political battle against the Bank of the United States, but only after ugly conflict. As for the impact of the controversy on his subsequent judicial attitudes, his desire to narrow the scope of federal judicial power and to leave vast power of unchecked constitutional interpretation in Congress may have yielded to greater confidence in judicial power when men of his own political and social philosophy came to dominate the Supreme Court—as witness the reaching-out for judicial power in the *Dred Scott* case. But the experience deepened his conviction that economic power should be exerted through local units rather than through gigantic concentrations of power whether supported by state or federal authority. He contended that governmental power, even when exercised to create private corporations, should have as its central aim promotion of the public welfare. He drove this point home in a memorandum drafted for the President shortly after his confirmation as Chief Justice in connection with the chartering of banks in the District of Columbia:

Every charter granted by a state or by the United States, to a bank or to any other company for the purposes of trade or manufacture, is a grant of peculiar privileges, and gives to the individuals who compose the corporation rights and privileges which are not possessed by other members of the community. It would be against the spirit of our free institutions, by which equal rights are intended to be secured to all, to grant peculiar franchises and privileges to a body of individuals merely for the purpose of enabling them more conveniently and effectually to advance their own private interests. No charter could rightfully be granted on that ground. The considerations upon which alone such peculiar privileges can be granted is the expectation and prospect of promoting thereby some public interest, and it follows from these principles that in every case where it is proposed to grant or to renew a charter the interests or wishes of the individuals who desire to be incorporated, ought not to influence the decision of the government. The only inquiry which the constituted authorities can properly make on such an application, is whether the charter applied for is likely to produce any real benefit to the community, and whether that benefit is sufficient to justify the grant.[14]

The same emphasis on the rights of the community and on the need for limiting the scope of government gift of privileges through incorporation appears in Taney's opinion in the *Charles River Bridge* case,[15] decided during his first term as Chief Justice. There, speaking for a majority of the Court, he rejected the plea of Daniel Webster and others for a broad interpretation of the charter so as to give a bridge company monopoly rights over transportation across the Charles River in the Boston area. With an eye upon a corporation that had gleaned rich profits from the Boston community he established the position that charter rights as against the state were to be construed narrowly. He declared:

... [T]he object and end of all government is to promote the happiness and prosperity of the community by which it is established; and it can never be assumed that the government intended to diminish its power of accomplishing the end for which it was created. And in a country like ours ... new channels of communication are daily found necessary, both for travel and trade, and are essential to the comfort, convenience and prosperity of the people. A state ought never to be presumed to surrender this power, because, like the taxing power, the whole community have an interest in preserving it undiminished.[16]

After elaborating the position that the flexibility of state action must not be presumed away through the broad interpretation of corporation charters he stated as follows his conviction that there must be a limit to the shaping of law for protection of existing rights of property: "While the rights of private property are sacredly guarded, we must not forget that the community also have rights, and that the happiness and well being of every citizen depends on their faithful preservation."[17]

One important implication of these materials and others to be presented hereafter is that in matters of legal and social philosophy Taney the Chief Justice was very much the same as Taney the citizen of Maryland and Attorney General of the United States. He was a man of deep convictions, convictions developed and established by his whole pattern of experience. Whether for good or evil, those convictions were basic to his interpretation of constitutional law.

Taney's constitutional attitudes found restatement in opinions as to the scope of the Commerce Clause. The commerce cases dealt primarily, not with the constitutionality of acts of Congress, but with the restraint which the grant of power to Congress implied for the exercise of state power over commerce. Were the states debarred from regulating interstate and foreign commerce even though Congress had not exercised its own power? Or was the power concurrent, so that a state might regulate interstate commerce within its borders so long as its regulations did not interfere with those of Congress? Was the carrying of persons commerce within the meaning of the Constitution? If it was commerce, might a state prohibit or restrict the immigration of aliens? Might it in the exercise of ts alleged concurrent power over interstate commerce stop at its borders slaves from other states? If not in the exercise of its commerce power, might a state exclude slaves from other states in the exercise of what were loosely called its police powers? In the exercise of one or the other of these types of power might a state, to preserve order among its own slaves, exclude free Negroes from other states, even in the face of the constitutional provision that citizens of each state should be entitled to the privileges and immunities of citizens of the several states?

These questions were all interrelated and they involved the underlying constitutional issues in which Taney was most deeply interested. To summarize his positions briefly, we can say that he believed a state had a substantive power to regulate interstate commerce; that the label of "police power" was not needed to validate state legislation in this field; that persons were not "subjects of commerce" within the meaning of the Constitution; that a state might exclude aliens; that a state might exclude slaves from other states; and that Negroes, even when free, were not "citizens" within the meaning of the Constitution and hence were not entitled to the constitutional privilege of going to and residing in other states.

Taney did not deny that the federal government protected important individual rights. Evidently speaking only of white people, he noted that "for all the great purposes for which the federal government was formed, we are one people, with one common country. We are all citizens of the United States; and, as members of the same community, must have the right to pass and repass through every part of it without interruption, as freely as in our own states."[18] But he contended that Congress could not prevent a state from expelling, and hence could not compel it initially to receive, "any person, or class of persons, whom it might deem dangerous to its peace, or likely to produce a physical or moral evil among its citizens. . . ."[19] In his interpretation of the "police powers" of the states, a term nowhere used in the Constitution and not hitherto much used in constitutional law, Taney seems to have wavered and shown some inconsistency,[20] developing a firm position only as he sensed the multiple implications of the use of the term. What may be regarded as his settled position was stated in the *License Cases*,[21] decided in 1847. He was defending there his position that the states had a substantive power to regulate interstate commerce within their borders in the absence of conflicting federal legislation. He objected to the contention that state quarantine and health laws were to be classified as passed "not by virtue of a power to regulate commerce, but by virtue of their police powers."[22] He objected to the distinction but thought that in any event the distinction was largely without substance. He explained as follows:

But what are the police powers of a state? They are nothing more or less than the powers of government inherent in every sovereignty to the extent of its dominions. And whether a state passes a quarantine law, or a law to punish offenses, or to establish courts of justice, or requiring certain instruments to be recorded, or to regulate commerce within its own limits, in every case it exercises the same power; that is to say, the power of sovereignty, the power to govern men and things within the limits of its dominion. It is by virtue of this power that it legislates; and its authority to make regulations of commerce is as absolute as its power to pass health laws, except insofar as it has been restricted by the Constitution of the United States. And when the validity of a state law making regulations of commerce is drawn into question in a judicial tribunal, the authority to pass it cannot be made to depend upon motives that may be supposed to have influenced the legislature, nor can the court inquire whether it was intended to guard the citizens of the state from pestilence and disease, or to make regulations of commerce for the interests and convenience of trade.[23]

Taney was saying, in short, that within the range of its reserved powers a state might enact constitutional laws without reference to the sanctifying label of "police power," or that if that label were to be used, it could be interpreted to cover not merely statutes dealing with preserving health and public order but all legislation deriving from the state's sovereign power. His major concern was in preserving the broad powers of the states as he conceived of those powers. He was trying to protect the states against the conscious or unconscious efforts of nationalists to drive them into the position of governments with merely delegated powers, powers labeled as "police." The full implication of that which he feared did not become apparent until some decades after the end of his term of office, when the concept of police power was used to protect such residue of state powers as judges sought to preserve, not merely against the federal commerce power but, more important, against the Due Process Clause of the Fourteenth Amendment.

In appearance at least, and probably with full sincerity, Taney as Chief Justice adhered to the position taken in 1832 that an interpretation of the Constitution given by the Supreme Court at a particular time was not necessarily binding for all the future. When in 1849 certain of the Justices challenged the validity of an opinion of the Court written in 1837, Taney remarked that he was "quite willing that it be regarded hereafter as the law of this court, that its opinion upon the construction of the Constitution is always open to discussion when it is supposed to have been founded in error, and that its judicial authority should hereafter depend altogether on the force of the reasoning by which it is supported."[24] But however much the Court might reconsider what it had previously said about the meaning of the Constitution, any changes that took place were changes merely in judicial positions, and not changes in the meaning of the Constitution itself. For Taney the Constitution was not an evolving document. In the *Dred Scott* case he said flatly that, while the Constitution remained unaltered, "it must be construed now as it was understood at the time of its adoption. It is not only the same in words, but the same in meaning . . . and as long as it continues to exist in its present form, it speaks not only in the same words, but with the same meaning and intent with which it spoke when it came from the hands of its framers, and was voted on and adopted by the people of the United States."[25]

We may note that at this time, in 1857, the Constitution was used to guard the rights of the states and particularly the rights of the South. In 1859, in the *Booth* cases,[26] it was used in defense of the powers of the federal government, on the one hand, and the rights of the South, on the other, when the state of Wisconsin attempted nullification of the federal fugitive slave law. In speaking for the Court, Taney presented a fine portrayal of our federal system—something he was eminently well equipped to do when not handicapped by the pressure of local loyalties. His picture was that of the people of the states working harmoniously together, acting through the states in local matters and through the federal government in matters delegated to it—in which the return of fugitive slaves was included. No mention was made of the issues of the Hartford Convention of more than forty years earlier, which had so enraged Taney, or of the South Carolina nullification threat when Taney was Attorney General, about which he had made no public commitment. The decision, based on a concept of balanced federalism, was a brilliant and clear elucidation of the federal system.

Yet enemy though he was of nullification or secession on the part of northern states or groups of states, Taney at times expressed the fear that secession in the South would not be attempted or would not be successful. In 1856, speculating on the possibility that Buchanan might be defeated for the Presidency, he thought it mattered little whether Fremont or Fillmore would be elected. He lamented the fact that

there will be no dissolution of the Union in either event. The Constitution will undoubtedly be trampled under foot, and the Union will be one of power and weakness, like the Union of England and Ireland or Russia and Poland. But how can the southern states divide, with any hope of success . . . with a powerful enemy in their midst? I grieve over this condition of things, but it is my deliberate opinion that the South is doomed, and that nothing but a firm united action, nearly unanimous in every state, can check northern insult and northern aggression.[27]

In 1861, after military hostilities had begun, Taney expressed to Franklin Pierce the hope "that the North, as well as the South, will see that a peaceful separation, with free institutions in each section, is far better than the union of all the present states under a military government, and a reign of terror preceded too by a civil war with all its horrors, and which end as it may will prove ruinous to the victors as well as to the vanquished."[28]

In his opinion in the *Merryman* case[29] in 1861, holding that the President had no power to suspend the privilege of the writ of habeas corpus, Taney delivered a magnificent portrayal of liberty as defended under the constitutional system. In his message to the special session of Congress called to support the war cause, President Lincoln replied indirectly, noting the protest that one sworn to execute the laws should not himself violate them. He thought there had been no violation. But, he explained:

> The whole of the laws which were required to be faithfully executed were being resisted and failing of execution in nearly one-third of the states. Must they be allowed to finally fail of execution, even had it been perfectly clear that by the means necessary to their execution some single law, made in such extreme tenderness of the citizen's liberty that practically it relieves more of the guilty than of the innocent, should to a very limited extent be violated?[30]

In their respective ways, both the Chief Justice and the President were defenders of the Constitution. Taney clearly expounded a doctrine of constitutional restraint on the arbitrary exercise of governmental power. Believing that the federal government had already destroyed or was about to destroy the Union as a union of states with local sovereignty in local matters, and that northern military coercion of the South would violate the very essence of the constitutional system, he could in apparently good conscience remain as Chief Justice of the United States while hoping that secession of the South would be accepted. To Lincoln there could be no Constitution without the Union. Preservation of the Union came first, to be followed by all possible effort to apply the principles of the Constitution for defense of the rights of all the people in all the states. Although Lincoln did not believe that the nation could permanently survive half slave and half free, and he believed passionately that freedom was the more desirable goal, he had had no intention of making a governmental on-slaught on the institution of slavery; and whatever steps he might have taken in that direction in the absence of a civil war would have been taken in harmony with constitutional principles—as he understood those principles. But, faced with a war and possible destruction of the Union, he was deter-mined to save the Union by any means necessary to that end, apparently believing that when survival of the Union was at stake almost any means was constitutional. Given their differ-ing assumptions, it is not surprising that neither the Chief Justice nor the President could see the constitutional issues through the eyes of the other.

In the face of the war issues, Taney lacked that dispassion-ateness which we consider an ideal for the Supreme Court. He showed the same zest for conflict that had characterized his struggle with the Bank of the United States in the 1830's. Reading the criticism of his *Dred Scott* opinion and learning that some lower federal courts were refusing to accept his holding that Negroes could not be citizens within the meaning of the Constitution, he wrote a long supplement to the opinion, which was published many years later in his authorized biog-raphy.[31] Although few of the important constitutional issues of the war reached the Court during his time, he formed opinions on some of them and even wrote out those opinions, either to clarify his own thinking or to have statements ready for use should cases come before the Court. One of his unused docu-ments found the Legal Tender Acts unconstitutional. Another held the conscription law unconstitutional. Another dealt simi-larly with the Proclamation of Emancipation.[32] He was com-pletely out of sympathy with the expansion of governmental power for the purpose of winning the war, and he would have used his judicial position to curb that expansion had it been possible to do so.

How, then, in final analysis, are we to appraise Taney as

Chief Justice of the United States? We can say that he brought to the Supreme Court a preoccupation with local welfare and local rights that had not hitherto characterized it. He believed in a federal system which gave to the federal government genuine authority but not authority enough to coerce a uniform pattern of life. He believed in regionalism within the national pattern and apparently assumed that the essence of good living, which the Constitution was intended to protect, was to be found in the relations of people in their local communities. Had he been able to embody such political and social theory in Supreme Court opinions without involvement in the almost frantically emotional issue of slavery, he would have made a great contribution to our constitutional laws. Even in spite of the passions involved in the slavery issue, the emphasis which he and his brethren placed on state and local government provided a healthy antidote for the emphasis on nationalism in the Marshall Court. This is not to imply that either emphasis was wrong. Rather it implies that both were needed and that they were probably needed most in the order in which they made their appearance.

Taney's conception of the judicial function is subject to challenge insofar as it led him to employ the judicial process—as in the *Dred Scott* case—to attempt settlement of issues on which the people were fundamentally divided. We may contend that where discretion exists the judicial process should be used to apply only those principles and to effect only those settlements to which the people have given or may be expected to give support, at least to the extent of general acquiescence, and that fundamental division should be left to resolution by the political process. We may say that the Court, although the guardian of the constitutional system and of the liberties and rights conferred or protected under that system, should ordinarily leave resolution of rapidly changing issues to other branches of the government, reserving its own energies for the articulation of the constitutional pattern out of the deeper and more settled sentiments of the people. But if in this respect Taney and his brethren made too much effort to be timely, if they took or yearned to take upon themselves the settlement of current issues which they thought neglected or badly handled by other government agencies, they did not in this respect greatly differ from Justices in other eras, including that in which we now find ourselves. Others have assumed, as did Taney, that destiny has laid upon them vast current responsibilities—responsibilities which have proved too broad for exercise from within the limits of judicial office. This comment is not made for the purpose of exonerating Taney but to emphasize the fact that the essential nature of the judicial function and the limits of that function require periodic redefinition and restatement, for the benefit of judges as well as of the people.

We are compelled to look at the conflict of loyalties that led Taney to prefer the dissolution of the Union to its maintenance under the conditions then existing, and to remain in the office of Chief Justice while holding that preference. It may help to remember this: Taney lived in an era not yet ended—if such an era can ever end—wherein it was believed that behind and beneath the language of the Constitution, undefined but perceptible to the man of character and training and insight, lay a body of principles from which the correct interpretations of the Constitution and of all sound law were to be derived. William H. Seward characterized this body of principles as a "higher law than the Constitution." I have found in Taney's writings no quotations of similar import, but the broad pattern of his diverse opinions implies a similar belief in a natural law pattern of rightness. Taney's conduct in his later years is understandable primarily in terms of his conviction that not the South but the North violated principles of natural law and hence of the Constitution itself, making inevitable the attempt at disunion. It has seemed to me that his convictions were held in competition with an unadmitted sense of some kind of guilt; but if that guilt was there, it is impossible to tell whether it resulted from conflicts basically within himself or from the psychological pressures of a powerful and determined majority who disagreed with him—the kind of pressures that may create a combined sense of frustration and guilt in even the most self-righteous of defensive minorities.

We may well differ among ourselves with respect to Taney's acts and attitudes affecting slavery and disunion. It is hard to find stature in an American public figure who advocated or seemed to advocate the preservation of the South's "peculiar institution" of human slavery. We are convinced that freedom gives the maximum of opportunity for a good life and that the ownership of one person by another is always bad. It is hard for us to envisage the peacefulness and the richness of living, for black people and white people alike, that characterized life in the ancestral home of the Taneys and many other plantations of the South. But it is also hard to comprehend the seemingly self-willed blindness of Taney and other paternalistic Southerners who refused to look away from peaceful residential plantations to mass-production plantations of other kinds where Negroes were worked to death under the lash of ruthless overseers. To us it simply refuses to make ethical and moral sense, and we cannot see how it could have made sense to intelligent and honest people a century ago.

Another difficulty stands in the way of discriminating appraisal. The victorious tradition is rooted in Daniel Webster's eloquent peroration in the Webster-Hayne debate, "Liberty and Union, now and forever, one and inseparable." Believing in that tradition, we believe in the absolute rightness of our existence as an independent nation with jurisdiction over all the continental territory we have ever possessed. Although disastrous world crises drive us in the direction of leagues or unions of nations, we accept nations almost unquestioningly as the appropriate units for exercise of sovereignty over peoples. We develop uneasiness when we see the linkage between nationalism and the ugly phenomenon of communism in the world and when in the Orient we see it linked with western-developed technology to produce concentrations of power that may eventually destroy us; but for ourselves nationalism and centralized strength, developed and maintained at almost any cost, seem the primary desideratum. It is therefore hard for us to look into the mind of a Jefferson or a Taney and weigh sympathetically the belief that human welfare might be better served if differing communities lived together merely as good neighbors and not as areas subordinate to strong central power.

In his own time the country found Taney wrong, or at any rate the victorious and more articulate part of the country so found him. History condemned him, by incomplete quotation, as the Chief Justice who had said that the black man had no rights that the white man was bound to respect. By some he was condemned as the deliberate betrayer of the Union. The pall of condemnation hung over his name for many decades and has not altogether subsided to this day. I should like hesitantly to suggest that in addition to criticisms directly voiced we can sense evidence of unconscious condemnation even in the selection of pictures of Taney picked for public use. Although he was not a handsome man, there are portraits available that do not give the observer cold chills, portraits that do not remind one, as a colleague of mine at the Johns Hopkins University put it, of an "old goat,"[33] portraits that do not set a very human and in important respects a very worthy American statesman beyond the pale. Whatever the exact measure of Taney's desserts, that measure is well above the level suggested by the drooping and bedraggled figure in the usual portrait. For all the limitations of his training, his outlook, and his performance, he had outstanding qualities of statesmanship that demand respect. His limitations derived from a provincialism too rigid to expand to the scope of full national vision. That provincialism was more than narrowly shared; it flowered throughout a section large enough that it almost defeated the armed forces of the Union. His strength lay in his ability to see law not merely in terms of abstract and nationally applied principles but in terms also of the intimate life of the diverse communities which made up the United States of his day. Such vision is one of the vital needs of peoples all the time and everywhere. In this respect Taney as Chief Justice had upon him the mark of true greatness.

CARL BRENT SWISHER *is Thomas P. Stran Professor of Political Science at Johns Hopkins University. He has been a Walgreen Lecturer at the University of Chicago, Commonwealth Lecturer at University College, London, and Bacon Lecturer on the Constitution of the United States at Boston University. Among his books are* Stephen J. Field, *1930;* Roger B. Taney, *1935;* Selected Papers of Homer Cummings, *1939;* American Constitutional Development, *1943 (2d ed., 1954);* Growth of Constitutional Power in the United States, *1946;* Theory and Practice of American National Government, *1951;* The Supreme Court in Modern Role, *1958;* Historic Decisions of the Supreme Court, *1958.*

NOTES

1. *Cong. Globe,* 38th Cong., 2d sess., 1012 (1865).
2. P. 113 (1950).
3. Tyler, *Memoir of Roger Brooke Taney, LL.D.* (1872), p. 20.
4. *Ibid.,* p. 80.
5. Bank War Manuscript, Library of Congress.
6. Swisher, *Roger B. Taney* (1935), p. 148.
7. 2 Ops. Atty. Gen. 475 (1831).
8. Swisher, *op. cit.,* p. 152.
9. *Worcester* v. *Georgia,* 6 Pet. 515 (1832). See also *The Cherokee Nation* v. *Georgia,* 5 Pet. 1 (1831).
10. Hogan, *The Role of Chief Justice Taney in the Decision of the Dred Scott Case,* 58 CAS. & COM. 3 (1953).
11. *Dred Scott* v. *Sandford,* 19 How. 393, 404–5, 407 (1857).
12. 4 Wheat. 316 (1819).
13. See Swisher, *op. cit.,* pp. 190–93.

14. Jackson Manuscripts, under date of June 20, 1836, Library of Congress.

15. *Charles River Bridge* v. *Warren Bridge,* 11 Pet. 420 (1837).

16. *Ibid.* at 547–48.

17. *Ibid.* at 548.

18. *Passenger Cases,* 7 How. 283, 492 (1849).

19. *Ibid.* at 466.

20. See Crosskey, *Politics and the Constitution in the History of the United States* (1953), I, 154–55.

21. 5 How. 504, 582 (1847).

22. *Ibid.*

23. *Ibid.* at 583.

24. *Passenger Cases,* 7 How. 283, 470 (1849).

25. 19 How. at 426.

26. *Ableman* v. *Booth,* 21 How. 506 (1859).

27. Taney to J. Mason Campbell, October 2, 1856. The letter is set forth at greater length in Swisher, *op. cit.,* pp. 492–93.

28. *Ibid.,* p. 554.

29. Ex parte *Merryman,* Fed. Cas. No. 9,487 (1861).

30. Richardson, *Messages and Papers of the Presidents* (1900), VI, 25.

31. Tyler, *op. cit.,* pp. 578–605.

32. See Swisher, *op. cit.,* pp. 564–72.

33. [For less "goatlike" portraits than the one facing p. 35, see Swisher, *op. cit.*—EDS.]

Courtesy of Harris & Ewing

MR. JUSTICE BRADLEY

Mr. Justice Bradley

By
CHARLES FAIRMAN

In *The Formative Period of American Law,* published in 1938, Dean Pound listed the ten judges that he ranked higher than all others in American judicial history: John Marshall, James Kent, Joseph Story, John Bannister Gibson, Lemuel Shaw, Thomas Ruffin, Thomas McIntyre Cooley, Charles Doe, Oliver Wendell Holmes, and Benjamin Nathan Cardozo. Ten years later Professor Willard Hurst observed that it was always those ten names that cropped up in addresses to lawyers; he had an "uneasy suspicion that all of the solemn judgments . . . come back to that one list which Dean Pound gave us."[1]

Pound's belief in the intellectual validity of studying legal history and judicial biography and Hurst's chiding of lawyers for not interpreting such history and biography anew ought to give pause to those who have neglected it. The reading of judicial history and biography is, I think, worth the while not merely of lawyers, to whom it is a part of mastering their profession, but also of intelligent, responsible citizens in general, by whom the history of a nation under constitutional law cannot be completely understood otherwise.

It is important to learn what has been said and done by and about the influential jurists, but it is equally important to reinterpret their history in a contemporary context. To understand how law has responded to changing human needs is to understand how new policies, in Justice McKenna's phrase, "pass from militancy to triumph or from question to repeal."[2] He who does understand is better able to evaluate contemporary

65

tendencies and to avoid the lament, common in every generation, "The Constitution as we knew it is gone!" Moreover, an
idea of the strength—and limitations—of American judges leads
to an appreciation of the quality of American justice.

The practical question, how or if judicial history is to be
taught in the schools, need not be answered or even asked
here. So many men have acquired an expert's familiarity with
matters in which they have never been tutored! The practical
reward of knowing judicial biography is obvious: the great
jurists are wise counsellors.

Such a man was Justice Joseph P. Bradley, one of the three
most important figures in a crucial period of the Supreme
Court's history. He sat on the Court from 1870 to 1892, Justice
Samuel Freeman Miller, the second of the three, from 1862 to
1890, and Stephen J. Field, the third, from 1863 to 1897. They
were the giants of those days. After the Civil War came the
western railroads and an economic expansion from which
many of our Commerce Clause problems spring. Bradley was
a strong nationalist and a great figure in the law of the Commerce Clause. Out of the war came the Reconstruction amendments—notably the Fourteenth—the interpretive history of
which has recently become a lively topic within the Court and
without. Chief Justice Warren, speaking for all the Justices in
the *School Segregation* cases,[3] pointed out the "inconclusive
nature of the Amendment's history" with respect to the question
there involved.

For eleven years Justice Bradley held the Fifth Circuit—ex-
tending then as now from Georgia to Texas—and there met
many of the hardest Reconstruction cases, including the
Slaughter House case,[4] in first instance. The decade of the
seventies was a period when Republican Congresses created
new federal rights and opened the federal courts more widely
to litigants. Bradley never held back from the expansion of
federal justice. Later, when Justice Holmes was attacking the
doctrine of *Swift* v. *Tyson*,[5] an effort that ultimately triumphed

in *Erie Railroad* v. *Tompkins*,[6] he rightly looked back upon Bradley as having perpetuated and extended the doctrine.[7] In the vigor of his intellect, in his complete mastery of his profession, and in the wide range of his thought, Bradley was a great Justice. There have been few from whom one can learn so much.

Bradley was born on March 14, 1813, on a farm in the Helderberg Mountains, sixteen miles west of Albany, New York. His forebears were of early Colonial stock. His parents had married at seventeen; Joe was the eldest of their twelve children. Here was a tightly knit family group of four generations living on small, adjacent farms. At his grandparents' hearth the lad listened to stories of the Revolution and imbibed the Bible and the Book of Common Prayer in the conversation of the household. He shared in the plowing and sowing, the mowing and pitching, that were the routine of the farm. In his early teens he helped to clear the land and to market the charcoal and the tanbark thus produced. (I am paraphrasing and summarizing an autobiographical sketch he wrote for his children.)

In the midst of it all, he read books—histories, travel, narratives, theology, mathematics. An uncle, three or four miles away, kept the town library, and there Joe Bradley would often spend his Sundays. He learned practical surveying, at which he made a dollar a day when he was employed.

An incident that became, as he looked back, one of the significant episodes of his life is described in the autobiographical sketch:

When I was fourteen or fifteen years of age a mathematical question went the round of our country schools and nobody could solve it—or, in our parlance, nobody could "*do the sum.*" Now "*to do any sum*" that was propounded was one of the objects of my highest ambition. But this one long defied my skill. . . . It was really an Algebraical problem, not properly solvable by Arithmetic. I worked upon it at spare times, for more than a year; and, at last, solved it, and propounded the rule for solving all like questions. . . . I was naturally very much elated. Amongst my country friends,

I had one a few years older than myself, who had the good fortune to be a student in the Albany Academy. In my simplicity, I sent the problem to him, asking him to propose it there. To my utter surprise and mortification, by the return mail came a letter from him with an algebraical solution. . . . I said to myself, if Algebra is such a wonderful thing as this . . . I will know something about it. A relative had recently purchased Bonnycastle's Algebra at a book stand in Albany. I heard of it, and walked five miles to borrow it; and hardly ate, drank or slept until I knew that book from beginning to end. This was in December, 1828, whilst I was engaged in teaching my first school.

The experience confirmed him in one of the most marked traits of his character, the habit of pursuing every question to the ultimate truth of the matter. Whatever the challenge, he wrestled until he prevailed. No wonder, as Cortland Parker said in his memorial remarks, throughout life Justice Bradley had "little or no deference for the mere opinion of others."[8]

I sometimes reflect upon what, it seems to me, is a significant contrast in the practice of the law. In the courtroom the law imposes severe tests in its insistence upon the most reliable evidence. Yet in some other aspects of the law, how credulous lawyers are. One writes a book, and lo, he becomes an authority. How often a court is invited to accept some professor's statement about the past, based, perhaps, upon shaky evidence that would never stand up against rigorous examination. Too readily the reader studying a decision accepts the court's summary of a statute involved without looking to the full text as set out in the session laws. How much supposing and theorizing is done about great cases, by commentators who have never studied the transcript of record, never examined the briefs to see what counsel had been urging, never felt any curiosity why this particular case was brought up at this time, never related the litigation to the objectives—usually economic objectives—of the interested parties. Often I surmise that if they could hear the conclusions imagined by writers who never schooled themselves to get to the bottom, the Justices of the past, like the dumbfounded Mortimer Snerd, might exclaim "No!"

To realize Bradley as a skeptical, tough, relentless person, pushing to the very truth and reason of things, consider farm life in the 1820's. All the food was raised at home: breadstuffs, meat, even sugar, which was drawn from the maple trees. So too all articles of clothing. When Joe Bradley went to college, he wore a homespun suit cut out and made by his mother. As Cortland Parker recalled of Bradley's first day at Rutgers, "Lincoln himself in his early youth was not much stranger. . . ."[9] It was a moneyless economy, isolated and self-contained. To realize how different it was from the present economic life, one has only to recall the plight of New York farmers in the depression of the 1930's, a hundred years after Bradley. Specialized as dairy farmers by that time, they suffered because security was beyond the control of the individual, as it is today. In the autobiographical sketch, Bradley tells how he made his own way in the age of individualism:

Whilst my father and I were threshing out the buckwheat crop one day [in the autumn of 1831] the desire for an education became so strong that I broke out in a way I had never done before to my poor father. I told him that my life was being wasted . . . that I felt that I *must* have an education. He said, "I cannot afford to give you an education." I said, I did not expect him to do it; but if he would let me go (I was then over 18) I would somehow obtain an education myself; and I would fully make up to him the loss of my unexpired time before coming of age. . . .

Bradley went down to Albany to take the boat to New York, where he hoped to find a clerkship and save enough money to return to the academy at Albany. At that moment the river froze! Bradley remained at Albany a few days. He poured over volumes in the state library. He visited the legislature, and heard John C. Spencer, a fine lawyer and later a member of the Cabinet, discuss the Revised Statutes. "I was greatly charmed by his clear logic and elegant diction," Bradley recalled. "It was my first initiation into the mysteries of the law."

So the lad took the stage back to Berne, where he was received into the home of the "dominie" of the Reformed Dutch Church, to be prepared for college. This meant mastering Latin and Greek. In 1833 he entered Rutgers, where he distinguished himself and in three years graduated in the same class with Frederick T. Frelinghuysen, the future Senator and Secretary of State, and Cortland Parker, who became the leader of the New Jersey bar and in 1883 president of the American Bar Association.

The three youths read law at Newark with Frelinghuysen's Uncle Theodore, the "Christian Statesman" and Whig leader. Bradley supported himself by working in a lawyer's office. "On Wednesday evening, November 13, 1839," so he recorded, "I was examined, at Trenton, before the Justices of the Supreme Court of New Jersey, on application for license to practice law; and on the next day, licensed and admitted to practice as an attorney at law and solicitor in chancery. . . ."[10]

How had Bradley prepared for his profession? "I adopted my own course of study," he recalled, "and frequently had mutual examinations with Frelinghuysen. Of course we mastered Blackstone and Kent."[11] Of the various works Bradley listed, Kent's *Commentaries* was the only one written on the American side of the Atlantic. There is no mention of Story: his treatises, in the main, came too late for Bradley's clerkship. For real property, he relied on Blackstone, but he had constantly at hand Cruise's Digest, Coke on Littleton, and the Statutes and Reports of New Jersey. "[T]he true mode of treating legal subjects," Cruise had written in his preface, "is by a systematic distribution of abstract principles, illustrated and supported by adjudged cases." So the holdings were woven into the text, the cases were cited in the margin, and certainly Bradley looked them up. Chitty on Contracts and Chitty on Bills and Notes were studied; also "many of the articles in Bacon's Abridgement," presumably the first American edition, of 1811. On the procedural side, the studies were heavy with antique learning. With New Jersey Statutes and Reports at hand for comparison, he worked through such then standard books as Sergeant Sellon's *Practice,* in the Preface of which, if he had the 1823 edition, doubtless he read that "[t]he obscurity and expense which necessarily attend the conduct of a *Suit at Law* . . . have long been the subject of complaints" by clients and by conscientious practitioners. Bradley was ever a black-letter man, and I suppose that his concern as a student was rather to master the intricacies of procedure than to imagine rational reforms. "Old Chief Baron Gilbert's little work on *Evidence* I not only studied and re-studied, but made a careful analysis and index of the work."[12] Gilbert's book first appeared in 1754. Perhaps Bradley used the seventh edition, Philadelphia, 1805. How much more rapid is the course of law today than it was when Bradley was an apprentice; how old were many of the books he used, as contrasted with the frequent revisions of materials and the still more frequent pocket supplements of today.

Bradley studied the Roman law as well as the works of modern civilians such as Pothier on Obligations. Kent's eclectic discussion invited such comparative study. Hoffman's influential book, *A Course of Legal Study,* urged that a knowledge of Roman law was "essential to legal preeminence," and reported a growing interest "among some young students of expanded views, and of liberal education."[13] Bradley certainly had "expanded views." His commonplace books were filled with annotations, wherein he sought an underlying reason and principle by drawing together the Roman and the common-law authorities. Through the years of clerkship and then of practice he made revisions and transferred the improved notes to a new journal. Recall the sentence, "I adopted my own course of study." Only by assuming a personal responsibility for one's own education, I suggest, can one ultimately attain a real mastery.

Early in 1839, while still reading law, Bradley made a visit to Washington, where of course he attended the Supreme Court. That was early in Taney's Chief Justiceship. By good fortune he heard the argument in *Bank of Augusta* v. *Earle*,[14] the great case on the position of an out-of-state corporation. He heard David B. Ogden, John Sergeant, Charles J. Ingersoll, Daniel Webster—the very distinguished counsel engaged in that case. (Exactly seventeen years later, in 1856, Bradley himself stood before the Court to argue his first case at that bar: *Murray* v. *Hoboken Land Co.*,[15] made memorable by Justice Curtis' discussion of the meaning of due process.)

Where was he to hang his shingle? Bradley decided to remain at Newark, where he was offered a junior partnership by the secretary and attorney of the New Jersey Railroad. "I never lacked employment in my profession," he records. "My connection with railroad cases took its origin from that partnership, and brought me to the notice of the Camden and Amboy, and Morris and Essex Companies,—from which I afterwards received frequent employment."

Thus Bradley became a "railroad lawyer." From the beginning of his career until his appointment to the Court, his most important client was Camden and Amboy.[16] He was drawn into the management as well as the legal work, being made secretary of the board and member of the executive committee. "Camden and Amboy" was a hateful name throughout the land, for it represented a monopoly in transportation across New Jersey and it represented privilege accorded to the Stevens and Stockton families by a docile and managed legislature. When the Civil War came, and greater facilities were demanded for movement between New York and Washington, powerful rival interests sought a federal right of way across New Jersey. Bradley was kept busy before congressional committees and in the courts warding off this threat. The Pennsylvania Railroad, seeking access to New York, was obliged to depend upon the New Jersey facilities. In 1871, the Pennsylvania obtained this property on a lease for 999 years; but in 1870, when Bradley's nomination came before the Senate, Pennsylvania's interest had not been made secure. Senator Cameron, representing Pennsylvania and the Pennsylvania Railroad, was unwilling to see the Camden and Amboy lawyer go on the Court unless Bradley would commit himself as supporting congressional power on certain points. Bradley was confirmed over Cameron's opposition, and his confirmation was the true root of a great to-do over "packing the Court," about which a lot of ill-considered things were said by politicians and later by historians.

When young Bradley began practice, Newark was an expanding city. In 1845, just as the earliest life insurance companies in the United States were getting started, the Mutual Benefit Company was established at Newark. For twelve years Bradley served as its mathematician. There were novel actuarial problems to solve, but his command of mathematics was adequate to their solution. Manufacturers were thriving. Newark produced for the southern market, and in political sympathy it was Democratic. Bradley, surrounded in Newark by factories, followed intelligently the progress of applied mechanics. Because of his wide experience—in transportation, in insurance, in business and industry—he later brought to the Court a fine working acquaintance with practical affairs. Only Justice Brandeis, I suppose, has been his equal in that respect.

Bradley practiced extensively in the federal courts. Justice Grier, who had the Third Circuit, held him in high esteem; and when Grier finally had to retire—an event he fended off for years—he was well content to anticipate having Bradley as his successor. In a half-dozen cases Bradley appeared before the Supreme Court. In addition to participating in *Murray* v. *Hoboken Land Co.*, Bradley took part in *Milnor* v. *New Jersey R.R.*,[17] which tested the validity of state legislation authorizing a bridge over a navigable stream. Bradley, defending the statute, had won Judge Grier's decision in the Circuit Court;

the Supreme Court, equally divided, affirmed without opinion. In 1866, in *Gilman* v. *Philadelphia*,[18] the Court established the validity of state bridge laws. It had been one of the hard problems of the Commerce Clause.

"Not slothful in business; fervent in spirit . . ."—the young lawyer observed both branches of the biblical injunction. From the moment he had money to spend, he bought really good books—chiefly history and literature, ancient and modern—and knew them as the records of human aspiration. In 1844 he was married to the youngest daughter of Joseph C. Hornblower, Chief Justice of New Jersey. Home life was as he had pictured it: a growing family; evenings and Sundays given to good reading and serious conversation; a refuge from the world's striving. It was Mary Bradley who made this happiness; she devoted herself to a husband who never learned to be patient. Professional success made increasing demands. In 1857 Bradley's account was: "My days are filled with toil and anxiety. Of business I have as much as I can do, and more. . . . The Spirit life, I fear, is not as prosperous as the worldly life. . . ."[19]

A lawyer is expected, on occasion, to make speeches, and his speeches record soundings of depth or shallowness. Bradley's measure may be taken by the manuscripts and notes he saved form the late forties and early fifties. What has America done? he asked in a Fourth of July address at Newark. It has sought, through law and government, "the unimpeded, unrestrained, free, development of the *individual man.*" It has sought to protect each man in "the enjoyment of all the natural liberty compatible with mutual security." It is pertinent to recall that speech when one considers the *Slaughter House* cases. This pursuit of individual improvement requires enlightenment, toward which he emphasized universal public education as a cardinal principle. He gave his conception of religious liberty and of civil liberty: "In religion each man is to be and ought to be his own judge of what is right and wrong. With civil liberty it is not so. In society every man's conduct concerns and affects others as well as himself. To make each one judge of his own case would be impossible, and wrong." These were not rationalizations of the interests of great corporate clients, for property was not a theme on which he dwelt. He stressed the importance of mutual security under government: every man's conduct affects his fellows.

The principle was practiced when Bradley played a major part in the decision of *Munn* v. *Illinois*,[20] sustaining rate regulation in the grain elevators at Chicago. Among the dangers that Bradley saw threatening American institutions was "Corruption in social life," under which he noted these points: Luxury; Effeminancy; the conception of "Born Gentlemen." Another danger was "Corruption in politics," in relation to which one may cite Bradley's fine opinion in Ex parte *Siebold*,[21] in 1880, sustaining the power of Congress to lay its own penalties upon state election officers who act corruptly in national elections. It was "an incontrovertible principle," he said, that the government of the United States may "execute on every foot of American soil the powers and functions that belong to it." This sustained the first comprehensive federal legislation to regulate elections.

Although Justice Bradley had a just appreciation of the great monuments of English law, he venerated the institutions of Rome. (This stood him in good stead when on his circuit he had occasion to apply the civil law.) As to the England of his own day, he deplored its pomp and splendor, its landed aristocracy, and its "more than Tyrian wealth" that caused misery and ignorance among the classes oppressed by the unjust social system. (Today, a century later, an American can no longer complain that the English are laggard in social reform!)

Bradley looked forward to the great American nation that would draw from "so many traditions and grand histories" that it would achieve "a fusion of the best laws and institutions of all lands—the Hebrew, the Indian, the Greek, the Roman, and the Gothic—embracing the Divine Law, the Law of Nations, and the Civil, Common, and Canon Laws."[22] His spirit responded to the "splendid passage" from Cicero's *Republic:* "There is a true law, a right reason, conformable to nature, given to all men . . . neither the Senate nor the People can absolve from its dictates. . . . It is not one thing at Rome and another at Athens, one thing today and another tomorrow; but it is one uniform, perpetual, immutable law, comprehending all peoples, at all times. . . ."[23] This last sentence had been adopted by Justice Story, via Lord Mansfield, in *Swift* v. *Tyson.*[24] In fact, Bradley copied out the passage from Cicero and sent it for the instruction of his youngest son at a moment when there had been submitted to the Court a commercial law case[25] in which presently the Justices reaffirmed the doctrine of *Swift* v. *Tyson.*

With the coming of the Civil War, Bradley's public speaking was directed to the great issues of that struggle. His central theme was the complete adequacy of the national government to all the exigencies of the conflict and its aftermath. In 1862 he ran unsuccessfully for Congress in a strongly Democratic district. In the election of 1868 he was a candidate for presidential elector and defended "the measures of the great Union party," with specific mention of "the National legal tender."

The course of appointment to the Supreme Court seldom runs smooth. Bradley's case was especially complicated, as I have traced elsewhere.[26] President Grant had two vacancies to fill, and he nominated William Strong of Pennsylvania and Bradley. Strong was confirmed first and asigned to the Third Circuit. Eight southern Republicans opposed Bradley, hoping for the nomination of some Republican from the South. Senator Cameron of Pennsylvania opposed for the practical reasons I have indicated. They were the only ones who voted against confirmation.

In *Hepburn* v. *Griswold,*[27] decided on the very day when Strong and Bradley were nominated, the Court, by vote of four to three, held the Legal Tender Act unconstitutional.

When the two new Justices came on the bench, Attorney-General Hoar sought, in cases awaiting decision, to obtain a prompt overruling. In the *Hepburn* opinion the reasoning of the majority dwelt upon the consideration that this was a debt contracted prior to the passage of the Legal Tender Act. They stressed the injustice of a legal tender law as it applies to pre-existing debts. But on the basic question of the power of Congress to give its paper money the quality of legal tender, surely the hardship of its operation did not go to the existence of the power. A declaration of war works even greater hardship. The five Justices of the new majority profoundly believed that the constitutional power of the national government did extend to the enactment of a legal tender law. They stood firm. Here is what Justice Miller wrote in a private letter one month after Bradley's confirmation:

> We have had a desperate struggle in the secret conference of the court for three weeks over two cases involving the legal tender question. The Chief Justice [Chase] has resorted to all the stratagems of the lowest political trickery to prevent their being heard, and the fight has been bitter in the conference room. Finally the new judges and the minority in Hepburn v. Griswold having withstood all assaults public and private, when the cases were called for argument yesterday, the Appellants dismissed their appeal. . . .
>
> The excitement has nearly used me up. It has been fearful; and my own position as leader in marshalling my forces, and keeping up their courage, against a domineering Chief, and a party in court who have been accustomed to carry everything their own way, has been such a strain on my brain and nervous system as I never wish to encounter again.[28]

In *Knox* v. *Lee*,[29] decided on May 1, 1871, the legal tender question was reopened, and the power of Congress was established by the new majority. On mature consideration, in 1884 the Court sustained the power of Congress to pass a legal tender law even without the aid of the war power.[30]

There were two distinct problems before the new majority of five. One was the constitutionality of the legal tender law. A good argument could be made on either side of that question, but the five were firm in believing theirs was the better view, and, on that, history has confirmed. But then there was a further question of judicial prudence: Should the Justices of the new majority submerge their own strong views in deference to the *Hepburn* precedent? That case had been decided by only four of seven Justices, on a day when there were two vacancies. Consistently with the practice announced by Marshall in 1834,[31] it was improper to declare the law invalid by the vote of less than the majority of a full bench. In truth, the four Justices had sought to snatch a quick decision, well knowing that the two new appointees—whoever they might be—would probably be disposed to sustain the war measure. Thus on the question of judicial propriety, I think it was the four, not the five, who should be blamed for the unfortunate incident.

While poking in closets, one may as well take up the Electoral Commission of 1877. There were rival returns from some states. Should the electoral votes for Hayes be counted, or those for Tilden? A commission was created to decide: five Senators; five Representatives; four Justices designated by Circuit and a fifth to be selected by the four. The fifth would no doubt have been Justice David Davis, had not the Democrats of the Illinois legislature suddenly caused him to be elected to the Senate. Thus the unwelcome task was cast upon Bradley. In the outcome, on substantive questions he voted with the Republicans. There was a commotion, but if the decision had been for Tilden, there would have been a commotion anyway. In all the discussion of the event, hardly any serious attention had been given to the question on which Justice Bradley had to make up his mind: What was the law of the case? One must go back to determine, according to the law of the state, what is the organ by which the state declares its vote. But the Democrats—normally the states' rights party—took a lofty national view and argued that federal authority should go beyond state authority in determining the nature of that organ.

I must not attempt here to explore the legal question that has been neglected since 1877. I will merely quote a letter written by Justice Bradley on October 28, 1882—a letter that has never, so far as I know, appeared in print. He was replying to Henry B. Dawson, a disappointed ex-Republican, a free-lance historian of "revisionist" tendencies, and a pugnacious gentleman. Here is Bradley's reply:

DEAR SIR:

I admire your out and out spoken manner of expressing your sentiments with regard to the Electoral Commission. But I want to put in a word in my own vindication. So far as I was concerned I took the subject up for consideration as a pure judicial question. I envied the other members who all, seven on one side, and seven on the other, seemed to have no difficulty in reaching a conclusion; whilst to me the questions raised were perplexing and difficult in the highest degree. I gained all the time for examination and reflection which I decently could. I heard every member (in the private conference) express their views at large; and then, in a short opinion, which you will find in the book, gave the conclusions to which I had come. I believe Justice Clifford read his opinion after mine; but we all knew what his opinion was. I speak now of the Florida case, which was the first and the test case. The great question was, whether the members of the two houses, when assembled to hear the count of votes for President and Vice President, could go behind the returns, (not of the electors), but of the elections of the electors, and institute a scrutiny into the original elections; or, whether the action of the state authorities on that subject was final. I came to the latter conclusion. So far as I am capable of judging my own motives, I did not allow political, that is, party, considerations to have any weight whatever in forming my conclusion. I know that it is difficult for men of the world to believe this, but I know it, and that is enough for me. And upon a careful review of the whole subject, I am still of the opinion that my conclusion was right. And, moreover, I have had the assurances of eminent Democrats that they concurred with me in my opinion.

During the anxious period that the Commission was in session, I allowed no one to approach me upon the subjects under discussion, except on one or two occasions Judge Field, a member of the

Commission, called at my house on a Sunday, and adverted to the questions at issue, but we entered into no extended discussion. I received almost every day, after delivering the first opinion, threatening letters of the coarsest and most vengeful character. But I did not feel any great alarm, because I supposed that dogs which bite do not usually bark.

I have now given you a very brief, but exact, description of my part in that great drama. I have done so because I do not like to be misunderstood and misjudged by those whose opinion I esteem.

But, let it pass. If I have the ill-fortune to be unjustly judged, I am not the first who has been in that predicament. We must take the world as it is, and having done what we conceived to be our duty, trust the rest to a higher power than that [that] rules the ordinary affairs of man in society.

In 1878, on the eighth anniversary of his coming to the bench, Bradley wrote this comment to his sister: "They have been eight years of hard work for poor pay, and immense gratuitous and unfounded abuse. Public life, in this country, is a gauntlet through which one passes subject to be struck at by every villain that chooses to do it."[32]

Early in May, 1870—as soon as the Supreme Court adjourned—Bradley started on his circuit. He held his first court at Galveston. The impression he left is preserved in the words of the leader of the local bar, William P. Ballinger, who wrote to his brother-in-law Justice Miller:

Justice Bradley held court here nearly three weeks. . . . [H]e did a great deal of business, holding court several days until nearly dark. He was a new dispensation to us—contrasting very strongly with our manner of judges for a long time past. I like him extremely—and that was the sentiment of the Bar. He is a thorough ready lawyer, and the most complete *business man* I have ever seen on the bench—becomes the perfect master of the case, down to its minutiae, with a facility and dexterity very admirable. His anxiety to get through here rendered him a little impatient in some instances; but he seemed ready to admit any mistake into which he might fall, and commanded the utmost confidence of the bar. We were unprepared—didn't expect him to do anything—and I was conscious that the Bar didn't show to good advantage, professionally, before him; but still I think, he was pleased with its deportment and judged favorably of its ability.

Ineptitude, clumsiness, fuzziness in conception or in performance—these to Bradley were cardinal sins. To illustrate,
I quote from a letter written from New Orleans to his daughter:

> I started to go to Church at Savannah, the first Sunday I was
> there, and not being able to walk the distance, took the horse car.
> I requested the driver to put me down at Broad Street, (in which
> the best Presbyterian preaching was to be had); but the stupid
> fool, (who makes me mad every time I think of him since) put me
> out at Broughton Street, which had nothing but an Episcopal
> Church in it. . . . This accident had such an effect on my temper,
> that I have not made the attempt to go to church since. . . .[33]

Four weeks had passed, but the Justice's Sabbath anger still
kept him from going to church! Bradley couldn't abide silly
errors, in himself or in others. Mrs. Bradley devoted her life
to protecting the Justice from irritation.

On this point—how unreasonable at times could be this
Justice who on the bench sought the perfection of reason—I
quote from the recollections of a distinguished Washington
lawyer, now dead:

> I remember Mr. James H. McKenney [the Clerk of the Supreme
> Court] telling me an amusing story about his irascible disposition.
> On one occasion he and Mrs. Bradley were going to the old Sixth
> Street Depot to take a Baltimore and Potomac train for New York.
> Mrs. Bradley kept the Justice waiting so that they missed the train
> by insisting that he change his clothes and put on a brand new pair
> of trousers. On the return to the house, he was found with a pen
> knife in his hand slashing the new trousers to shreds and mumbling
> "you will never compel me to miss another train."[34]

I return to Justice Bradley on his progress through his circuit, in 1870. At New Orleans he found the *Slaughter House*
litigation awaiting him. In 1869 the Republican legislature had
passed a law, ostensibly "to protect the health of the city of
New Orleans," whereby a favored group got a twenty-five-year
monopoly on the abattoir business. It was a thoroughly bad
carpetbag measure. Said the *New Orleans Picayune:*

> Those speculative gentlemen who framed the slaughter-house
> act, though they exhibited no little shrewdness in obtaining its

passage . . . forgot that it is always extremely hazardous to speculate on the necessities of a people, and that the people still have rights which it is impossible for a State Legislature to deprive them of.[35]

What rights, against the state legislation? John A. Campbell, who had left the Supreme Court when the South seceded, invoked the new Fourteenth Amendment. He sought to turn this shield about so that it would protect the people of the South against victimization by the Republican carpetbaggers. The state supreme court sustained the monopoly statute. Bradley, as Circuit Justice, allowed writs of error to the Supreme Court. That was on May 13, 1870. But the state courts did not recognize the allowance of those writs of error as effecting a supersedeas.[36] Thus when Bradley arrived in New Orleans, counsel for the butchers sought a federal injunction against further state court proceedings. That had to be denied: there was a statute forbidding it. Bradley seized the occasion, however, to deliver a formal opinion holding the monopoly to be obnoxious to the Privileges and Immunities Clause of the Fourteenth Amendement. It was "the first case in which the subject was fully considered."[37] What were the essential privileges guaranteed by the new amendment? Bradley replied:

It may be difficult to enumerate or define them . . . but so far as relates to the question in hand, we may safely say that it is one of the privileges of every American citizen to adopt and follow such lawful industrial pursuit—not injurious to the community—as he may see fit, without unreasonable regulation or molestation, and without being restricted by any of those unjust, oppressive and odious monopolies, or exclusive privileges which have been condemned by all free governments. . . .[38]

A *"liberty of pursuit,"*[39] a "sacred right of labor,"[40] which Bradley found to be "one of the fundamental principles of a free government, as well as one of the fundamental privileges of an American citizen."[41]

In the cases that went up from the state court, the Supreme Court held that the Fourteenth Amendment afforded no relief against the monopoly statute.[42] Bradley dissented, as did Field, Swayne, and Chief Justice Chase. To Justice Miller and the four who stood with him to make the majority, the great concern was to preserve the essentials of the federal system; iniquitous as they all knew the monopoly to be, they were unwilling to see the Supreme Court become the censor of the wisdom of state laws.

Bradley figured largely in the Supreme Court decision on *Munn* v. *Illinois*[43] and the other so-called *Granger* cases in 1877. Illinois had regulated the charges in grain elevators at Chicago. Wisconsin, Minnesota, and Iowa had regulated railroad rates. (So, too, had Illinois, but no Illinois railroad case went up at that time.) Had the legislatures taken property without due process? The effort was, not to show that the statutory rates were unreasonably low, but to induce the Court to hold that rate-fixing was beyond the legislative power. Extreme, all-or-nothing arguments were used. Upon mature consideration, the Court sustained the power to fix rates. Field and Strong dissented. Chief Justice Waite gave the opinion; this has been the basis for giving him special mention as the defender of the public interest. Actually, I believe, Bradley—the former railroad lawyer—had a greater influence in establishing the doctrine of the case than did Waite. I have set out the record in a long article that contains the text of Bradley's "Outline of my views" and his "Principles for decision in the Granger cases." Waite used the memorandum, and returned it indorsed: "With many thanks. . . . Had it not been for the within I could never have won your approbation of my own. . . ." I summarize Bradley's points:

Whenever an employment affects the general public, so that compensation for its exercise operates as a common charge on the citizen, it may be regulated by the legislature. . . . Whether an employment comes within the category of those which affect the general public and create a common charge is to be determined by its nature and its relation to public wants.[44]

The same considerations that had caused the charges of mills, ferries, turnpikes, hackmen, and the like to be limited in times past, would sustain the new regulatory statutes. The decision was a landmark. In 1934, in *Nebbia* v. *New York*,[45] where New York's regulation of milk prices was sustained, the Supreme Court restated the doctrine of the *Munn* case in clear language truly expressing Bradley's thought. Had Waite assigned the case to Bradley, the opinion would have been more tightly fashioned in the first place.

The drive and direction of the fight against regulation in this group of eight cases came from lawyers who practiced or often appeared in Chicago: Burton C. Cook, Charles B. Lawrence, John W. Cary, Orville H. Browning, William C. Goudy, and, sturdiest of all, John N. Jewett. In an alarming discourse, Jewett told the Court that only the judiciary could frustrate "the efforts of radical politicians and crazy communists."[46] Other counsel had sought to distinguish the troublesome instances of rate regulation at common law: the innkeeper, the common carrier, the money-lender, etc. Not so Jewett: he charged straight on. He said that they were all hateful institutions of England, where "the subject was the slave of government, and living in daily apprehension of the worst acts of tyranny and oppression." Our Revolutionary forefathers, he maintained, had fought to put a stop to all that. For Jewett, examples of rate regulation at common law had no place in America.

(Every time I read Mr. Jewett's oral argument in *Munn* v. *Illinois,* I have a peculiar psychic experience: familiar accents come to my ear, the expressions fall into a cadence I have heard before—I have the sensation that I am listening to station WGN and hearing one of those instructional addresses once featured on the "Chicago Theater of the Air"!)

Bradley stuck by the *Granger* cases to the end of his career. In *Wabash Railway* v. *Illinois* in 1886,[47] the question was

whether the railroads were subject to state control of interstate rates, Congress not yet having occupied the field. The
majority held that they were not, and thereupon Congress
created the Interstate Commerce Commission. Bradley had
dissented: so solicitous was he to preserve some regulation
that, in the silence of Congress, he would have sustained the
state authority. In 1890 in *Chicago, Milwaukee and St. Paul
Railway* v. *Minnesota*,[48] the majority declared the reasonable-
ness of rates to be a judicial question. The opinion was foggy;
one can't say exactly what was meant, but its consequences
make a long and unhappy story. Bradley dissented sharply.
The decision, he said, "practically overrules *Munn* v. *Illinois*";
that rate regulation is a legislative prerogative was, he said,
"a principle which I regard as of great importance."[49]

He did not mean that the federal judiciary had no power of
supervision as to what procedure the state legislature might
set up. In *Davidson* v. *New Orleans*,[50] in a concurring opinion
of 1878, he had said that in enforcing the Due Process Clause
of the Fourteenth Amendment the Court should inquire, if
need be, whether the procedure created by the legislature was
"suitable" and "admissible" in the particular matter, or on the
contrary was "arbitrary, oppressive and unjust." "Such an examination may be made without interfering with that large
discretion which every legislative power has of making wide
modifications in the forms of procedure,"[51] to meet the habits
and preferences of the people.

It is pertinent while examining Bradley's views on legal
questions touching railroads to mention his opinion in *Railroad
Co.* v. *Lockwood*[52] in 1873. It is the great case establishing
the doctrine that a common carrier's stipulation for exemption
from liability for negligence is contrary to public policy. "The
carrier and his customer do not stand on a footing of equality."[53] That railroads should not be allowed to abdicate their
essential duties was Bradley's point. This great opinion had

a tremendous influence upon the state courts, for in those days the Supreme Court was an important fountain of the common law.

In the law of the Commerce Clause, Bradley set up some of the great landmarks, such as *Coe* v. *Errol*[54] and *Brown* v. *Houston*[55] on state taxation of goods once in transit. *Robbins* v. *Shelby County*,[56] in 1887, is the head of the long line of "drummer cases": "In the matter of interstate commerce, the United States are but one country."[57] This body of the law has now been profoundly affected by the introduction of sales and use taxes; yet the *Robbins* case was expressly reaffirmed in 1946.[58]

Two memorable dissents where Bradley took advanced national ground may be mentioned because they became the law of the Court after he had gone. In 1871 he argued that the federal income tax was constitutionally applicable to a state officer's salary.[59] In 1877 he argued that a corporation's resort to the federal court could not be made the basis for a state's revocation of its license.[60] He did not allow himself to be caught in the argument that the greater—the state's power wholly to deny admission—must include the less.

On some opinions history has not looked so kindly, for example in the case of Chicago's great woman lawyer, Myra Bradwell. The Illinois Supreme Court denied her admission to the bar. The United States Supreme Court said that no privilege or immunity under the Fourteenth Amendment was involved.[61] The case comes immediately after *Slaughter House* in the Reports. Bradley concurred, in an opinion dwelling upon the "natural and proper timidity and delicacy which belongs to the female sex," unfitting woman for the practice of the law. (Eventually Myra Bradwell was admitted to the bar of the Supreme Court, on March 28, 1892, but Justice Bradley had died two months before.)

To say that Bradley spoke for the Court in the *Civil Rights Cases*[62] confers no accolade—at least not in the North. That decision held invalid the Civil Rights Act of 1875, the statute wherein Congress forbade discrimination on grounds of color in inns, public conveyances, and places of public amusement. The Thirteenth Amendment forbids slavery: but the with-holding of equal enjoyment of inns, etc., was not a badge of slavery, said the Court. The Fourteenth Amendment provides, *"No State* shall," but the *state* had not acted; therefore the matter was beyond the reach of Congress. Justice Harlan dis-sented, with even more than usual vigor. His strongest point, it seems to me, was this: innkeepers and common carriers are under a common-law duty to serve all; they perform public offices. This was enough, Harlan argued, to make what they did state action within the reach of the Fourteenth Amend-ment. Our conceptions are broadening nowadays. The pro-hibition "No State shall . . ." is now broad enough to mean that no state shall by its courts specifically enforce a restrictive covenant based on race,[63] nor shall its courts even award damages for a breach.[64] If a state were entirely to hand over the function of education to private schools, it is not difficult to foresee that discrimination by such schools would be state action. It goes somewhat further to say that discrimination by an innkeeper is state action; yet we know that the law, in accord with the public conscience, is moving. We may hear more of Justice Harlan's dissent. It is almost eighty years since the *Civil Rights* cases were decided. All those who care for the law ought to take satisfaction in the knowledge that con-ditions have improved so greatly as to make them feel un-happy about that old case.

Much of the present law on civil liberties had no existence until quite recent times. It was seldom that the Court in Brad-ley's day had a case on civil liberty. However, one can cite *Boyd* v. *United States*,[65] in 1886, wherein Bradley, for the Court, gave the first great exposition of the Searches and Seizures provision of the Fourth Amendment. He there picked up and elaborated a major theme of the period of the Revolution: "Constitutional provisions for the security of person and property should be liberally construed";[66] "[i]t is the duty of courts to be watchful for the constitutional rights of the citizen, and against any stealthy encroachments thereon."[67] "The *Boyd* opinion has been the guide to the interpretation of the Fourth Amendment to which the Court has most frequently recurred."[68]

At the close of sixty-nine years—Bradley always marked anniversaries—he wrote down this comment: *"Life—all of one's life—is the only preparation for death. He that has lived faithfully and honestly, need not fear death. . . .* [E]very part of life [is] important."[69] In summing up Bradley's life, it can be said that every period of his life was a season of greatness: college, reading for the bar, early years in practice.

He exemplified the virtue of professional detachment: he gave to his great railroad client all the fidelity that is owed by an advocate and counsel, but he maintained an entire independence of judgment. Professional detachment is a great virtue, one that becomes rarer as economic interests become more highly concentrated and lines of conflict are more sharply drawn.

He completely mastered his profession: there was a craftsmanship in all Bradley's work, a tightness and tidiness, a wide resourcefulness, that is wholly admirable. People tend nowadays to score a Justice's performance by the impressionistic standards of the commentators. Bradley's work, however, stands the test of time, because he had disciplined himself in his craft.

Professional competence, nevertheless, is not the greatest quality to be expected of a Justice of the Supreme Court. The office demands statesmanship. That is the Court's highest function. This is not the place to debate whether the Court holds its high powers by a good title. Indeed it is too late in our history to treat that as an open question. The Court, with its traditional powers, is with us. Justices have varied in their adequacy. There have been seasons when the Court has served America ill. On balance, however, I believe that the nation has been greatly strengthened by an institution that has stood for reason and justice and an honest weighing of interests. At this juncture of national life Americans can afford to place a high value on those judicial qualities. The magistrate I have presented to you ranks high among the exemplars of the Court's best wisdom.

CHARLES FAIRMAN *taught at Harvard, Williams, Stanford, and Washington Universities. Now engaged in the preparation of a biography of Justice Bradley and a volume on the history of the Supreme Court, he is the author of* The Law of Martial Rule, *1930 (2d ed., 1943),* Justice Miller and the Supreme Court, *1862–1890, 1939, and numerous articles in law reviews. He is professor emeritus of law at Harvard Law School.*

NOTES

1. *Who Is the "Great" Appellate Judge?* 24 IND. L.J. 394, 397 (1949).
2. *Bunting* v. *Oregon,* 243 U.S. 426, 438 (1917).
3. *Brown* v. *Board of Education,* 347 U.S. 483, 489 (1954).
4. *Live-Stock Dealers' and Butchers' Assn.* v. *Crescent City Live-Stock Larding and Slaughter-House Co.,* 15 Fed. Cas. No. 8408; 1 Woods 21 (C.C.La., 1870).
5. 16 Pet. 1 (1842).
6. 304 U.S. 64 (1938).
7. *Holmes-Pollock Letters* (Howe ed., 1941), II, 215.
8. "Mr. Justice Bradley of the United States Supreme Court," address to the Historical Society of New Jersey, Jan. 24, 1893, p. 14.
9. *Ibid.,* p. 7.
10. *Miscellaneous Writings of the Late Hon. Joseph P. Bradley* (1902), p. 79.
11. I have set out the entire passage in *The Education of a Justice,* 1 STANF. L. REV. 217, 230 (1949).
12. *Ibid.*
13. Pp. 249, 484–85 (2d ed., 1836).
14. 13 Pet. 519.
15. 18 How. 272.
16. For brevity, sacrificing rigorous accuracy, I speak simply of "Camden and Amboy" without explaining its relationship with the

"Joint Companies" and later the "United Companies." The details are set forth in *Mr. Justice Bradley's Appointment to the Supreme Court and the Legal Tender Cases*, 54 HARV. L. REV., 977, 1128 (1941).

17. 3 Wall, App. 782 (C.C.N.J., 1857, aff'd, 1862).

18. 3 Wall. 713.

19. Letter of Aug. 6, 1857, to his sister, Mrs. Ambrose W. Palmer.

20. 94 U.S. 113 (1877).

21. 100 U.S. 371, 395.

22. Letter of June 4, 1876, to his son Charles.

23. Book iii. 22.

24. 16 Pet. 1, 19 (1842).

25. *Brooklyn City and Newton R.R. Co.* v. *National Bank of the Republic*, 102 U.S. 14 (1880).

26. See note 16, *supra*.

27. 8 Wall. 603 (1870).

28. Charles Fairman, *Mr. Justice Miller and the Supreme Court, 1862–1890* (1939), pp. 170–71.

29. 12 Wall. 457.

30. *Juillard* v. *Greenman*, 110 U.S. 421.

31. *Briscoe* v. *Bank of Kentucky*; *Mayor of New York* v. *Miln*, 8 Pet. 118, 122.

32. Letter of Mar. 21, 1878, to Mrs. Ambrose W. Palmer.

33. Letter of June 4, 1871, to Caroline Bradley.

34. Letter of John Spalding Flannery, Dec. 3, 1951.

35. June 8, 1870, p. 1, col. 3.

36. See *Slaughter House Case*, 1 Woods 21, 24 (1870), 10 Wall. 273 (1870).

37. Judge Woods at 1 Woods 21, 22.

38. 1 Woods at 28–29, 15 Fed. Cas. at 652.

39. 1 Woods at 31, 15 Fed. Cas. at 653.

40. 1 Woods at 29, 15 Fed. Cas. at 652.

41. 1 Woods at 31. The reference to "fundamental principles of free government" does not appear in the passage as recorded in 15 Fed. Cas. at 652.

42. 16 Wall. 36 (1873).

43. 94 U.S. 113.

44. *The So-Called Granger Cases, Lord Hale and Justice Bradley*, 5 STANF. L. REV. 587 (1953).

45. 291 U.S. 502, 532 *et seq.*

46. 5 STANF. L. REV. 650.

47. 118 U.S. 418.

48. 134 U.S. 418.

49. *Ibid.* at 461.

50. 96 U.S. 97.

51. *Ibid.* at 107–8.

52. 17 Wall. 357.

53. *Ibid.* at 379.

54. 116 U.S. 517 (1886).

55. 114 U.S. 622 (1885).

56. 120 U.S. 489.

57. *Ibid.* at 494.

58. *Nippert* v. *City of Richmond,* 327 U.S. 416 (1946).

59. *Collector* v. *Day,* 11 Wall. 113; overruled in *Graves* v. *O'Keefe,* 306 U.S. 466 (1939).

60. *Doyle* v. *Continental Insurance Co.,* 94 U.S. 535; overruled in *Terral* v. *Burke Construction Co.,* 257 U.S. 529 (1922).

61. *Bradwell* v. *State,* 16 Wall. 130 (1873).

62. 109 U.S. 3 (1883).

63. *Shelley* v. *Kraemer,* 334 U.S. 1 (1948).

64. *Barrows* v. *Jackson,* 346 U.S. 249 (1953).

65. 116 U.S. 616.

66. *Ibid.* at 635.

67. *Ibid.*

68. Justice Frankfurter, dissenting, in *Harris* v. *United States,* 331 U.S. 145, 155, 160 (1947).

69. Letter of Mar. 13, 1882, to Mrs. Ambrose W. Palmer.

MR. JUSTICE HARLAN

Mr. Justice Harlan

By
ALAN F. WESTIN

In 1833, the Bluegrass State of John Marshall Harlan's birth
was borderland. Once a stronghold of Jeffersonian Republicanism, Kentucky had swung into the Whig columns in 1824 under the creative leadership of Henry Clay, to remain there for
more than a quarter-century.[1] With his father a close friend of
"Prince Hal" and a dominant figure in Kentucky's Whig coun-
cils, John Harlan was imbued with the Whig credo as his natural faith. Growing up in the manorial Ashland District, with
Clays, Crittendens, and Breckinridges as neighbors and a
household staffed with Negro slaves, Harlan's youth exemplified the southern Whig tradition. As a boy, Harlan recalled
later, he stood among the audience in picnic groves and torch-
light parades listening to Henry Clay expound the gospel of a
national bank, a national tariff, and a supreme law of the land.
His father defended the same Whig tenets in his successful
campaigns for Secretary of State and Attorney General of Kentucky and Congressman from his home district. As a student at
Centre College in Danville, Harlan joined the young Kentucky
gentlemen sent to learn their Presbyterian fundamentals, beginning a lifelong devotion to Sabbath observance, temper-
ance, and Bible-study at this school where "the moral and
religious culture of the youth has always been regarded by the
officers of the College as their most important object." At seventeen Harlan left Centre to study law at Transylvania University, "the Harvard of the West." Under the guidance of
teachers like Judges George Robertson and Thomas Marshall

of the Kentucky Court of Appeals, Harlan dipped into Coke, Blackstone, and Littleton, read Kent and Story, and, above all, absorbed the nationalist philosophy of his namesake, Chief Justice John Marshall. It was on a note of allegiance to that faith that Harlan left Transylvania. With secession rumbling in the eaves in the early 1850's, Judge Robertson delivered an address in 1852 to the senior class at Transylvania, defending the supremacy of the Constitution against the "pernicious errors" of the secessionists and expounding the ideas of Washington, Hamilton, Marshall, and Clay. Heading a three-man petition to publish the address was the signature of John Marshall Harlan. The petition condemned "the monstrous doctrines of nullification and secession, which threaten, ere long, unless firmly resisted by the patriotic intelligence of the people, to undermine the fabric of our Government. . . ."

Harlan was admitted to the bar in 1853, ready and eager to move into the legal and political world of the Kentucky Whigs. At that moment his party was about to begin fifteen years of wandering in a political wasteland, too nationalist to merge with the Democrats and too Southern to join the Free-Soilers or Republicans. With the deaths of Clay and Webster in 1852, the smoldering conflict over slavery flared up to divide the Whig Party into a Northern and a Southern camp; in Kentucky and elsewhere the local Whigs tried to side-step the slavery issue temporarily by raising the banner of American nativism. This took the form of the semi-secret Know-Nothing movement. Harlan joined it because his father and the most prominent Whig leader of Frankfort were the sponsors of the local Know-Nothings. In later life he suggested that he had been so uncomfortable about its anti-Catholicism and the oath to vote only for native-born Americans that he almost refused to join.

Once in the party, the strapping six-foot, two-inch redhead plunged with gusto into the political campaigns of the 1850's. As a stump-speaker for the American ticket in the 1855 state elections, canvasser for the Know-Nothing Party's presidential nominee in 1856 (Millard Fillmore), and successful candidate for judge of Franklin County in 1858, John Harlan flashed into prominence as one of the most able young orators in the Blue-grass. Traveling on horseback from town to town and living out of a pair of saddle bags, debating Democratic speakers twice his age, Harlan began attracting huge audiences for his appearances. He was billed as the "young giant of the American Party," and his speeches were described, approvingly, as "orthodox . . . Know-Nothing scripture"—anti-foreign, pro-slavery, and anti-Catholic in just the right proportions. But Harlan's efforts were rendered on behalf of a waning party. Although the Americans won the state election of 1855, they failed to carry the state for Fillmore in the 1856 presidential contest and lost decisively in the state elections of 1857 and 1858. Kentucky voters might have been worried, in a general way, about the future of "Romanism" in America, but it was slavery that they were most wrought up about, and on that score, the Democrats promised the most vigorous pro-slavery course.

Harlan's attitude toward slavery was shaped by family, regional, and political factors. The Harlans owned about a dozen slaves, inherited by James Harlan and his wife from their parents. These were house servants, not field hands in plantation style. James Harlan hated slave trading, freed several of his slaves and helped them get a start in life, and joined Henry Clay in emancipation activities such as the African Colonization Society. The Harlans were strongly anti-abolitionist, however, believing that freeing all the slaves in their uneducated condition would be disastrous, while any forced emancipation would be a violation of the property rights of American citizens. As the 1850's brought increased anti-slavery pressure from Northern abolitionists and Kentucky anti-slavers like Cassius Clay, the Harlans became increasingly committed to the defense of property rights in slaves, the right of the states to deal with slavery as they saw fit, and the obligation of the national government to protect slave property in the new territories. This was Harlan's perspective in the late 1850's, and it was to remain basically the same for over a decade.

Harlan's spectacular success as a campaigner in the 1855, 1856, and 1858 elections resulted in the nomination of the twenty-six-year-old county judge as the candidate of the Opposition Party (the latest Whig-American title) for Congress. He was defeated after a hard campaign in which he attacked domestic and foreign policies of the Buchanan administration and defended property rights in slavery. Harlan particularly supported the *Dred Scott* case as right and just. Harlan lost the Ashland congressional election by fifty votes, in what was widely regarded throughout Kentucky as a case of ballot-stuffing by the Democrats. Although his friends raised a $10,000 purse to pay for a recount, he decided that it would be wiser, in the long run, to enjoy the sympathy of the fair-minded voters and not to contest the election.

Between 1859 and 1861 the steady pressure of events reluctantly pushed Harlan and the Kentucky Whigs from the politics of evasion to the final hard choice between slavery-with-secession and support of the Union. In 1860 the Harlans, as most Kentucky Whigs, backed Bell for President on the Constitutional Union ticket, dedicated to the noble and ambivalent goals of "The Union, the Constitution, and the Enforcement of the Laws." Following Lincoln's inauguration and the secession movements, John Harlan was among those trying desperately to stave off a war. Once Fort Sumter was fired upon, however, the pro-Union men in Kentucky realized peace efforts were finished and they turned to saving Kentucky from falling into the Confederate camp. This was not an easy task, since many of the state's business and family ties were linked to the South, and the state administration was pro-Confederate.

During May, June, and July of 1861, Harlan and a few friends hired brass bands and stood on store boxes on the pavements of Louisville each afternoon telling everyone who would listen of the importance of Kentucky remaining in the Union. The threat of Confederate invasion led Harlan to join a home-guard unit formed by Unionists, as Captain of the Crittenden Union Zouaves. Other adventures followed, from his role in the smuggling of "Lincoln Guns" into Kentucky to a remarkable episode in which Harlan virtually took over the Louisville *Journal* from its editor and kept the paper from swinging to the Southern camp. By the fall of 1861 Harlan realized he must "join the Volunteer Union forces and become something more than a speaker for the Union cause in public halls or on the stump." He raised an infantry regiment, called on those to join him who were for the Union and against those who had "invaded" Kentucky for a "foreign government," and was commissioned, at 28, as Colonel of the 10th Kentucky Volunteers. As head of the 10th, Harlan was under General George Thomas (the famous Virginia commander who cast his fortunes with the North). John Harlan saw action in Kentucky, Mississippi, and Tennessee. He outmaneuvered Morgan's Raiders at Rolling Fork Bridge in Kentucky during September of 1861, which not only earned him a commendation from Brigadier General Speed S. Fry for saving the Union railway lines and breaking Morgan's hold on Tennessee, but established him as something of a military hero at home, where victories were few in this period.

Harlan's close contact during the war with the German immigrants and Kentucky mountaineers of his regiment and his respect for their soldierly devotion led the young scion of Ashland to write glowingly in his dispatches of his men's "willingness, even eagerness, to endure any fatigue or make any sacrifice. . . ." In later years, this bond with the men who wielded the bayonets buttressed Harlan's egalitarian instincts. "When war menaced the country," Harlan observed, "it was the poor and sons of the poor who sprang to its defense." They "deserve the thanks of the country for the cheerfulness with which, with insufficient food and rest, they bore up under the severest pri-

vations. . . ." Also, the qualities of men as men were brought
home to Harlan, to wash away the nativistic aspect of his an-
tagonism to Catholics and immigrants. Writing of the "many
Catholics in my regiment," Harlan noted:

It was a magnificent sight to see how the boys struggled through
mud and rain to reach the field of battle. The ground was so wet
and muddy under them that their feet slipped at every step. I see
now with great distinctness old Father Nash pushing along on
foot with the boys. Equally earnest with him was a Catholic priest
from Washington county, who had come with Catholic soldiers
from that county.

In February of 1863, Harlan's father died suddenly. John
was the only one who could handle the estate, the law business, and support his mother, wife, and family. This forced him
to resign from service, and issue a letter that made clear that
he still supported the Union cause with all "the warmest sympathies of [his] heart." After receiving a testimonial from his
regiment, Harlan returned to Louisville and civilian life in
March of 1863. His retirement did not mean a complete dis-
engagement from service, however, for during the entire war
Kentucky stood in a constant state of invasion, occupation, and
unease. In the fall of 1864, for example, Harlan took a prominent part in defending Frankfort against a guerrilla raid led
by Confederate General John H. Morgan.

Harlan arrived in Kentucky just as the state election campaign of 1863 was about to begin. The Kentucky Unionists
approached him immediately and asked him to accept the
nomination for Attorney General. "The suggestion was not disapproved by me," Harlan wrote, "principally because if elected I
would be required to remove to the capitol of the State where
my father lived at the time of his death, and where I was compelled to be in order to wind up his business and estate."
Harlan was nominated and he joined the Kentucky Unionists
in making the "dangerous policies" of President Lincoln the
dominant issue of the campaign. Defending slavery and constitutional liberty at the same time, Harlan attacked Lincoln's

promulgation of the Emancipation Proclamation and his suspension of the writ of habeas corpus. This was in keeping with Harlan's later observation that "the Kentucky Unionists, as a general rule, did not approve of all the methods suggested by the Union men of the Northern States for the prosecution of the war, particularly those relating to the institution of slavery." This note was exactly right as far as political sentiment in Kentucky was concerned. With Federal troops policing the election, the Union Party trounced the Peace Democrats; John Harlan received a 50,000-vote plurality over his opponent.

Harlan's activities during his four-year term as Attorney General were multifold. Since the job was a part-time one, he was able to maintain an active law practice, first with his brother James and then alone, appearing in the state and federal courts, particularly in the matter of claims against the United States and Kentucky governments, and especially for slaves enlisted or drafted in the army.

As Attorney General, Harlan argued over 60 appellate cases for the Commonwealth, including cases defending property rights in slaves. In one revealing case, *Bowlin* v. *Commonwealth*,[2] a lower state court, in light of the Federal Civil Rights Act of 1866, had allowed Negro testimony against a white defendant indicted for larceny, despite a Kentucky law forbidding Negro testimony against white persons. True to his strong convictions and his political position, Harlan filed a special "Suggestion for the Commonwealth" that declared:

The only question on this appeal is as to the propriety of the court admitting the testimony of a Negro against a white person. Not feeling at liberty, according to my views of that question considered as a legal proposition, to uphold the judgment of the court below, the case is respectfully submitted to the court without argument on behalf of the Com'th.

The Kentucky Court of Appeals shared Harlan's view and promptly reversed the conviction.

With Kentucky for the Union but dismayed by emancipationist measures, Harlan, like many former Whigs, supported General George McClellan for the presidency in 1864 and bitterly attacked the Lincoln administration. In one of his speeches, Harlan condemned the Republican party as

. . . based upon the single idea of hate and hostility to the social institution of one section of our country; its candidate having been elected in accordance with the Constitution, he was entitled to be respected as President.

The disunionists of the South, however, were not content to await the slow processes of the ballot box. They fired upon the flag of the United States and then aroused the entire people of the North, including those who have felt and believed that the Abolitionists could have averted the terrible calamity of civil war had they been actuated by that spirit of conciliation and compromise in which the Constitution was framed by our Fathers.

But for what purpose did the people of the North rise as one man? It was to maintain the Union, and the Constitution which was the only bond of that Union. It was for the high and noble purpose of asserting the binding authority of our laws over every part of this land. It was not for the purpose of giving freedom to the Negro. . . .

Since Lincoln was now "warring chiefly for the freedom of the African race," a true Unionist like McClellan was needed by the country.

Meanwhile, Harlan settled the family estate by freeing the slaves held by his father and making himself responsible for their value. This was done to prevent their being sold "down river." During 1864, John and Mollie Harlan had a Negro slave as cook, purchased from her owners, who was set free because of differences in the kitchen between Mrs. Harlan and "Aunt" Fannie.

Between 1865 and 1867 Harlan was a leader of the Conservative Union Party, a middle-of-the-road group that tried to steer a course between the two major groups in Kentucky, the Democrats (Confederates) and the Radicals (supporters of President Johnson's administration). The Conservatives, whose leaders were the same Whig-Americans who tried to attack both abolitionists and secessionists in the years just before the Civil War, tried to strike the same type of compromise position. In the 1865 elections for state legislature, the dominant issues were the Thirteenth Amendment and Reconstruction policy in Kentucky, and on these issues the Conservatives swung close to the Democratic side. Harlan made a series of speeches in which he condemned General John Palmer for enlisting large numbers of Negroes to effect their emancipation, since this resulted in the creation "of large bodies of Negro men, women, and children in this State, [living] at the expense of the Nation and [receiving] a watchful care which has never been exhibited for the wives and families of white soldiers of Kentucky." The operation of the Freedman's Bureau and federal coercion of the state authorities was attacked by Harlan, who predicted only chaos from the situation in which the state is denied the power "to effect the removal of the blacks to other localities or protect her white citizens from the ruinous effects of such a violent change in our social system." In times like these, Harlan wrote to a fellow-Conservative, there had to be "a thorough union of all citizens who . . . are opposed to the admission of the Negro to the ballot-box or to the enjoyment of other political advantages." Harlan regarded the Thirteenth Amendment as outrageous. It was not only "a flagrant invasion of the right of self government" and a breach of promise to the loyal slave-holders of Kentucky, but it also gave to "a bare majority in Congress" the power to wipe out property rights guaranteed by the Constitution. As in 1861, Harlan affirmed that he remained "opposed to the dissolution of the Union in any event," and he tried to suggest a compromise solution to the slavery issue, offering the proposal that Kentucky itself should undertake a gradual abolition of slavery over the next seven years.

The Democrats scored a solid victory in the 1865 elections. The following year the Conservatives swung into an alliance with the Radicals, the two parties supporting E. H. Hobson, a distinguished Union General, as their joint gubernatorial nominee. The exultant Democrats hammered away at this uneasy coalition in the 1866 canvass, while Radical policies in Washington grew even more distasteful to Kentuckians. The Conservatives (including Harlan) attacked the proposed constitutional amendments and, at the same time, the "heresies of secession and rebellion" championed by the Democrats.

Again the Democrats swept the polls over the combined Radical-Conservative ticket, this time by a 38,000 vote margin. The victory, one newspaper wrote, was a triumph of gray over blue. The leaders of the Conservative Party met in Frankfort in March of 1867, surveyed their failure, and emerged with a reconstructed movement they dubbed the Conservative Union Democrats, or "Third Party." The manifesto of the new party announced that it was the real Democratic party in Kentucky, standing against the usurpations of Congress and the divisive efforts of the Confederates. John Marshall Harlan was the party's nominee for Attorney General. The regular Kentucky Democrats were not impressed by this name-stealing, however, and they went on to pile up smashing victories in both the congressional and state elections of 1867. The fact was, as the Cincinnati *Weekly Gazette* had observed: "There are but two parties in Kentucky. You must go to the one or to the other. . . . If you choose to attempt a middle party, well and good. In some places the rebels will beat you; in others, the Radicals."

In 1868, the Conservatives simply evaporated. Many of its leaders, encouraged by overtures from the Democrats, went over to that party. A smaller group, including Harlan, chose the other road.

The resounding defeat of the Conservatives in 1867 convinced Harlan that a third party could accomplish nothing in Kentucky. Bred in the tradition that no honorable man was without a party affiliation and living in an era when the practice of law was inescapably intertwined with politics, Harlan began to consider a new political allegiance. At just this moment, he moved from the fiercely anti-Negro and pro-Democratic stronghold of Frankfort to the more cosmopolitan city of Louisville, which lay close to the staunch Republican stronghold of Indiana. When he opened his law office in Louisville, Harlan's closest contacts were with the leading Radicals, primarily because much of Harlan's attention in 1867 and 1868 was with the split in the Kentucky Presbyterian Church. As a devoted and active Presbyterian layman, Harlan had endorsed the pro-Union position adopted during the war by the General Assembly of the Presbyterian Church in the United States. In 1866, in keeping with the postwar swing of Kentucky sentiment to the Southern cause, a revolt took place among Kentucky Presbyterians, and a majority of the communicants, headed by the Democratic party leaders, broke away from the national church and from the uncompromisingly pro-Union leadership of the dominant figure in the Kentucky church, Rev. Robert J. Breckinridge. Harlan became a leader of the Northern group. In 1867 the Southern group tried to seize control of Centre College by means of a bill in the Kentucky legislature putting the college under the jurisdiction of the Southern Synod. John Harlan was chosen to present the case against the bill to the Judiciary Committee, and, through his efforts, the Breckinridge group managed to kill the measure.

Harlan was also the counsel for the Breckinridge faction in several bitter court fights in which the Southern adherents tried to win title to church property held by pro-Northern congregations. For Harlan the result of these religious conflicts was to add the stain of heresy and schism to the Democratic cause and to make allegiance with the Southern leaders impossible. His closest friends and legal associates were now Northern-Presbyterian, pro-Radical figures such as United States Attorney G. F. Wharton, District Judge Brand Ballard, General W. C. Goodloe, and the influential Benjamin Bristow, with whom Harlan soon entered into a law partnership.

On the political front, it had become clear by 1868 that only the Republican and Democratic parties were viable in national

politics and the same two-party pattern began to emerge
in Kentucky after the decade of confused multi-party politics.
At both state and national levels Harlan found himself unable
to stomach the Democrats. His gravitation to the Republicans
was accelerated when, in 1868, General Ulysses S. Grant was
chosen as the Republican standard-bearer. General Grant had
been an acquaintance of Colonel Harlan during the war; he
stood for defense of the Union victory against the resurgent
forces of the secessionist democracy; and he was unconnected
personally with the struggles over the War Amendments and
reconstruction. By this time Harlan accepted the War Amendments as a *fait accompli* and felt that this was the sensible
course to adopt if Kentucky and the South were to move forward economically and socially in the postwar decades. Thus
the autumn months of 1868 found Harlan campaigning in Kentucky for General Grant and in Indiana for the Republican
Governor, Oliver P. Morton. In both places, his main attack
was on the Democratic party for its ante-bellum intransigence.
Significantly, during his speeches, he defended the Republican
party for having sponsored the Thirteenth and Fourteenth
Amendments.

Between 1868 and 1871 Harlan plunged happily into law
problems in his new firm of Harlan, Newman & Bristow. He
also took hold of the newly formed and still overwhelmed Republican party of Kentucky, corresponding extensively with
party leaders throughout the state and carrying his personal
following into the new organization. The most important development he pondered during this period was the impending
enfranchisement of the Negro, and what this meant for Republican party hopes in Kentucky. As the leading historian of
Kentucky during reconstruction has written,

It was the Negroes on whom the Radicals now began to pin
their faith for ultimate victory. . . . It was predicted that there
would be 100,000 Negro voters; and with considerable elation the
Louisville Commercial [a leading Republican paper] declared that
elections thereafter would not be "the one-sided affairs of 1867,
1868, and 1869."[3]

The Republicans set out to attract the new voters, holding picnics and organizational meetings and stressing the indebtedness of the Negro to the party of "Honest Abe" and Charles Sumner. The first real test of Negro strength at the polls, apart from a premature contest in 1870, was the election of state officers in 1871. The Republicans, anxious to present a fresh candidate, chose John Marshall Harlan as their gubernatorial nominee and party leader.

Harlan's leadership of the Republicans provided, according to most students of Kentucky political history, "[t]he real beginning of an intelligent opposition to the Democrats . . . and it can be truly said that the Republican Party in Kentucky was born [in 1871]."[4] Harlan championed a comprehensive program for the expansion of the Kentucky economy and thundered at the Democrats for choking the state's growth by their continued backward perspective and race hatred. He struck out at the Democratic-supported monopoly of the Louisville & Nashville Railroad and urged the voters to back Republican plans to franchise a line of the Cincinnati Southern Railway. His speeches were filled with pleas that Kentucky should build up "rivals" to the Louisville & Nashville monopoly "and every other monopoly in this commonwealth." Harlan warned that monopolies not only "stifled the powers of industry and national health" but had the effect of "absorbing the capital of the state and controlling its politics." The Democrats replied by branding the railway bond proposal as a scheme to run up a huge "Radical rule" debt and " 'do' the people of Kentucky out of forty or fifty millions," as had been done in Louisiana under the Republicans. Harlan also came out for a state-sponsored program of inviting immigrants to Kentucky, from Germany and other countries of Europe, so that the state's rich "agricultural, mineral, and manufacturing resources may be developed." But when Harlan attacked the Democratic legislature for failing to assist a German-immigration society with funds and for driving immigration "to other states," the Democrats came to the debating platforms carrying clippings of

Harlan's speeches in the 1850's attacking foreigners and opposing any further immigration. The Democrats continued to
read Harlan's "Know-Nothing scripture" throughout the campaign. Another theme developed by Harlan was a plan to substitute an income tax for the Democrats' property tax as a
means of paying the Civil War debt of the state. The Democratic policy, he explained to voters, taxed "your farms, houses,
land, implements, and tools" at the same level that it taxed
"the incomes . . . of the wealthy." In place of this, Harlan proposed the equivalent of the federal tax system. Congress, realizing "that the poor man would have to fight the battles of the
country . . . determined to make the rich man pay the taxes.
. . . The lawyer and the physician were taxed on their income
over and above $2000, but the poor mechanic who only made
$1000, or $1500, a year was not taxed on his income at all."
Harlan also urged that, in place of the new state law that
raised school deficits by assessing local families in proportion
to the children they enrolled in school, there should be a general property tax for school maintenance. Praising the poor
men who had fought courageously in the Civil War, Harlan
said that "the rich owed it to the poor to contribute to the
education of the latter."

Harlan's turn to anti-monopoly and neo-Jacksonian issues
seems to have been caused not simply by the rise of strong
Granger and populist sentiment in Kentucky, but also by an
interest that he developed in the early 1870's in the future of
the Kentucky mountaineers, men he had grown to know and
respect in his regiment. Mrs. Harlan noted in her memoirs that
during the 1871 and 1875 campaign, "The sturdy mountaineers, in particular, became a most interesting study to him. He
predicted a great future for them, because of the opportunity
for education that was then opening to them and the new
ambition that seemed then to be stirring in them."

However important the new issues of the 1871 campaign
proved to be in shaping the economic philosophy of Mr. Justice

Harlan, the issue that overrode everything else was the Negro question. For the Democrats, civil rights was the rallying cry by which they would keep their anti-Negro coalition together; for the Republicans, the new Negro voters represented the only chance, as a matter of strict arithmetic, to break Democratic hegemony in Kentucky. In the three years since his move into the Republican Party, Harlan had been forced to reconsider his attitude toward the civil rights problem. The War Amendments whose ratification he had opposed were now a part of the Constitution of the United States and their repeal was impossible to visualize. In the eyes of the fundamental law, Negroes were no longer chattels like horses and houses but were human beings, entitled to every right of a free American given by the supreme law of the land. To some Southerners, this investing of the mass of uneducated Negro slaves with civil rights was a call to violence against the law or to the beginning of a cynical evasion of the amendments. To Harlan, however, a man who held the Constitution alongside the Bible as a document to which unswerving allegiance was owed, and who believed there was "no safety in this land of ours except in rigid adherence to the law," the adoption of the War Amendments could not be brushed off that easily. Perhaps grudgingly at first, perhaps with the feeling that too much had been done too fast, Harlan began to look realistically, with a constitutional perspective, at the needs of reconstructing the Union and at the position of the Negro in Kentucky. Slavery was ended. Negroes were working for wages or in trades and were going to schools. Negroes were looking about for a party in Kentucky to which they could give their allegiance, and they were going to have ballots equal in weight to those of the whites. Most important, the continued agitation of the secessionists and irreconcilables to repeal the War Amendments had encouraged elements in Kentucky to take the law into their own hands. As Professor Coulter has described the scene, "Calling themselves 'Regulators,' 'Rowzee's Band,'

'Skagg's Men' and various other names, bands of men set about a veritable reign of terror in various parts of the state."⁵ Any white man who incurred the displeasure of the bands could expect sudden death. The main effort of the bands, of course, was directed at Negroes:

> In the course of a few days lynch law ran riot on negroes charged with rape in Bardstown, Frankfort, and Owensboro; "Skagg's Men" raided twenty negro houses near Lebanon and robbed and maltreated the occupants; a mob removed a negro's family from the Danville jail and hanged him in a graveyard; the "Regulators" hanged two negroes in Washington County; . . . "Regulators" grotesquely garbed broke up a religious meeting of negroes, shot one and beat many. Thus the story went. In western Kentucky, the "Regulators" gave notice to the negroes to leave the county and warned landowners not to rent to negroes on the peril of having their houses burned.⁶

Perhaps more than anywhere else, the lynchings, floggings, robberies and terrorizing that swept through Kentucky, and the failure of the Democratic administration to control this, made Harlan re-examine his ideas. He became convinced that the only way to bring peace was to accept the results of the war, recognize the legal rights of the new freedmen, and end the reign of violence, even if it took federal intervention to do the job. By the time of the 1871 campaign, it was a new Harlan that mounted the platform to give his views on the "Negro question." Addressing a rally in Livermore on July 26, Harlan announced that he gave wholehearted support to the War Amendments and Negro civil rights:

> It is true fellow citizens that almost the entire people of Kentucky, at one period in their history, were opposed to freedom, citizenship and suffrage of the Colored race. It is true that I was at one time in my life opposed to conferring these privileges upon them, but I have lived long enough to feel and declare, as I do this night, that the most perfect despotism that ever existed on this earth was the institution of African slavery. It was an enemy to free speech; it was an enemy to good government; it was an enemy to a free press.
> The time was, and not long ago in Kentucky, when any declaration, such as I now make, against the institution of slavery, would

have imperiled my life in many portions of the State. With slavery it was death or tribute. It knew no compromise, it tolerated no middle course. I rejoice that it is gone; I rejoice that the Sun of American Liberty does not this day shine upon a single human slave upon this continent; I rejoice that these human beings are now in possession of freedom, and that that freedom is secured to them in the fundamental law of the land, beyond the control of any state.

It seemed wise to the majority of the people of this nation, not only to secure them their freedom in this way, but also to secure them the rights of citizenship, and the rights of suffrage; and I am now thoroughly persuaded that the only mode by which the nation could liberate itself from the conflicts and passions engendered by the war in connection with the institution of African slavery was to pass these Constitutional Amendments, and to place it beyond the power of any State to interfere with or diminish the results of the war now embodied in these Amendments. They are irrevocable results of the War; and because the Republicans of the State of Kentucky now acquiesce in those Amendments, or now declare them to be legitimate and proper, it is not just or candid to charge them with inconsistency.

Let it be said that I am right rather than consistent.

Harlan's new civil rights position included several direct attacks on the Democrats for their opposition to civil rights measures. Defending the Federal Civil Rights Act of 1866 and condemning the failure of the Kentucky Legislature to allow Negro testimony in the state courts, Harlan explained:

Had the Federal Government, after conferring freedom on the slaves, left them to the tender mercies of those who were unwilling to protect them in life, liberty and property, it would have deserved the contempt of freemen the world over. It was due to humanity that some effort should be made to counteract the unjust and cruel policy which excited outrages upon their lives, liberty and property, and closed the courts against all remedy for such offenses, except where the proof [came from white witnesses]. . . .

Harlan went on to condemn the bands of Regulators and Klansmen who were terrorizing Kentucky, and he attacked the Democratic administration for failing to take strong measures to halt the breakdown of order:

For myself, I say that I have no terms to make with that band of murderers and assassins, denominated Ku Klux; Nor shall I have any terms to make with them, if I shall have the honor to become the Chief Magistrate of the Commonwealth; Nor has the Government of the United States any terms to make with them. If they cannot be reached in any other way, if the state authorities, who can act more efficiently than any others, will not protect its citizens in the enjoyment of their inalienable rights; if our courts are to be intimidated, and the laws trampled under foot by a band of cut-throats and murderers, I trust that some power will prove itself sufficiently strong to grapple with such monsters.

When questioned about the constitutionality of the recently enacted Federal "Anti-Klan" Act of 1871, Harlan replied, "I have carefully examined that Kuklux Bill, and while I entertain some doubts as to the constitutionality of one of the provisions in that bill, I see nothing in it to create any serious alarm among the law-abiding citizens of Kentucky." In another speech, he discussed his attitude toward states' rights by saying that he belonged "to that school of politicians, which teaches me, that I owe a paramount allegiance to the Government of the Nation. . . ." Although he respected "the just authority of the State," he could never forget that the Constitution and all laws made in pursuance thereof "are the supreme laws of the land, anything in the Constitution or the laws of the States to the contrary notwithstanding." He called on the people of Kentucky to submit to the War Amendments on that basis, for any attempt to disturb them would isolate Kentucky from the rest of the country.

If quotations from Harlan's former Know-Nothing speeches made good reading to the voters in reply to Harlan's immigration proposals, the Democrats found ten times the ammunition in Harlan's earlier civil rights statements, and Democratic campaigners laughed away Harlan's explanation that he would rather be "right than consistent." Harlan's opponent, Preston H. Leslie, stated that Harlan had assured the people that Republican civil rights policies were "revolutionary, and if carried out would result in the destruction of our free government." "That was a correct view of it," Leslie said.

Throughout the campaign Democratic orators branded Harlan a "political weathercock" and printed his earlier statements in opposition to the War Amendments, congressional civil rights acts, and Negro suffrage. They also advanced the argument, much as Harlan had put it in 1865, that the Republicans were advocating "social equality" between whites and Negroes. Harlan's reaction to the charge was to deny it. "What do they mean by this cry of Negro equality? Do you suppose that any law of the State can regulate social intercourse of the citizen? . . . We do not declare as the Democratic orators well know, in favor of social equality. No law ever can or will regulate such relations. Social equality can never exist between the two races in Kentucky." Stressing that what he advocated was the full legal equality of Negroes with whites, Harlan illustrated the distinction by saying that, in the public schools, it was obviously "right and proper" to keep "whites and blacks separate."

Harlan had not expected to win the governorship and he did not. He did succeed in piling up 89,000 votes for the "New Republicanism," 63,000 more than the party had received in the prior state election. As one Republican observed, "the long, dark, dreary night of Republicanism in Kentucky" was over. While the Republican party would not carry Kentucky for the presidency or governorship until 1896, it was a revitalized and united party that Harlan had built, and the Republicans were to play an important role in the political and economic life of the state, a role which the old Radicals had never been able to manage.

In 1872 the Republican state convention chose Harlan as its favorite-son nominee for Vice-President of the United States, and, once Grant and Wilson had been nominated, Harlan went through Kentucky and the surrounding states speaking for the Republican ticket. During the presidential campaign Harlan received a telegram from Senator James G. Blaine, asking him to come to Maine to speak for the ticket there.

Accepting the invitation, Harlan found himself one of fifteen or twenty speakers from different states who had been assembled by Blaine for a two-week, "whirlwind" campaign. The following year Harlan was appointed by Attorney General George H. Williams "to assist in prosecutions for violations of the Enforcement Acts of Congress." Harlan took the oath of office at once and participated in civil rights cases arising in the federal district of Kentucky.

In 1875 Harlan was chosen again by the Republicans as their gubernatorial nominee, over Harlan's "earnest protest." Again, Harlan waged a vigorous campaign, this time against James B. McCreary for the Democrats. Early in the campaign it became clear that the civil rights issue was still at the forefront in the minds of Kentucky voters, and that the Democrats intended to continue their attack on Harlan's pro-civil rights position.

One of the Democrats' main issues in the campaign was the Federal Civil Rights Act of 1875, which had prohibited discrimination against Negroes in inns, theaters, and public carriers. Charging that this gave Negroes greater privileges and legal rights than whites enjoyed (again a theme which Harlan had sounded himself in 1865), the Democrats challenged Harlan to state where he stood on the congressional act. Harlan responded, throughout the campaign, by denying that the act meant what the Democrats said it did and by accusing his opponents of trying to arouse racial prejudice. "The clear and manifest purpose of the Act," Harlan said, "as seen upon its face, was to secure equal, not superior, privileges to the colored race. Whatever rule or usage was applicable to whites in the manner of public conveyances, was intended by that bill, to be made applicable alike to the colored race." Harlan added that, independent of the Civil Rights Act, he believed that "under the law of Kentucky today, any one of the colored men within the sound of my voice has the same right . . . that any white man possesses to ride in one of your cars from here to the city of Louisville." Harlan seemed to be uncomfortable, however, with the act's application to private individuals, just as he had felt uneasy about "one provision" of the Anti-Klan Act of 1871. In discussing the 1875 act, Harlan called the attention of his listeners to a ruling that had just been made by the federal circuit judge for the district in which Kentucky was located. The grand jurors had asked Judge Emmons whether the act of 1875 required them to indict private persons who denied accommodations to Negroes, and Emmons had instructed them that it did not, since Congress had no power under the Thirteenth or Fourteenth Amendments to regulate discrimination by other than state governments. Harlan announced:

> In the conclusion which that distinguished Republican jurist reached, I concur, I do not believe that the Amendments to the Constitution authorize the Federal Government to interfere with the internal regulations of theater managers, hotel keepers or common carriers within the states in reference to the colored man, any more than it does in regard to white people. . . . These are matters of local concern, to be determined and regulated by local authority. . . .

To Harlan, the Civil Rights Act of 1875 had "ceased to have a practical importance in this State" after the Emmons ruling. The Negro people, he said, had not sought to cause racial trouble "in reference to the matters covered by the last Civil Rights bill," and it was only the attempt by the Democrats "to excite the people" over the act that was creating difficulties.

Following in the mold of the 1871 campaign, Harlan's speeches were defenses of emancipation and the War Amendments, of the Civil Rights Act of 1866 and the use of Negro testimony in state courts, of the full employment of legal rights by Negroes and the distinction between legal and social rights. Harlan again called for an end to race-politics and anti-Negro agitation.

As in 1871, the Democrats lashed out at Harlan the chameleon. The Louisville *Courier-Journal* remarked that "no one can laugh off inconsistency better than he, for his youth, the passions of the time, for which he was not responsible, are always at hand to excuse positions that to his present view are incorrect." In 1875 Harlan continued to urge the economic progress and social reform program which he had framed in the previous election, particularly the theme that "each and every citizen should be made to bear the burdens of the government in proportion to his ability to pay." His platform called for the spread of public education, the encouragement of immigration, a state antimonopoly program, and similar measures. The Democratic tide and the hold of war issues were too strong for the Kentucky Republicans, however; Harlan was defeated, although he continued to raise the Republican vote in the state.

During 1875 and 1876 Harlan spent most of his spare time marshaling support to secure the 1876 presidential nomination for his law partner, Benjamin Bristow, then Secretary of the Treasury. As head of the Kentucky delegation to the Republican Convention of 1876, Harlan made a nominating speech for Bristow which, in keeping with the nomination of a Southerner for the Republican ticket, dwelt almost entirely on Bristow's record of support for the War Amendments, the federal civil rights acts, free schools for whites and blacks to be paid for by a general property tax, and suppression of the Ku Klux Klan. On all these issues, the implication was clear; John Marshall Harlan stood alongside his nominee.

When it became apparent to the Kentucky delegation that Bristow could not be nominated and there was danger that James G. Blaine, whom the delegation did not favor, might sweep the nomination, Harlan threw the Kentucky votes to Rutherford B. Hayes and started the drive that won Hayes the nomination. Harlan stumped the border states vigorously for Hayes during the 1876 campaign. When Hayes was elected, it was a simple fact of political life that General Harlan—leader of the Kentucky Republican Party, a powerful Republican campaigner from Maine to Tennessee, and the man who had started the Hayes bandwagon in the Convention—had a major claim upon the new Republican administration. His position with Hayes was strengthened by his excellent work as one of the five commissioners sent by the President to Louisiana, in the spring of 1877, to decide which of two rival state administrations was the lawful regime. While the commission's finding for the Democratic claimants angered congressional Republicans, it greatly assisted Hayes in his settlement of reconstruction. In July of 1877 Harlan visited Hayes to discuss appointments for several Kentucky Republicans. Hayes brought up the question of Harlan's future and asked him, "Would a first class foreign mission tempt your ambition?" making it clear that this included "the very best Mission we have—the English Mission." Harlan said he thought not, but took three weeks to think over the offer, "because due respect to the President required that I should not appear to treat his offer lightly." When he saw the President again, Harlan expressed his profound gratitude for the President's offer but stated, as he wrote in a diary, "I could not, at my age of life, afford to live four years in Europe. My family was large and fortune limited, and to surrender my profession for any such public service was impossible."

In March of 1877 Hayes began consideration of a successor to Justice David Davis, who had resigned from the Court to become United States Senator from Illinois. Hayes determined to appoint a "Southern man" and spent the usual period entertaining suggestions, sifting candidates, and assessing political claims. By September, Hayes wrote to a close friend, "Confidentially and on the whole, is not Harlan the man? Of the right age, able, of noble character, industrious, fine manners, temper and appearance. Who beats him?" Convinced that there was no one who did "beat him," Hayes sent Harlan's name to the Senate on October 16, 1877, for confirmation as Associate Justice of the Supreme Court.

But Harlan was not yet a Justice. A set of complicated factors, focusing around the hostility of congressional Republicans to President Hayes's reconstruction policies and anger at the pro-Democratic report of the Louisiana Commission, caused the Senate Judiciary Committee to delay Harlan's confirmation and begin hearings on his suitability for the Court. Among the charges made to the Committee by anti-Harlan spokesmen was the allegation that he was not a "real Republican." One letter to the Committee warned:

I think that some little effort ought to be made to save the Supreme Court from passing into the hands of the late enemies of the Gov't & their allies. I think that a man who spends months personely [sic] electioneering for a place on the Bench ought to be rejected. I think a man who is by his own confession a particeps [sic] criminis to the late debauchery & revolution at New Orleans will be a dishonor to the bench. I think a man who opposed all the late Cons' amendments is a dangerous man to trust on the bench. . . .

Harlan had been warned about these arguments against his nomination by a member of the judiciary committee who was strongly supporting him, James B. Beck, Democratic Senator from Kentucky. To defend himself, Harlan wrote to Senator Beck on October 31, reviewing his political life and his changes of position, and enclosing extracts from his published speeches showing his support for civil rights measures. Division within the judiciary committee and concerted opposition to Harlan from two Senators prolonged the hearings until November 26, when the committee announced to the Senate that Harlan's nomination would be reported favorably. He was confirmed by the Senate and took the oath of office as an Associate Justice on December 10, 1877.

One important fact should be kept in mind when considering Harlan's career as a Supreme Court Justice, that his tenure on the Supreme Court—34 years—spanned at least three distinct periods in American constitutional history. When Harlan joined the Court, until the mid-1880's, the Court under Chief

Justice Waite was still attuned to pre–Civil War, Jacksonian ideas about the legitimacy of government's role in the economy and in civic affairs. It was also influenced by strong Unionist conceptions of the nation-states relationship, and by the idea that the Civil War Amendments had meant to create substantial federal rights for the new Negro freemen. The second period, from the mid-1880's until about 1904–6, saw the Supreme Court take on fully the ideology and mood of American capitalism in the age of enterprise, a time when business was the nation's idol, government was weak and often corrupt, and control of "alien forces" again began to preoccupy the white, Anglo-Saxon Protestant forces of middle-class America. During this era, the Court's majority raised property and contract rights to near-absolute status in American public law; reduced government to a negative, "night-watchman" function in society; regarded labor unions and farmer-protest groups as "interferences" with the free market and social Darwinism; and stripped away most of the meaning of the Civil War Amendments so far as the Negro in America was concerned. In the final period of Harlan's tenure, from 1904 to 1906 until his death, in 1911, the Court moved into a mildly progressive phase, reflecting the impact of Theodore Roosevelt's presidency, the muckrakers, the rise of city reformers, and what was to culminate in Woodrow Wilson's reform administration in 1912.

Justice Harlan participated in 14,226 cases during his years on the Court. In 745 of these, he delivered the opinion of the Court, wrote concurrences in 27, and joined the majority in 13,074. In 380 cases, Harlan dissented, 137 times with written opinions, 82 times joining in the dissenting opinions of other Justices, and 161 times registering a dissent without opinion. In the limited space available, a full review of his constitutional doctrines is impossible. A review of the themes from his decisions that are most revealing about Harlan as a Justice and as an ideological spokesman is both possible and appropriate for this volume.

One way to characterize Harlan (the way most commentators have tended to see him) is as a premature New Dealer, a man whose thundering dissents from the muscle-flexing conservatism of the Court majority were to become, again and again after 1930, the supreme law of the land. This portrait of Harlan as a consistent liberal draws support from many of his leading opinions.

In the realm of economic affairs, for example, Harlan protested when the Supreme Court declared, in 1905, that New York's law setting a ten-hour working day for bakers was unconstitutional as an unreasonable restraint on freedom of contract between employer and employee.[7] He dissented when the Court gave a restrictive reading to the Federal Pure Food and Drug Act, narrowing the protection that Congress meant to give to consumers by that legislation.[8] Justice Harlan wanted the Court's fellow-servant rule narrowed so that employees injured at work could recover for negligence chargeable to employers,[9] and he protested vigorously when the Supreme Court struck down the Federal Employer's Liability Act as constituting a burden upon interstate commerce.[10] He affirmed the right of working men to quit work simultaneously, and while on circuit, he rewrote broad antistrike injunctions issued by the federal district courts.[11]

In case after case, he attacked the Supreme Court's restrictive reading of the Interstate Commerce Act of 1887, and spoke out against decisions stripping the Interstate Commerce Commission of its rate-setting and regulatory functions.[12] He considered the Court's invalidation of the federal income tax to be a "disaster" and a "judicial revolution."[13] He opposed the Court's rulings in trust cases, maintaining that the Sherman Anti-Trust Law had been enacted to cover monopolies in manufacture which affected interstate commerce.[14] And he denounced the "sophistical" "rule of reason" developed by the Court in the *Standard Oil* and *American Tobacco Company* trust prosecutions.[15] He protested against doctrines under the

Commerce Clause that seemed to let corporations escape from fair taxation in the state where they did business,[16] protesting as well against the fact that state police power regulations enacted in the interest of health and morals were being struck down whenever these laws "touched interstate traffic."[17] Time and again, he warned that the Supreme Court was acting as a super-legislature over economic affairs, enacting its own notions of public policy through judicial legislation, and denying the right of state and national lawmakers to perform their constitutionally assigned function.[18]

When it came to civil rights, Justice Harlan bitterly condemned the Court's emasculation of the Civil War Amendments,[19] attacked the constitutionality of legalized segregation with its separate-but-equal foundation,[20] and in case after case insisted that the majority of his brethren were denying full constitutional protection to persecuted minorities in the nation—Negro, Indian, and Chinese.[21] He maintained that the protections of the Civil Rights Act applied not only to citizens but sheltered also the alien lawfully in this country.[22] It was John Harlan alone who struck out at seamen's work contracts that were so feudal in character and high-handed in operation that they constituted involuntary servitude prohibited by the Thirteenth Amendment.[23]

In the area of civil liberties, Justice Harlan held free speech and free press to be so central to the core of a democratic society that the Supreme Court should give them special protection against majority-will restrictions, and he was often led to condemn majority doctrines that seemed to set up "public welfare" as an easy justification for repressions of speech and press.[24] He insisted that the Fourteenth Amendment incorporated as rights against the states those fundamental guarantees of the Bill of Rights that protected civil liberty and due process.[25] His dissents, often solitary complaints, marked many rulings that he felt cut into these rights, as in cases involving the right to indictment by grand jury,[26] confrontation of accusing witnesses,[27] the privilege against self-incrimination,[28] the right to trial by petit jury,[29] and decisions which Harlan felt to ignore the constitutional prohibitions against cruel and unusual punishments[30] or ex post facto laws.[31] When the United States acquired Hawaii, Puerto Rico, and the Philippines, Justice Harlan challenged Supreme Court decisions that held that the Constitution did not "follow the flag"—that the standard civil liberties guarantees for American citizens did not extend to the inhabitants of these insular territories of the United States.[32]

Behind his dissenting opinions, John Harlan had private views on imperialism, labor, protective tariffs, civil rights, Republican Party strategy, and similar issues that were also in dissent from the dominant social thought of his day. John Harlan's view of corporations and captains of industry can serve to illustrate this strain of his credo. Writing in 1905 to his close friend and former law partner in Kentucky, Augustus Willson, Harlan expressed his deep concern over the need to check "the great railroad systems which threaten to dominate the country." Warming to his subject, Harlan observed:

> Indeed, the greatest injury to the integrity of our social organization comes from the enormous power of corporations. We must have corporations. We could not get along without them, but we must see that they do not corrupt our government and its institutions. Men in charge of corporations will use their money in ways and for purposes that would not be practised by them in respect to their own money. We had reached that point in the management of politics when educated men, being at the head of national and State committees would be willing to receive from officers of corporations money for political purposes which they knew was practically stolen from stockholders and policyholders.
>
> We are now passing through a crisis upon this subject of private and public honesty. The American people have determined to have a thorough house cleaning, the end of which will be elimination from our public life of many who are now influential and are deemed respectable.[33]

This cool view of the leaders of commerce and finance was deeply held by the Justice. Harlan wrote to his sons in 1896, speaking of Russell Sage, that "any such unmitigated scamp who loves money more than he does all else on earth, cannot appreciate or will not appreciate that anything else on earth is entitled to consideration in our government except . . . invested personal property."[34] In the same letter, Harlan lashed out at "that prince of railroad wreckers and corruptionists, C. P. Huntington, president of the Southern Pacific Railroad Company, and one of the monster swindlers of this age of money getting." These harsh opinions of the "money getters" were widely known to the public as well. An angry item in the *Illustrated American* noted:

Justice Harlan, of the United States Supreme Court, recently observed in a promiscuous company, that in his opinion half of the men in Wall Street should be in State's Prison. Certain men of prominence in Wall Street endeavored to get from Judge Harlan a denial of the remark attributed to him, but he declined to retract his ugly words.[35]

Perhaps the most fundamental concern that Harlan felt over corporate domination of American life was revealed when business spokesmen condemned his dissent in the income tax case. Stung by editorial denunciations of him for having "waved the red flag of Socialism"[36] and "expounded the Marx gospel from the bench,"[37] Harlan wrote to then Governor Willson:

The financial gamblers and their agents, and the holders of immense properties who object to paying taxes, are mad at me because my dissent drew the lines sharply and gave the country a true idea of the situation. I read my dissent with all the earnestness I felt, and my earnestness in this matter was quite as sharp as when the flag was fired upon at Sumter. . . . Slave property sought to dominate the freeman of America [then], and we know the result. Now, the effort of accumulated capital is to escape the burden of just taxation, and put all the burdens of government on those least able to bear it—those who are the vital forces of the country and who fight its battles when the country is at war.[38]

The difficulty with any full-dress portrait of Harlan as an orthodox liberal, however, is that other decisions he handed down, including several of the most important cases that Harlan and the Court passed upon in these periods, do not square with the liberal pattern. Consider these contrasts, for example. It was the liberal Harlan—the foe of due process omnicompetence and judicial legislation—who said in *Atkin* v. *Kansas*,[39] sustaining a state eight-hour workday law for public employees:

No evils arising from such legislation could be more farreaching than those that might come to our system of government if the judiciary, abandoning the sphere assigned to it by the fundamental law, should enter the domain of legislation, and upon grounds merely of justice or reason or wisdom, annul statutes that had received the sanction of the people's representatives.

Yet this same Justice Harlan declared in *Smyth* v. *Ames*,[40] that it was a matter for "judicial inquiry" rather than for state legislation or expert commissioners' judgment whether reasonable transportation rates had been set by the states. This duty was one from which "the court cannot shrink," and with a Fieldian basso, John Harlan declared:

The idea that any legislature, state or Federal, can determine for the people and for the courts that what it enacts in the form of law, or what it authorizes its agents to do, is consistent with the fundamental law, is in opposition to the theory of our institutions. . . . The perpetuity of our institutions and the liberty which is enjoyed under them depend, in no small degree, upon the power given to the judiciary to declare null and void all legislation that is clearly repugnant to the supreme law of the land.[41]

Consider the issue of labor contracts as another example. The same Harlan who dissented in *Lochner* v. *New York*,[42] condemning the majority's elevation of "liberty of contract" over the public health and safety interests in setting ten hours for hazardous bakery work, was the Justice who wrote a ringing Spencerian opinion in *Adair* v. *United States*[43] striking down a federal statute that prohibited interstate transportation companies from discharging workers solely because they joined a union after contracting not to do so. Said Harlan:

The right to purchase or to sell labor is part of the liberty protected by [the Fourteenth Amendment] . . . labor organizations
have nothing to do with interstate commerce as such . . . [This
Act] arbitrarily sanctions an illegal invasion of the personal liberty
as well as the right of property of the defendant. . . .[44]

Framing the central problem, Harlan stated:

. . . the employer and the employé have equality of right, and
any legislation that disturbs that equality is an arbitrary interference with the liberty of contract which no government can legally
justify in a free land.[45]

Many more examples could be given of Harlan's unpredic-
table judicial intervention in behalf of property rights, from
state bond repayment cases to the rights of patentees, from
rate regulation cases to taxation matters. But, as the two contrasting sets of cases just used as illustrations suggest, Harlan
had little of the consistency of a Field, a Bradley, a Hughes,
a Black, or a Warren about him, even allowing for minor de-
viations on the part of those men.

The answer—indeed, the central key to Harlan's judicial
philosophy—is that he did not believe that liberty issues and
property issues were separate or conflicting matters. In the tradition of Locke and Clay, he saw these as twin values, indis-
solubly united. He became as outraged by "improper" government interference with an employer, a bondholder, or a corporation, as he did with government injustice toward the
Negro, the Chinese, merchant seamen, or persons accused of
crime. While quotations could be supplied from dozens of his
civil liberties and civil rights decisions, it is, significantly, a
comment from a dissent against the right of a patentee that
captures perfectly Harlan's attitude:

I am of opinion that every officer of the government, however
high his position, may be prevented by injunction, operating directly upon him, from illegally injuring or destroying the property
rights of the citizen. . . . In my judgement it is not possible to con-
ceive of any case, arising under our system of constitutional government, in which the courts may not, in some effective mode, and
properly, protect the rights of the citizen against illegal aggression,

and to that end, if need be, stay the hands of the aggressor, even if he be a public officer, who acts in the interest or by the direction of the government.[46]

Thus, Harlan would dissent fiercely from majority decisions that he branded as "judicial legislation," but he never accepted the validity of that charge when he believed that "precious constitutional rights" were being violated. In this sense, he was oriented toward results, and if his idea of the just results has become popular among liberal constitutional historians and political scientists today, it should be noted that this is because such commentators take the parts of Harlan they approve and dismiss as anachronistic those doctrines that do not fit the present age. Such is the fate of many public figures, and, given our need for both continuity and public folk-heroes, the only real damage done is to truth and history, which have been victims in this game for thousands of years.

When Harlan died, in harness, in 1911, the Supreme Court lost a man who had followed both Henry Clay and Theodore Roosevelt; who had gone from slave holder and foe of the Civil War Amendments to the single consistent champion of Negro civil rights on the Supreme Court in his day; whose devotion to individualism was sometimes Arcadian but always rooted in the American dream; whose belief in absolute equality before the law could spread over both corporations and unions, black and white; and whose anti-capitalist impulses were tempered by an absolute regard for a fundamentalist Protestantism and an equally fundamentalist Constitution. A liberal he was, on balance, but neither an aristocratic liberal like Holmes (and without Holmes's intellectual heights as a logician and judge) nor a philosophical social reformer like Brandeis (and lacking the latter's self-control and self-consciousness in using the judicial function). Rather, Harlan was a man with first-class polemical skill and a powerful sense of the moral quality of American constitutional justice. From 1877 to 1911, in an era of getting and spending when men built America of bold visions and human wreckage, and when American politics was too often a game of boodle, Harlan voiced the protest of the Old America of the Jacksonian age, and carried the themes through the bleak years until the voice of American progressivism was heard again in the 1900's.

Today, with race relations transfixing American society and politics, his dissents in the field of civil rights are remembered above all else. In 1963, during congressional debates over public accommodation practices, his dissent in the *Civil Rights Cases* was urged as the proper view for Court and country, just as his dissent in *Plessy* v. *Ferguson* had been invoked and accepted by the Supreme Court in striking down the "separate but equal doctrine" in the *Segregation Cases* of 1954. Let the *New York Times* editorial written after that 1954 ruling, "Justice Harlan Concurring," serve as a fitting conclusion to this sketch of Harlan:

It is eighty-six years since the Fourteenth Amendment was proclaimed a part of the United States Constitution. It is fifty-eight years since the Supreme Court, with Justice Harlan dissenting, established the doctrine of "separate but equal" provision for the white and Negro races on interstate carriers. It is forty-three years since John Marshall Harlan passed from this earth. Now the words he used in his lonely dissent in an 8-to-1 decision in the case of Plessy v. Ferguson in 1896 have become in effect by last Monday's unanimous decision of the Supreme Court a part of the law of the land.

Justice Harlan said: "Our Constitution is color-blind and neither knows nor tolerates classes among citizens. . . . The arbitrary separation of citizens on the basis of race . . . is a badge of servitude wholly inconsistent with the civil freedom and the equality before the law established by the Constitution."

Last Monday's case dealt solely with segregation in the schools, but there was not one word in Chief Justice Warren's opinion that was inconsistent with the earlier views of Justice Harlan. This is an instance in which the voice crying in the wilderness finally becomes the expression of a people's will and in which justice overtakes and thrusts aside a timorous expediency.[47]

ALAN F. WESTIN *is associate professor of public law and government, at Columbia University. He has been a member of the Harvard, Yale, and Cornell faculties and the recipient of fellowships from the Rockefeller, Ford, and New World Foundations. He is engaged in the preparation of a full-length biography of Mr. Justice Harlan and a volume on the history of the Supreme Court, 1877–1911. Among his previous publications are* The Anatomy of a Constitutional Law Case (*1958*); The Supreme Court: Views from Inside (*1961*); The Uses of Power (*1962*); The Third Branch of Government (*1963*); *and* An Autobiography of the Supreme Court (*1963*).

NOTES

1. The biographical portion of this article is adapted from an earlier article by the author: *John Marshall Harlan and the Constitutional Rights of Negroes: The Transformation of a Southerner*, 66 YALE L.J. 637 (1957). For the continued use of the Harlan papers for work on a full biography, I remain indebted to the present Mr. Justice John M. Harlan, as well as to the Dean and Librarian of the University of Louisville Law School, where another portion of the Harlan papers are deposited. Footnotes to original sources for the biographical discussion can be found in the *Yale Law Journal* article. We are grateful to the *Yale Law Journal* for permission to use materials first published there.

2. 65 Ky. 5 (1867).

3. Coulter, *The Civil War and Readjustment in Kentucky* (1926), 422.

4. *Ibid.* at 433.

5. *Ibid.* at 359.

6. *Ibid.* at 360.

7. *Lochner* v. *New York*, 198 U.S. 45, 65 (1905).

8. *United States* v. *Johnson*, 221 U.S. 488, 499 (1911).

9. *New England R. Co.* v. *Conroy*, 175 U.S. 323, 347 (1899); *Martin* v. *Atchison, Topeka & Sante Fe R. Co.*, 166 U.S. 399, 404 (1897).

10. *Employers' Liability Cases*, 207 U.S. 463, 540 (1908).

11. *Arthur* v. *Oakes*, 63 Fed. 310 (C.A. 7th 1894).

12. *Texas & Pacific R. Co.* v. *I.C.C.*, 162 U.S. 197, 239 (1896); *I.C.C.* v. *Alabama Midland R. Co.*, 168 U.S. 144, 176 (1897); *Harriman* v. *I.C.C.*, 211 U.S. 407, 423, 429 (1908).

13. *Pollock* v. *Farmer's Loan & Trust Co.*, 157 U.S. 429, 608 (1895), rehearing 158 U.S. 601, 638 (1895).

14. *United States* v. *E. C. Knight Co.*, 156 U.S. 1, 18 (1895); *Anderson* v. *United States*, 171 U.S. 604, 620 (1898).

15. *Standard Oil Co.* v. *United States,* 221 U.S. 1, 82 (1911); *United States* v. *American Tobacco Co.,* 221 U.S. 106, 189 (1911).

16. See, e.g., *Galveston, H. & S. A. R. Co.* v. *Texas,* 210 U.S. 217, 228 (1908).

17. See, e.g., *Bowman* v. *Chicago & Northwestern R. Co.,* 125 U.S. 465, 509 (1888); *Rhodes* v. *Iowa,* 170 U.S. 412, 426 (1898).

18. Harlan's first dissent on the Court, in *United States* v. *Clark,* 96 U.S. 37, 44 (1877), and his last dissents, in the *Standard Oil* and *Tobacco* trust cases, *supra,* were each protests against "judicial legislation."

19. *Civil Rights Cases,* 109 U.S. 3, 26 (1883).

20. See, e.g., *Plessy* v. *Ferguson,* 163 U.S. 537, 552 (1896); *Berea College* v. *Kentucky,* 211 U.S. 45, 58 (1908).

21. For the Negro cases, see notes 19 and 20, *supra;* for a Chinese case, see *United States* v. *Wong Kim Ark,* 169 U.S. 649, 705 (1898); for an Indian case, see *Elk* v. *Wilkins,* 112 U.S. 94, 110 (1884).

22. *Baldwin* v. *Franks,* 120 U.S. 678, 694 (1887).

23. *Robertson* v. *Baldwin,* 165 U.S. 275, 288 (1897).

24. *Patterson* v. *Colorado* ex rel. *Attorney General,* 205 U.S. 454, 463 (1907).

25. See *Hurtado* v. *California,* 110 U.S. 516, 538 (1884); *Maxwell* v. *Dow,* 176 U.S. 581, 605 (1900); *Twining* v. *New Jersey,* 211 U.S. 78, 114 (1908).

26. *Maxwell* and *Hurtado,* note 25, *supra.*

27. *West* v. *Louisiana,* 194 U.S. 258, 267 (1904).

28. *Twining,* note 25, *supra.*

29. *Schick* v. *United States,* 195 U.S. 65, 72 (1904).

30. *O'Neil* v. *Vermont,* 144 U.S. 323, 366 (1892).

31. *Hawker* v. *New York,* 170 U.S. 189, 200 (1898).

32. *Hawaii* v. *Mankichi,* 190 U.S. 197, 226 (1903); *Downes* v. *Bidwell,* 182 U.S. 244, 375 (1901); *Dorr* v. *United States,* 195 U.S. 138, 154 (1904); *Trono* v. *United States,* 199 U.S. 521, 535 (1905).

33. Harlan to Augustus Willson, Washington, D.C., Dec. 1, 1905; Willson papers, Felson Club, Louisville, Ky.

34. Harlan to James and John Harlan, Washington, D.C., May 24, 1895, Harlan papers, author's possession.

35. Mother's scrapbook, undated clipping, Harlan papers.

36. *New York Sun,* May 22, 1895.

37. 60 *Nation* 394 (1895).

38. Harlan to Willson, Washington, D.C., June 1, 1895, Willson papers, *op. cit. supra* note 33.

39. 191 U.S. 207, 223 (1903).

40. 169 U.S. 466 (1898).

41. *Ibid.* at 527–28.

42. 198 U.S. 45, 65 (1905).

43. 208 U.S. 161 (1908).

44. *Ibid.* at 173, 178, 180.

45. *Ibid.* at 175.

46. *International Postal Supply Co.* v. *Bruce,* 194 U.S. 601, 606, 616–17 (1904).

47. *New York Times,* May 23, 1954, § 4, p. 10, cols. 1, 2.

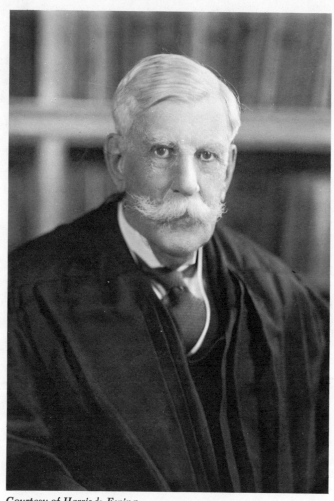

MR. JUSTICE HOLMES

Mr. Justice Holmes

By
FRANCIS BIDDLE

My observations about Justice Oliver Wendell Holmes are
made with the hope of catching and holding for a fleeting moment of memory the characteristics that were peculiarly his
and that are worth handing down to a generation of young
Americans. Such a re-creation—if I can achieve it—seems to me
to have an uncommon value. We Americans tend to live so
eagerly in the future that we have few links with the past. And
if the future enlarges the actuality of the present, the memory
of our own heroes can banish our historical insecurity and
strengthen the direction of our national aim. They can lift us
by the sense of their nobility.

Holmes's contributions to American life reached from his
days as a soldier, when he left Harvard College to enlist in the
Massachusetts Twentieth to fight for the Union in the Civil
War, through the first World War and a dozen years beyond.
That is a long span, seventy years of active life, and he was
busy from the first: turning to law after he was mustered out
on July 17, 1864, a lieutenant colonel; practicing in Boston for
a dozen years before he published *The Common Law* in 1881;
joining the Supreme Judicial Court of Massachusetts the next
year, against the advice of President Eliot of Harvard and
Professor Ames who wanted him to stay on in the Harvard
Law School—here was his *métier,* they argued, he was essentially a scholar and teacher. But he was eager to be closer to

the actualities of life, and he could not be content with the detached vision of the student's closet. After twenty years on the Massachusetts Supreme Judicial Court, the last three as Chief Justice, Holmes was appointed by President Theodore Roosevelt to the United States Supreme Court. There he served for nearly thirty years, resigning in 1932, when he was ninety-one.

The events of his life after the adventure of the war (he was wounded three times) were not dramatic. His personal life—serene, happy, normal—affords little material to the historian. More than most public men, even members of the Court on which he sat, his whole career was centered in his profession—twenty years as a student and scholar, nearly fifty as a judge. Yet his life from beginning to end gives one the sense of the passion and urgency of a man of great action. "On the whole," he wrote to Lady Pollock, "I am on the side of the unregenerate who affirm the worth of life as an end in itself as against the saints who deny it."[1] With this vigorous faith he enjoyed life hugely, enjoyed his work, enjoyed his friends; cared about good talk, knew the rare and lonely excitement of reaching into thought before expressing a conclusion in words which perhaps might touch the ultimate; felt, as he once told a group of Harvard undergraduates, "the secret isolated joy of the thinker, who knows that, a hundred years after he is dead and forgotten, men who never heard of him will be moving to the measure of his thought."[2]

That sense of hitching his wagon to the star of greatness, of never accepting the second best, runs through his utterances. He was the child of the flowering of New England, as Van Wyck Brooks has called that region's renaissance. He knew his father's friends and in turn took his place in the famous Saturday Club of Boston among Louis Agassiz, Richard H. Dana, Lowell, Longfellow, Whittier, Prescott the historian, Charles Eliot Norton, and Charles Francis Adams. Like them, he remained to his marrow and bone a New Englander—salty, cautious about money, not given to the new reform "nostrums" as he called them, loving the wind-swept downs and little inland farms of the country about Manchester where he spent his summers; sober, intrinsic, a sound mind in a sound body; self-disciplined; rugged in health. There was nothing of the modern American Bedouin about him. His roots were deep in his own soil, and he cherished his roots with a continuous sense of the overlap of history.

But being a man of a larger and richer world, he loved the complexity and range of life, himself a complex human being. He was full of contradictions, so much so that the easy classification of the casual critic whose ear is caught by some heady aphorism of the judge is seldom accurate. Holmes would have been amused—I don't think often annoyed—by these half-baked generalities which tried to catch and pin him down, a museum piece in a glass case for the crowd to gaze at. Thus he has been called the Great Dissenter; yet his major dissents have now become the law. It is said that he teaches that might makes right, that morality is blind preference, and that truth is what the dominant majority wants. His skepticism is thought to be his greatest sin, for skepticism, they say, allows neither faith nor compassion.

Such suggestions come from those who believe in absolute systems, which in the realm of law they call "natural law." Holmes disliked the phrase, and particularly the implicit suggestion that *law* was separate from an act of sovereign power, from something that could be enforced. His nature rebelled against the assumption that the preferences of a single group of the community, whether or not accepted by other groups, became law by a sort of laying-on of hands, and against this revealed test of moral assumption by this sanction alone contrary to the will and choice of the community. His was the instinct and outlook of a whole man—a contemporary in his own world. He was skeptical of all generalities, although he loved to make them. Were not facts, he liked to ask, interesting only to bring out the beauty of some theory of life, some new *aperçu,* like the necklace of a pretty woman? Skepticism, after all, was a part of the approach to his world of the eighteenth-century American democrat who, brought up on the separation of church and state, refused to recognize personal beliefs of the spirit in the public domain of the community.

He was a completely religious skeptic, disbelieving, as I have suggested, in static, and revealed concepts. The object of his great book *The Common Law*—a new edition was published only last year—was to present a view of the common law for which he believed other tools than logic were needed. "The life of the law," he wrote, "has not been logic: it has been experience. The felt necessities of the time, the prevalent moral and political theories [and] intuitions of public policy . . . have had a good deal more to do than the syllogism in determining the rules by which men should be governed. The law embodies the story of a nation's development through many centuries, and it cannot be dealt with as if it contained only the axioms and corollaries of a book of mathematics."[3] His approach was historic and eclectic. He tried to penetrate below the symbols of an established order to find the psychological or convenient reasons for their acceptance. To Holmes law was the expression of life, and like life was ever changing and growing, "always approaching, and never reaching, consistency."[4] Behind all law was the sense of the community. Thus in explaining the development of the law of liability, he said: "Every important principle which is developed by litigation is in fact and at bottom the result of more or less definitely understood views of public policy."[5] Of military conscription he remarked: "No society has ever admitted that it could not sacrifice individual welfare to its own existence."[6]

Holmes would have scoffed at the idea that he was a pragmatist if by that word it was suggested that he held, like his old friend William James, a metaphysical view which could be handily used to improve the universe. The historians Morison and Commager, when describing the pragmatic movement in the United States which began after the turn of the century, repeat the Italian Papini's remark that pragmatism was really less of a philosophy than a method of doing without one.[7] Holmes would have accepted the dictum to cover his rejection of absolute truths and his feeling for the organic evolution of law rather than reference to some abstract measure of judgment lingering in the bosom of Abraham. Such an approach sprang naturally from the American experience, with its shifting and progressive character and its inclination to put all ideas to the test of utility.

Even fundamental law was "an organic growth that must be molded to the changing needs of a changing society," according to Morison and Commager. Historical jurisprudence was being supplanted by sociological jurisprudence, a change which Roscoe Pound characterized as an "adjustment of principles and doctrines to the human conditions they are to govern rather than to assumed first principles."[8] This scientific approach to law as an evolution rather than an abstraction was reflected in the introduction of the case system into the law schools. It made possible the reinterpretation of the American Constitution, which came no longer to be regarded "as scholastic theologians" regarded "the sacred scriptures."[9] In a famous dissent in the *Lochner* case,[10] where the majority had held that a New York law limiting the hours of work in bakeries to ten a day was unconstitutional—the absolute was, of course, the sacred freedom to contract—Holmes dissented. "The Fourteenth Amendment," he observed, "does not enact Mr. Herbert Spencer's Social Statics. . . . A constitution is not intended to embody a particular economic theory, whether of paternalism . . . or of *laissez faire*."

It was not surprising that skepticism and pragmatism, branded as twin evils, were vigorously attacked by those who based their thinking as well as the conduct of their lives on absolutes; nor was it remarkable that in a society where so many revolutionary changes were taking place so fast, empha-

sis should be pointed to the blessings of continuity rather than
of change. Today many critics of Holmes's point of view, most
of them believers in the doctrine of natural law, call it pragmatism, a philosophical movement which, according to Professor Walter B. Kennedy of the Fordham Law School, "tends to
uproot all ideals, principles and concepts of the legal order."[11]
Kennedy by insisting that the principle of *stare decisis* has
been abandoned by the United States Supreme Court, which
no longer looks for certainty and continuity in law, seems to
forget that *stare decisis* grew up on the experimental and
pragmatic empiricism of the common law, that it rejects absolutes, and that it owes none of its life to such rigid conceptions
as natural law.

If these critics of Holmes could better understand him and
realize his apparent contradictions, they would learn, perhaps,
to reconcile the need for change with the necessity of continuity in a world that is not forced to choose between such
harsh dichotomies. That the American taste for gadgets has
turned a little sour in our throats, thus forcing our attention
beyond the monotonous efficiency of the assembly lines, does
not mean that Indians or Egyptians should be denied these
satisfactions as a partial way of life. Skepticism and faith can
exist together, and out of their balance a good life may be
obtained. The mind of Holmes, not his heart, was skeptical.
His zest for life was a faith in the reality of his own world and
his own country, which made him a wholly mature man. "Life
is an end in itself, and the only question as to whether it is
worth living is whether you have enough of it," he once said.[12]
His skepticism never wore off that fullness of living as it did in
other men of his generation. The doubts of Henry Adams were
not religious, but evidenced a mistrust in the value of life itself, which his aesthetic sensibility translated into a contempt
for the crude, raw, hurrying, and careless living of contemporary America—a turmoil and a rush which Holmes met with
his head up and a beating pulse. Is it corrupting for a man's

faith to be identified deeply with life because he discards a religious explanation of its variety and wonder? Holmes had his own beliefs, but he refused to call them eternal or to insist they must exclude the possibility of other vision. His skepticism never cooled the pattern of his loyalty to what for him counted as the ultimate.

His dissent in the *Abrams* case testified to his faith. Jacob Abrams, a poor and ignorant garment worker, had been sentenced to twenty years in prison for distributing a ragged little pamphlet which suggested in the usual hackneyed phrases that the workers of the world should arise to challenge an American expeditionary force to Siberia in 1917. ". . . when men have realized that time has upset many fighting faiths," wrote Holmes, "they may come to believe even more than they believe the very foundations of their own conduct that the ultimate good desired is better reached by free trade in ideas— that the best test of truth is the power of the thought to get itself accepted in the competition of the market, and that truth is the only ground upon which their wishes can be safely carried out. That, at any rate, is the theory of our Constitution. It is an experiment, as all life is an experiment. Every year if not every day we have to wager our salvation upon some prophecy based upon imperfect knowledge. While that experiment is part of our system I think that we should be eternally vigilant against attempts to check the expression of opinions that we loathe and believe to be fraught with death, unless they so imminently threaten immediate interference with the lawful and pressing purposes of the law that an immediate check is required to save the country."[13]

I have quoted this passage from the famous and moving dissent not only to show with what depths of belief Justice Holmes held his convictions but to indicate at the same time that the tolerantly rational turn of his mind would not permit him to confuse his own faith with any universal conception. It explains what at first appears to be a contradiction, the ancient predicament between faith and doubt. By indicating his major moral (and intellectual) premise, he would not allow his own belief to influence the reaches of his judgment. Here his deepest personal conviction coincided with the First Amendment—an experiment, as he felt impelled to describe it in order to make perfectly clear that even that great pronouncement was neither universal nor eternal. To many lawyers and judges, the idea that the American Constitution was an experiment instead of the expression of eternal verities must still be shocking.

Holmes never insisted that his preferences should be applied to others. Justice Frankfurter has written about them: "These opinions are the more significant in that, not infrequently, they come from a man who, as a judge, enforces statutes based upon economic and political theories which he does not share and of whose efficacy in action he is skeptical."[14]

This objective and judicious play of his mind did not spring from any lack of strong opinion about the economic and social experiments which, so often he felt bound to point out, did not offend the Constitution. He was a man of his age. He had been brought up on Malthus, Darwin, and John Stuart Mill, and he believed in them. Yet his inclination to keep the market without regulation did not incline him to damn constitutionally those legislative restrictions which in private life he termed nostrums. In 1910 he wrote Sir Frederick Pollock: "Of course I enforce whatever constitutional laws Congress or anybody else sees fit to pass—and do it in good faith to the best of my ability—but I don't disguise my belief that the Sherman Act is a humbug based on economic ignorance and incompetence."[15] Holmes was a liberal in the strict nineteenth-century sense, not in the meaning now usually attached to the word to designate an advocate of interference by the state to protect its people from the ferocity of the free enterprise to which the early philosophy of liberalism had led.

And occasionally he would lash out at the ameliorators, who

had a way of irritating him. In 1895 he said to the graduating class at Harvard: ". . . we have learned the doctrine that evil means pain, and the revolt against pain in all its forms has grown more and more marked. From societies for the prevention of cruelty to animals up to socialism, we express in numberless ways the notion that suffering is a wrong which can be and ought to be prevented, and a whole literature of sympathy has sprung into being which points out in story and in verse how hard it is to be wounded in the battle of life, how terrible, how unjust it is that anyone should fail."[16] He did not believe that you could legislate bliss. Once he remarked to his secretary that he saw no injustice in being born a toad rather than an eagle.

To the charge that Justice Holmes was pragmatic and skeptical is often added the accusation that he believed only in the brutality of force—that all law was founded on force. Reduced to its ultimate, one of his critics has recently remarked, this point of view is the negation of all ethics, teaching that might makes right, that morality is blind preference, and that truth is what the dominant majority wants.

Holmes, hating sentimentality and believing that it was healthy to remind the theorists and reformers now and then that law had no meaning unless it could be enforced, in one sense equated law and power. But such an attribute did not exhaust a conception; it described one of its essential attributes. Writing to J. C. H. Wu, a young Chinese graduate of the Michigan Law School, who had become a judge of the Shanghai Provisional Court—the letters reach over a dozen years— Holmes was eager to make Wu see just where he stood on the ultimate assumptions. He believed, he said, that there were no a priori ultimates—not even that man was an end in himself. "We march up a conscript with bayonets behind to die for a cause he doesn't believe in." Then came the sentence so often quoted with horror: "Our morality seems to me only a check on the ultimate domination of force, just as our politeness is a check on the impulse of every pig to put his feet in the trough."[17] But if by such aphorisms he liked to shock the bourgeois in all of us, particularly in young Professor Wu, whom Holmes had grown to love tenderly like a son, but who might not have, as Holmes had begun to suspect, the "fire in his belly," Holmes spent his life asserting the value of courage, of truth, and of tolerance. He had to point out now and then that these virtues were his personal preferences and that they ought not to be taken as eternal verities. He had come to learn and to insist on what Judge Learned Hand has called the agony of facing oneself. But if he doubted the ultimate values, his strong Puritan tradition would not permit him to question *his* values—health, hard work, courage amid doubt, an open mind and the will to achieve it. And sometimes he could outline his faith, rising above the doubts. In 1913, at a dinner of the Harvard Law School Association, he spoke of this faith—"the faith that I partly have expressed, faith in a universe not measured by our fears, a universe that has thought and more than thought inside of it."[18] And if to him life was "a roar of bargain and battle," he felt compelled immediately to add, "in the very heart of it there rises a mystic spiritual tone that gives meaning to the whole. . . . It suggests that even while we think that we are egotists we are living to ends outside ourselves."[19]

One cannot describe Holmes without recording the quality of his wit in talk as in writing, words and thought indistinguishable, so that his clarity, his freshness, and his poet's touch clothed his ideas in a style that made them sound inevitable. His irony was remorseless but accurate, often touching unpromising facts into incandescence, as, for instance, when the mayor of New Bedford was sued for discharging a policeman for political activities. The policeman, Holmes remarked in passing on his suit to be reinstated, might "have a constitutional right to talk politics, but he has no constitutional right to be a policeman."[20] That exactly was the essence of the case. In another opinion of the Massachusetts Supreme Court he concluded that: "A boy who is dull at fifteen probably was dull at fourteen."[21] With a polite yet satisfying irony in an opinion dealing with a will contest, he wrote: "If a single woman not otherwise distinguished should be minded to prolong the remembrance of her family name by a beautiful monument over her grave, we could not pronounce it unsuitable or improper as a matter of law."[22]

Now and then a rare side-remark from the bench would delight the brethren or any others who were within earshot. In the *Gavit* case a taxpayer had achieved a temporary victory in the Second Circuit, where the court had held that income from a trust fund was not taxable under the Revenue Act of 1913.[23] Holmes was interested, he said, because he enjoyed such an income. The taxpayer's argument passed the remark until the summation, when he ventured: "I hope, Mr. Justice Holmes, that the Statute of Limitations has not run in your case so that you will not be foreclosed from getting back the tax you have mistakenly paid to the Government." Everyone in the courtroom looked at the Justice. "Nothing you have said," he remarked with a deadly mildness, "nothing you have said, my dear sir, leads me to hope." He wrote the opinion reversing the judgment of the lower court.

Solicitor General James M. Beck, a Philadelphia lawyer, seldom resisted the temptation to quote Shakespeare at the end of an argument. On a particular occasion when the lawyer had indulged himself in a long bit from *Hamlet*, Holmes could not stand it any longer, and, poking Chief Justice Taft, who was comfortably asleep, whispered in his ear, by no means inaudibly: "I hope to God Mrs. Beck likes Shakespeare!"

Holmes's fame as a letter-writer adds luster to the extraordinary breadth and variety of his talents. Correspondence with Sir Frederick Pollock, the great English legal scholar and historian, records a friendship which began in 1874 when Holmes was thirty-three and with his wife spent a summer in

England. Admirably edited by Professor Mark DeWolfe Howe, who was Holmes's secretary in 1933–34, these letters run over a period of almost sixty years. Both men shared the same tradition of law, to which was added their interest in philosophy, in literature, and in art. Their reading covered an immense diversity—from Kant to Wodehouse. As they grew older, their interests broadened out on paper, and each year they let go a little more, particularly Holmes, who enjoyed thrusting the final shaft into a friend when the occasion was afforded. Of Henry Adams he wrote: "When I happened to fall in with him on the street he could be delightful, but when I called at his house and he was posing to himself as the old cardinal he would turn everything to dust and ashes."[24] Pollock criticized the stupidities of commentators on "the two greatest classics of our tongue, Shakespeare and the English Bible."[25] Holmes agreed, adding that the translators of the Bible "when they didn't exactly know what the old Jew was driving at had a general notion that it was something damned splendid and wrote taller talk than the honest Hebrew ever dreamed of."[26] The American's sense of continually balancing the complex in thought with the simple in most action is repeated in one earthy passage. A platitude, he wrote, had come home to him with a quasi-religious force as he was repining at the thought of his slow progress in new ideas, and it occurred to him to reflect how the greater part of life was wholly absorbed in living, in "victuals—procreation—rest and eternal terror." One had better "accept the common lot; an adequate vitality would say daily: 'God—what a good sleep I've had.' 'My eye, that was dinner.' 'Now for a rattling walk. . . .' Functioning is all there is—only our keenest pleasure is in what we call the higher sort. I wonder if cosmically an idea is any more important than the bowels."[27]

In 1953, the wonderful Holmes-Laski correspondence, also edited by Howe, was published. When the letters began, Holmes was seventy-seven, Laski "a frail stripling of twenty-three," to use Justice Frankfurter's phrase in the charming foreword. The letters continued until Holmes died, but before the end he could no longer give Laski's letters adequate answers, only "a few hesitating straggling words."[28] Holmes disagreed, he wrote Pollock, with Laski's direction, his "upward and onwardness," but he found among these young liberals an atmosphere of intellectual freedom in which he could breathe. And at least Laski "didn't believe that universal bliss would ensue if the world would only get a move on and obey when the *New Republic* says Hocus—Pocus—Presto-Chango."[29] In all these letters we get a sense of the man's style, not merely a neat phrase or felicitous approach, but texture and contour, a solid stamp of race below the surface. Young Laski felt it. "You can have a manner," he suggested to Holmes, "without having anything to say; but you can have style only when you have a *fond* of substance."[30] Only Holmes could have spoken of a "spontaneity taking an irrational pleasure in a moment of rational sequence";[31] or remarked that Bergson was forever "churning the void to make cheese";[32] or regretted that Dicey "could not think like a devil and therefore could not touch the complexities of the exquisite";[33] or pointed out to this talented and arrogant Englishman that "England with all its beauties and powers is Little Pedlington."[34]

Some day the definitive life of Justice Holmes will be completed;[35] and we shall have a chance at all the other unpublished letters: his long correspondence with Lewis Einstein, the diplomat; the letters to his friend, Mrs. John Chipman Gray; the great store of correspondence at the Harvard Law School. And he wrote them all in a longhand, often very hard to decipher, with meticulous care to say exactly what he meant—and to say it very well indeed.

If Justice Holmes had been asked to advise a young lawyer regarding his career, he might, I think, have said to him something like this: "I doubt whether I can be of much help to you, my lad. If you care enough you will achieve something.

But you must put everything you have into your work, the whole urge and flight of your soul—and then something more. You must hold only one standard—to live nobly if you are to practice a noble profession. As to your reading, don't spend your evenings dredging through the advanced reports of the courts. Read French novels, read poetry, read the things we once called the humanities. Above all, read contemporary books. No book after twenty-five or fifty years is worth anything—that is, generally speaking. Don't forget that when the Judgment Day comes you may be asked to recite on *The Decline and Fall.* . . . A good lawyer is a man of the world, first and last. A great lawyer is a man of the great world."

He would have paused, thinking his words sounded inadequate. How could he sum it all up in a sentence? Then he might have added, as he once wrote: And never forget, "Life is painting a picture, not doing a sum."[36]

FRANCIS BIDDLE, *a Philadelphia lawyer now resident in Washington, began his career in the law as law clerk to Justice Holmes during October term, 1911. He has held many posts of great importance in the national government, serving as Chairman of the National Labor Relations Board, 1934–35; Judge of the United States Court of Appeals for the Third Circuit, 1939–40; Solicitor General of the United States, 1940–41; Attorney General of the United States, 1941–45; and United States member of the International Military Tribunal, 1945–46. He is a prolific author whose writings include* The Llanfear Pattern, *1927;* Mr. Justice Holmes, *1942;* Democratic Thinking and the War, *1944;* The World's Best Hope, *1949;* The Fear of Freedom, *1951;* Justice Holmes, Natural Law, and the Supreme Court, *1961; and two volumes of autobiography,* A Casual Post, *1961, and* In Brief Authority, *1962.*

NOTES

1. *Holmes-Pollock Letters* (Howe ed., 1941), I, 101.

2. "The Profession of the Law," in *The Occasional Speeches of Justice Oliver Wendell Holmes* (Howe ed., 1962), p. 31.

3. *The Common Law* (Howe ed., 1963) p. 5.

4. *Ibid.*, p. 32.

5. *Ibid.*

6. *Ibid.*, p. 37.

7. *The Growth of the American Republic* (4th ed., 1950), II, 271.

8. *Ibid.*, p. 273.

9. *Ibid.*, p. 274.

10. *Lochner* v. *New York*, 198 U.S. 45, 75 (1905).

11. *Portrait of the New Supreme Court*, 13 FORD. L. REV. 1, 14 (1944).

12. "Speech to the Boston Bar Association, March 7, 1900," in *Speeches*, p. 122, at 126.

13. *Abrams* v. *United States*, 250 U.S. 616, 630 (1919).

14. "Mr. Justice Holmes and the Constitution," in *Mr. Justice Holmes*, ed. Felix Frankfurter (1931), p. 100.

15. *Holmes-Pollock Letters*, I, 163.

16. "The Soldier's Faith," in *Speeches*, p. 73, at 74.

17. *Book Notes, Uncollected Letters, Papers*, ed. Harry C. Schriver (1936), p. 187.

18. "Law and the Court," in *Speeches*, p. 168, at 174.

19. "The Class of '61," in *Speeches*, p. 160, at 162.

20. *McAuliffe* v. *New Bedford*, 155 Mass. 216, 220 (1892).

21. *Laplante* v. *Warren Cotton Mills*, 165 Mass. 487, 489 (1896).

22. *Davis* v. *Chase*, 181 Mass. 39, 41 (1902).

23. *Irwin* v. *Gavit*, 268 U.S. 161 (1925).

24. *Holmes-Pollock Letters*, II, 18.

25. *Ibid.*, p. 105.

26. *Ibid.*, p. 106.

27. *Ibid.*, p. 22.

28. *Holmes-Laski Letters*, ed. Mark Howe (1953), 1406.

29. *Ibid.*, p. 17.

30. *Ibid.*, p. 693.

31. *Ibid.*, p. 131.

32. *Holmes-Pollock Letters*, II, 75.

33. *Holmes-Laski Letters*, p. 712.

34. *Ibid.*, p. 745.

35. The first two volumes of Professor Howe's biography have been published: *Justice Oliver Wendell Holmes: The Shaping Years, 1841–1870* (1957), and *Justice Oliver Wendell Holmes: The Proving Years, 1870–1882* (1963).

36. "The Class of '61," in *Speeches*, p. 160, at 161.

MR. CHIEF JUSTICE HUGHES

By
MERLO J. PUSEY

Charles Evans Hughes's special qualifications for the exalted position of Chief Justice of the United States were recognized early in his career. While Hughes was still governor of New York in 1910, President William Howard Taft visited him at Albany and two days later confided to Archie Butt: "I don't know the man I admire more than Hughes. If ever I have the chance I shall offer him the Chief Justiceship."[1]

Taft did have an opportunity to carry out this intention, for a few months later the death of Melville W. Fuller left the Chief Justiceship vacant. Meanwhile, however, the President had named Governor Hughes to be an Associate Justice of the Supreme Court to succeed Justice David J. Brewer. In offering his friend this lesser position three months before Chief Justice Fuller's death, Taft had frankly informed Hughes of his wish to see him head the judiciary. Then as a second thought he had added in a postscript:

> Don't misunderstand me as to the Chief Justiceship. I mean that if that office were now open, I should offer it to you and it is probable that if it were to become vacant during my term, I should promote you to it; but, of course, conditions change, so that it would not be right for me to say by way of promise what I would do in the future. Nor, on the other hand, would I have you think that your declination now would prevent my offering you the higher place, should conditions remain as they are.[2]

Hughes had accepted the Associate Justiceship without giving any weight to Taft's desire to see him at the head of the

147

Court. "Should the vacancy occur during your term," he replied to Taft, "I, in common with all our citizens, should desire you to act freely and without embarrassment in accordance with your best judgment at that time."[3] Hughes did not immediately resign his governorship, however. When he took his seat as Associate Justice in October, 1910, Taft was still thinking of him for the Chief Justiceship, but the President did not come to a final decision until December.

Throughout this period it was widely assumed that the position would go to Hughes. Two of Taft's close associates then on the Supreme Bench, Justices Horace H. Lurton and William R. Day, told Hughes that they understood his promotion was assured.[4] The President is said to have gone so far as to place the nomination of Charles Evans Hughes to be Chief Justice of the United States into the hands of Vice-President James S. Sherman, asking only that it be held temporarily in abeyance because the President was about to discuss his choice with Senator Joe Bailey of Texas.[5] Other reports are to the effect that six members of the Senate Judiciary Committee called on the President and convinced him that it would cause friction in the Court to make the youngest member of that body its presiding officer.[6] In any event, Taft changed his mind and gave the seat under the bronzed eagle to Associate Justice Edward Douglass White.

Hughes was again considered for the Chief Justiceship in 1916. By this time his ability on the bench had been amply demonstrated, and his colleagues would probably have welcomed his promotion because of Chief Justice White's failing health and his lax methods of managing the conferences of the Justices. But the chief motive behind the linking of Hughes's name with the Chief Justiceship at this time appears to have been political—to keep him from resigning to run for the Presidency against Woodrow Wilson.

President Wilson's Secretary of the Interior, Franklin K. Lane, whispered to Justice Hughes at a dinner party that if he remained on the bench he would be in line for the Chief Justiceship.[7] Hughes thought Lane was joking. Then Chief Justice White, who had been a Democratic Senator from Louisiana, called at the Hughes home and said that he was going to retire and that Hughes would be his successor if he were still on the bench.

"Why," Hughes exclaimed in surprise, "President Wilson would never appoint me Chief Justice."

"Well," White replied, with the air of one who was weighing his words, "he wouldn't appoint anyone else, as I happen to know."[8]

Hughes dismissed the suggestion on the ground that any such appointment, following a refusal on his part to accept nomination for the Presidency by the Republican party, would be regarded as a deal. A few weeks later the Republican national convention did select him to run against Wilson, in spite of his efforts to discourage his nomination and his sincere desire to remain on the bench, and he resigned from the Court feeling that he had no honorable alternative.[9]

When Chief Justice White died in 1921, Hughes's name was prominent among those publicly mentioned as his probable successor. At that time, however, Hughes was Secretary of State, and the Irreconcilables in the Senate (who were angered by Hughes's efforts to get the United States into the League of Nations, without Article X) were trying to promote the idea of "kicking him upstairs." Hughes let President Harding know that if he should be offered the Chief Justiceship he would not accept it, and he would resign as Secretary of State.[10] Having set his hand to the plow as director of American foreign policy, he did not intend to turn back. He would have viewed the offer of any other position as an indication of lack of confidence in the work he was then doing.

It is interesting to note that when Harding named former President Taft to succeed Chief Justice White, Taft responded to Hughes's congratulations as follows: "I cannot but think that I am to sit in a seat that would have been yours by right, had you not responded to what you deemed the highest call of duty in two instances."[11]

One of those instances was obviously in 1910, and Taft seemed to be saying that if Hughes had not accepted the Associate Justiceship at that time he (Taft) would have named him Chief Justice. The other instance to which Taft refers was doubtless Hughes's rejection of the deal that he understood Chief Justice White to have offered him in 1916. In any event, the fact that Hughes was repeatedly considered for the Chief Justiceship over a period of two decades is indicative of his high standing in the legal profession and his eminence as a public servant. On all of these occasions his name was put forward without any connivance or even suggestion on his part. Indeed, Hughes never sought a public office of any sort, except to campaign for the governorship of New York and for the Presidency after being nominated with no effort on his part.

Certainly Hughes was uniquely prepared to be Chief Justice when President Hoover induced him to accept that office in February, 1930. To be sure, he protested that he was then too old to assume such a burden,[12] and after his nomination an irate faction in the Senate protested that he was too conservative. But both objections were lacking in substance. Hughes had probably passed the zenith of his powers (he was nearly sixty-eight), but he was still vigorous in mind and body and capable of outworking most men half his age. And his ripe experience as a practicing lawyer, investigator, governor, Justice, Secretary of State, Judge of the World Court, and civic leader gave him an advantage that no younger man could have matched.

Although he had never presided over a court before, Hughes took the reins with an easy grace and an appearance of mastery that gave him immediate and unquestioned leadership of the Court. This was of special importance because the Court was split into factions that were not only far apart in their views on basic constitutional issues but also personally antagonistic. On one side were Justice Pierce Butler, able, strong-minded, and outspoken former railroad attorney; Justice Willis Van Devanter, an amiable, bright jurist of the old school; Justice George Sutherland, former Senator from Utah, an exponent of laissez faire in economics but not in judging; and Justice James C. McReynolds, the narrow and crabbed former United States Attorney General from Tennessee. On the other side were Justice Louis D. Brandeis, the keen fact-finder and crusader for human rights; Justice Oliver Wendell Holmes, Jr., the aged philosopher of the bench, who was replaced in 1932 by the scholarly and judicial-minded Benjamin N. Cardozo; and Justice Harlan F. Stone, an able, experienced, and liberal-minded jurist who had been Coolidge's Attorney General and was later to be Chief Justice. Hughes stood about midway between these two groups, with Justice Owen J. Roberts somewhat to the right of him but also in a central position, and it was only the great respect of both factions for the "Chief," as they called him, that kept them working together in some degree of harmony.

Before his elevation to the office Hughes once wrote:

The Chief Justice as the head of the Court has an outstanding position, but in a small body of able men with equal authority in the making of decisions, it is evident that his actual influence will depend upon the strength of his character and the demonstration of his ability in the intimate relations of the judges. It is safe to say that no member of the Supreme Court is under any illusion as to the mental equipment of his brethren. Constant and close association discloses the strength and exposes the weaknesses of each. Courage of conviction, sound learning, familiarity with precedents, exact knowledge due to painstaking study of the cases under consideration cannot fail to command that profound respect which is always yielded to intellectual power conscientiously applied.[13]

Here we have the key to Hughes's success as Chief Justice. It was not so much the position he held as his own personality, his industry, and his keen intellect that made him the dominant figure in the Court.

Three distinct avenues of leadership are open to the Chief Justice. Although his vote counts for no more than that of any other member of the Court in the final decision of cases, he may exert a powerful influence (1) as the presiding officer over the open sessions of the Court, (2) as the moderator of the conferences in which the Justices make their decisions, and (3) as the assigner of cases to the Justices for the writing of opinions. Throughout his eleven years in the Chief Justiceship, Hughes took full advantage of these prerogatives to strengthen the Court as an institution and to lead it in the direction he thought it should take.

"In open court," Justice Felix Frankfurter tells us, "he [Hughes] exerted authority by the artistic mastery with which he presided."[14] No one in the history of our courts appears to have excelled Hughes in this phase of his work. His innate courtesy, his long experience in the practice of law, and his close study of proper conduct on the bench gave him a superb code of courtroom manners. His dignity, his resourcefulness and unflagging industry in analyzing the cases before the Court enabled him to meet every situation that arose. To see him in operation was to witness the administration of justice at its best.

In Hughes's eyes time was always precious. He opened court on the stroke of twelve o'clock, with never as much as a moment's delay in eleven years. As each lawyer began his argument, Hughes timed him with unvarying precision, using the ancient gold watch that his students had given him when he was teaching as a prize fellow at Columbia University in the eighties. No lawyer, however distinguished or vehement, was allowed to overrun his time. Once when counsel asked how much time remained, Hughes snapped, "Fourteen seconds." On another occasion he is said to have called time on a leader of the New York bar in the middle of the word "if."[15]

When argument in one case was completed, he would call another if only a few minutes remained before adjournment time. His determined effort to utilize every moment to full advantage irked some lawyers, but it helped to keep the Court abreast of its work and enhanced its reputation for efficiency and exactness.

The Chief was always reluctant to break into a lawyer's argument with questions. While at the bar himself, he disliked questions from the bench and developed in high degree the art of anticipating questions that would interrupt the orderly unfolding of a case. On the bench he remembered this. Yet if questions from the bench seemed necessary, Hughes did not hesitate to ask them.

Usually he got straightforward replies. The Chief Justice did not like to be told that a point raised by a member of the Court would be covered later in the argument. That reply suggested evasiveness. When counsel so responded to other members of the Court, Hughes often rephrased the question and got a responsive answer.

His faculty for sizing up lawyers "a split second after the first word was uttered"[16] was a notable aid to the Court. Because most of the lawyers who appear before the Supreme Court, except the Solicitor General, his staff, and a very few top practitioners, are strangers to it, Hughes made a special point of not letting their inadequacies or their unfamiliarity with the Court deprive the Justices of intelligent arguments on both sides of the case. If counsel wandered far afield, Hughes would bring him back to the chief points at issue by asking, "Isn't your argument so and so?" If the lawyer assented, the Chief Justice would say, "Now the Court would like to hear you on these other points," specifying precisely what he had in mind.

Occasionally Hughes almost took over the task of counsel before the Court. One day a lawyer completely lost the thread of his argument and began to talk recklessly and incoherently.

In his most kindly manner Hughes sought to refocus the lawyer's mind on the principal points of the case by asking questions, but counsel still babbled and stammered. At last Hughes took the brief and summed up the argument in masterly fashion, with the grateful assent of the bewildered lawyer.[17] Under his watchful eye no lawyer could stray very far from the gravamen of the case, but his interruptions were always courteous and helpful. "I know of no instance," Justice Roberts has said, "where a lawyer had reason to feel rebuked or hurt by anything that the Chief Justice said or did."[18]

As moderator of the conferences in which the Justices took their decisions, Hughes also exerted a powerful influence. Although he had never presided over a court before he became Chief Justice, he had learned the art by watching Chief Justice White in the days of his (Hughes's) Associate Justiceship. White was not an ideal presiding officer. Sometimes he left the Court without leadership. When he encountered a difficult case, he was likely to take it to conference with no solution to offer. "Here is a baffling case," he would say. "I don't know what to do with it. God help us!"[19] White's attitude encouraged rambling debate and needless controversy that were a source of irritation to the more efficient Justices on the Court. When Hughes later became Chief Justice, he was determined to avoid the mistakes that had handicapped his good friend and former chief, and in very large measure he succeeded in doing so.

Hughes's first precaution was to go to the conference thoroughly prepared. As petitions for certiorari, jurisdictional statements, and motions came in from the Clerk's office, they were studied by his law clerk. The Chief relied upon his law clerk for a comprehensive survey of these cases. With his clerk's notes on each case before him, he would then dip into the records and briefs and make concise notes of his own on all the cases that he believed to be of sufficient importance to merit discussion in the conference. Cases that seemed to merit no discussion went on a special list (the "deadlist" the clerks called it), and not more than half a dozen times in eleven years did any other Justice challenge the Chief's judgment to the extent of asking that one of these cases be brought into the conference for discussion.

The Chief would go to conference carrying his concise notes, his clerk's memoranda, his marked copies of records and briefs, and numerous lawbooks. Taking his seat at the head of the table with youthful exuberance, he was conspicuously prepared for any challenge that might arise. Edwin McElwain, the last law clerk who served him, concluded that Hughes's obvious and thorough preparation was a warning to anyone who might disagree with him to "know *all* the facts and know them well."[20]

With the Justices assembled at the conference table, Hughes would launch into case after case, succinctly stating the facts and his conclusions with scarcely a glance at his notes. His genius for stripping away nonessentials and going to the core of each controversy was strikingly in evidence. So accurate, fair, and complete were his statements to the conference that in many instances no other Justice would feel it necessary to add to what Hughes had said or to speak in opposition. Justice Roberts has told us:

So comprehensive was his knowledge of the petitions, briefs, and records, that if any question were raised by one of the brethren, the Chief Justice would reach for the printed book, which was full of white markers, turn to the appropriate place, and either summarize or read the material which supported the statement he had made. I do not remember an instance when he was found to have erred in his original statement.[21]

The discussion in conference was focused on about 40 per cent of the petitions for certiorari that came before the Court. Only about half of these survived the rigorous test that the Court applied. Soon the cases that were accepted came on for argument, and after the lawyers had had their say, Hughes carried these cases back to conference for decision on the merits. In preparation for this task he extended and, if necessary, revised the notes he had previously made in each case. His presentation of the argued cases to the conference was no less precise, although, of course, far more thorough than his outline of the "certs" had been. Once more Justice Roberts is the best witness of how Hughes handled this part of his assignment:

His presentation of the facts of a case was full and impartial. His summaries of the legal questions arising out of the facts were equally complete, dealing with the opposing contentions so as to make them stand out clearly. When this had been done, he would usually look up with a quizzical smile and say, "Now I will state where I come out," and would then outline what he thought the decision of the Court should be. Again in many cases his treatment was so complete that little, if anything, further could be added by any of the Justices. In close and difficult cases, where there were opposing views, the discussion would go round the table from the senior to the junior, each stating his views and the reasons for his concurrence or his difference with those outlined by the Chief. After the Chief Justice had finished his statement of the case and others took up the discussion, I have never known him to interrupt or to get into an argument with the Justice who was speaking. He would wait until the discussion had closed and then briefly and succinctly call attention to the matters developed in the discussion as to which he agreed or disagreed, giving his reasons. These conference sessions lasted from twelve o'clock sometimes until after six, sometimes until six-thirty in the evening, and sometimes the session had to be adjourned until Monday afternoon to finish the business on hand. It is not hard to understand that, at the close of such a conference, most of the Justices were weary. The sustained intellectual effort demanded was great. The way the Chief Justice came through these difficult conferences was always a matter of wonder and admiration to me.[22]

This thorough, objective, and forceful manner of presenting the cases to his fellow Justices accounts in large measure for Hughes's great influence in the Court. It must be remembered that his version of the case would be fully outlined before any other Justice had an opportunity to speak. The discussion would thus be centered upon the conclusions of the Chief Justice, and when the voting began, in the inverse order of seniority, the other members of the Court would be in effect voting with the Chief Justice or against him. As none of the brethren liked to differ from the Chief, the Court would be split only when deep convictions left no alternative.

Because Hughes's influence loomed so large within the Court, some casual observers have concluded that he was domineering. The reverse is true. To Hughes's way of thinking, dictation on the part of the Chief Justice would have been almost as obnoxious as dictation to the Court by the President or any other official. Moreover, he clearly recognized the impossibility of dominating such strong-minded men as Brandeis, Butler, and Roberts. A Court of independent Justices would respond to leadership based upon fair treatment, full discussion, and a thorough knowledge of the facts and the law, Hughes reasoned. But he knew that neither emotional pleas nor high-powered arguments could be effective, and he resorted to no such techniques.

Instead of trying to dominate his brethren, Hughes expended a good deal of energy in maintaining the confidence and good will of all members of the Court. Knowing that the conservative foursome—Justices Van Devanter, Butler, Sutherland, and McReynolds—frequently conferred together, the Chief Justice would neither join them nor sponsor a rival faction. While his door was always open to Justices who wished to discuss any sort of problem, he did not himself solicit the views of other members of the Court. Nor did he ask anyone else to support his views. With rare exceptions, no one knew what his decision in any given case would be until he expressed himself in conference with all the Justices present. "I am sure," Justice Roberts has written, "that this calculated course greatly strengthened his position and authority with the brethren."[23]

Hughes's attitude remained the same when President Roosevelt's nominees came to the Court in 1937 and after. Each was welcomed to the judicial fraternity with typical Hughesian affability. For example, when Justice Hugo Black took his seat in the fall of 1937, with a horde of critics still demanding his scalp because he had admitted one-time membership in the Ku Klux Klan, Hughes greeted him with warmth and courtesy befitting the most distinguished jurist in the land.[24] Justice Black when a Senator had also opposed confirmation of Hughes as Chief Justice and had fought tenaciously to pack the Court, but, so far as Hughes was concerned, Black's appointment as an Associate Justice entitled him to courtesy and respect. The Chief's congeniality and good will were not reserved for those who might agree with him. Consequently, Justice Black came to have a real affection for Hughes.[25]

It is sometimes said that Hughes, when various New Deal cases were under consideration, laid down the law to his brethren in the hope of averting retaliation against the Court. One rumor is to the effect that a newspaperman, standing in a corridor near the conference room while the AAA case[26] was being debated, heard Hughes remonstrate with the conservative Justices that they were not only ruining the country but also ruining the Court. Hughes wrote to his son that the report was "manifestly absurd."[27] Although he was deeply perturbed by some of the more reactionary decisions from which he dissented, he never lost his sense of proportion.

We also have Justice Roberts' word that there was no histrionism in the conference of the Justices:

Strong views were often expressed around the conference table, but never in eleven years did I see the Chief Justice lose his temper. Never did I hear him pass a personal remark. Never did I know him to raise his voice. Never did I witness his interrupting a Justice or getting into a controversy with him, and practically never did any one of his associates overstep the bounds of courtesy and propriety in opposing the views expressed by the Chief. The result was a feeling of personal cordiality and comradeship that I think was unique in a Court so seriously divided in its views on great matters of constitutional policy and law. Men whose views were as sharply opposed as those of Van Devanter and Brandeis, or those of Sutherland and Cardozo, were at one in their admiration and affectionate regard for their presiding officer.[28]

Rumor-mongers claimed also that Hughes changed his vote in the six-to-three decision that invalidated the Agricultural Adjustment Act. His motive, it was said, was to save the Court from the criticism to which another five-to-four decision might give rise. But this reckless bit of speculation did not even reflect intelligent guessing. Anyone familiar with Hughes's background knew that he would not alter his judgment in a case before the Court for the sake of expediency. Instead of lecturing his brethren and changing his vote in the AAA case, he outlined, in his presentation of the case to the conference, much of the reasoning that later went into Justice Roberts' opinion. This is one of the cases in which the Court is generally believed to have been wrong. In his retirement Hughes was well aware of the adverse judgment of the bar and of public opinion as to the Court's invalidation of the AAA, but he did not want anyone to suppose that he had taken the popular view and then altered his vote to minimize criticism of the Court. Short of voting against his convictions, however, the Chief spared no effort to achieve harmony within the Court on major constitutional issues.

In his exercise of the third great power of the Chief Justiceship, the assignment of opinions, Hughes also adhered to rules designed to strengthen the Court as an institution. It is true that he wrote many of the more important opinions himself. Occasionally he felt that the pronouncement of the Court was of such a momentous nature that the people would expect the Chief Justice to serve as spokesman. But he also took his share of the run-of-the-mine cases and attempted to make a fair distribution of the opinions likely to command public attention so as to avoid jealousies and to encourage the brethren to work together as a team. He wrote in his biographical notes: "My most delicate task was in the assignment of opinions. I endeavored to do this with due regard to the feelings of the senior Justices and to give to each Justice the same proportion of important cases while at the same time so far as possible equalizing the burden of work. Of course, in making assignments I often had in mind the special fitness of a Justice for writing in the particular case."[29]

At the end of the Saturday conference Hughes would sit down with his law clerk and make his assignments with the aid of a little chart showing the position each Justice had taken in each case. Usually he would try various combinations before he was satisfied. Then he would jot down the number of each case opposite the name of the Justice who was to write the opinion, and the clerk would deliver the assignments the same evening. There were two exceptions, however. Knowing that Justice Cardozo went to work on his opinions immediately after getting his assignment, the Chief withheld Cardozo's assignment slip until Sunday. Cardozo had suffered a heart attack before his nomination to the Supreme Court, and Hughes took this means of curbing his colleague's industry. In order to avoid suspicion that he was making an exception to shield Cardozo's health, he also withheld the assignments of Justice Van Devanter, who lived near Cardozo in a Connecticut Avenue apartment house.

With Van Devanter the Chief Justice followed a very different technique. Van Devanter had what his friend Justice Sutherland called "pen paralysis." In conference he spoke with remarkable fluency and clarity, but when he sat down to write an opinion, the words would not come. Van Devanter was often so slow in getting out his opinions that the Chief would have to withhold new assignments and occasionally to relieve the "pen paralyzed" jurist of a case to prevent procrastination from draining the substance out of justice. Hughes did it, however, with a fine flourish that avoided any ill-feelings. "Let me relieve you," he would say. "You are overworked."

In general Hughes frowned upon specialization by Justices.

To do his work properly, according to Hughes, a Justice had to be at home in tax law, admiralty, civil rights, and every other branch of the law. "Every Justice," he used to say, "should have a chance to demonstrate through the writings of opinions the wide range of his reasoning powers and not be kept before the public as an extremist or specialist working in one particular groove."[30] With this end in view, he made a regular practice of assigning conservative Justices to write liberal opinions and liberal Justices to write conservative opinions whenever the voting records made this possible.

When the Court was divided, Hughes also sought to avoid extremes by assigning the opinion to a Justice who had taken a middle-of-the-road view. That is why Roberts was chosen to write the opinion, in *United States* v. *Butler,* that brought the Agricultural Adjustment Administration to an end of its days. For the same reason plus his desire to make a fair distribution of the more important cases, Hughes originally intended to assign the *Gold Clause* cases[31] to Justice Stone. It was only after Stone dissented in part in one of the cases that the Chief Justice changed his mind and decided to write these opinions himself, for he was convinced that the three opinions should be written by the same Justice.

In writing his own opinions Hughes demonstrated both industry and dispatch. He could not tolerate the idea of the Court lagging far behind in its work, and he knew that the best means of keeping it abreast of its inexorable task was for him to set the pace in preparing his opinions and circulating them among the brethren for approval. This he did in spite of his extra administrative duties and the heavy burden of presenting each case in detail to the conference. Instead of being a place of repose for old men the Court under his leadership was a hive of industry.

Hughes's opinions were always worked out in accord with a routine formula. He first re-examined the set of notes he had used in presenting the case to the conference as well as any notes that he might have made as a result of the conference discussion. Secondly, he outlined the main points that he would cover and the order in which he would deal with them. Before he began to write, therefore, he knew precisely what he was going to say and the general form in which he would say it. With his conclusions thus formulated, he began to scratch out his first draft in longhand without regard for paragraphing, spelling, or punctuation. As soon as the first section was down on paper in this crude form, he would call his secretary, Wendell W. Mischler, and dictate from the script. The second segment would then be roughed out while Mischler was typing up the first, and this process would continue until the opinion was completed. This typed draft then went to the printer with such corrections as Hughes saw fit to make. Although the Chief made additional corrections on the proof sheets, he was not in the habit of rewriting opinions in proof, as some Justices have done.

Stylistically, Hughes adhered to some very definite ideas. Judicial opinions, he reasoned, have a special function—to make the judgment of the Court unmistakably plain to the bar and the lower courts.[32] Judges were not hired to write literature. Opinions abounding in catch phrases and sparkling classical allusions might be pleasing to read, but they were likely to be honeycombed with obscurities. Vagueness and confusion were the deadly sins of opinion writing. When Hughes sat down to write an opinion, his great struggle was for accuracy, clarity, conciseness, and power.

Feeling that every losing party should know precisely why he had lost, the Chief made it evident that he had weighed every important point. As he wrote, he used to imagine that he had a lawyer representing each party looking over his shoulder and saying, "Now, you 'son-of-a-gun,' don't dodge this point."[33] But his careful weighing of the issues resulted in no indecision. When the evaluating had been done, Hughes marshaled powerful arguments behind his conclusions. He be-

lieved that the decisions of the Court should be stated with all
the authority, power, and conviction that the writer of the
opinion could summon.

As to Chief Justice Hughes's contribution to the law, the
first factor that we should note is the judicial quality of his
mind. He has often been referred to as a statesman on the
bench, but that designation does him an injustice. In the roles
of governor of New York and of Secretary of State from 1921
to 1925 he demonstrated many qualities of statesmanship. On
the bench, however, he was strictly a judge. When he rendered
a decision, he was not primarily influenced by what he thought
might be best for the administration in power or popular with
the people or even in the national interest. Rather, he made a
sincere and conscientious effort to state the law as he found it
by judicially examining the Constitution, the statutes, and the
precedents in the light of the living society which the law must
serve.

Hughes was always keenly aware of the limitations that the
American political system places upon governments. "These
limitations were imposed," he used to say, "so as to safeguard
rights believed to be fundamental."[34] It was the inescapable
duty of the judge to maintain those barriers to arbitrary
power. Although he recognized the difficulty of the task, he insisted that the conscientious judge could not shrink from it. To
the end of his days he held firmly to that conviction.

At the same time he recognized the law as a living thing.
The Founding Fathers had not invented a strait-jacket but a
system under which free men could live as long as they might
retain the intelligence and restraint to respect its principles.
That system, he insisted, leaves ample room for change and
experimentation. In a speech he amplified that view as follows:

We must ever keep before our minds the illuminating phrase of
Marshall, "that it is a *constitution* we are expounding." That constitution was made, as Justice Matthews observed, "for an undefined
and expanding future, and for a people gathered and to be gathered from many nations and of many tongues." We should be faith-

less to our supreme obligation if we interpreted the great generalities of the Constitution so as to forbid flexibility in making adaptations to meet new conditions, and to prevent the correction of new abuses incident to the complexity of our life, or as crystallizing our own notions of policy, our personal views of economics and our theories of moral or social improvement.[35]

Deeply aware of this double duty of the judge—first, to hold to the fundamentals of the law and, second, to view those fundamentals in the light of current realities—Hughes distrusted the labels so frequently applied to Justices. He rejected classification either as a conservative or as a liberal. His basic loyalty on the bench was to the American political system and to the concept of justice itself. I do not, of course, contend that he attained complete objectivity. No human being can do that. But he probably attained as high a degree of judicial detachment as any man who ever sat on the bench in this country.

The "statesmanship" attributed to Hughes as a Justice is usually related to an alleged shift of views or to pressures applied to his brethren in 1937 to save the Court from being packed. The case most frequently cited to prove the point is *West Coast Hotel* v. *Parrish*,[36] in which the Court overthrew its previous decision that state minimum-wage laws were unconstitutional. In 1936 the Court had upset the New York minimum-wage law for women in *Morehead* v. *New York* ex rel. *Tipaldo*.[37] In the spring of 1937, after President Roosevelt had introduced his bill to add six new Justices to the Court if the Justices then over seventy years of age did not retire, the Court found a similar statute of the state of Washington to meet all the requirements of the Constitution. It was logical to assume—in the absence of facts to the contrary—that the Court had reversed itself under pressure.

Chief Justice Hughes disclosed in his biographical notes, however, that this momentous decision had been taken two months before any member of the Court had an inkling of the Court-packing plan. So far as Hughes himself was concerned, he needed no conversion on the point at issue. He had vigorously dissented when five members of the Court had struck down the New York minimum-wage law. Indeed, he had voted to uphold minimum-wage legislation during his first period of service on the Supreme Bench from 1910 to 1916.[38] When the *Tipaldo* decision was rendered, he felt that the Court had inflicted a grave wound upon itself. Consequently, he welcomed the *West Coast Hotel* case as an opportunity for the Court to correct its error. Although he argued vigorously for such action, he kept his presentation of the case to his brethren solely on a judicial plane, without any suggestion that the majority ought to yield to the public demand for a reversal of the *Tipaldo* precedent.

Hughes laid the *West Coast Hotel* case before the conference of the Justices in December, 1936. This time the Court divided four to four, with Hughes, Brandeis, Cardozo, and Roberts voting to uphold Washington's minimum wage law, and with Van Devanter, Butler, Sutherland, and McReynolds in opposition. Justice Roberts had changed his mind. When the Chief Justice learned of this shift, he almost hugged Roberts, but he had not hounded the younger Justice nor tried to alter his views.

The four-to-four vote would have saved the Washington statute as it had been held constitutional by the highest court of that state. But Hughes was reluctant to have such an important decision made by a tie vote. Knowing that Justice Stone, who was ill at the time, would vote with the liberal wing of the Court on his return, the Chief Justice decided to hold the case. Stone returned to the bench about February 1, and the Court then overturned the *Tipaldo* decision and the older precedents by a vote of five to four. Before Hughes finished writing his opinion, however, the Court-packing bombshell burst on February 5. When all the facts are known, there is nothing whatever in this incident to suggest that Hughes yielded to expediency. On the contrary, he held tenaciously to the finest tradition of an independent judiciary.

In so short an essay it is impossible to give any adequate impression of Hughes's impact on the legal thinking of his day. We can get some impression of his work on the bench, however, by looking at a few opinions in fields in which his influence has been especially felt—the fields of civil liberties and the Commerce Clause. It is interesting to note that Hughes's first great civil liberties opinion, known as *Bailey* v. *Alabama,*[39] which was handed down soon after he first joined the Court, brought him into collision with his very good friend, Justice Holmes. It was the case of a poor and ignorant Negro tenant farmer who had been sentenced to 136 days of hard labor under Alabama's peonage law. Hughes insisted that the law had the effect of punishing a man for debt and that it was therefore a violation of rights guaranteed by the Thirteenth Amendment. Holmes wrote a strong dissent that has ever since been a source of puzzlement to his admirers. For the most part, however, these two giants of the law were found side by side in demanding a broad and meaningful interpretation of the rights embedded in the Constitution.

When Hughes returned to the Supreme Bench as Chief Justice in 1930, there was much confusion as to whether freedom of speech, freedom of the press, and similar basic rights were secure against encroachments by the states. The First Amendment clearly forbade Congress to invade these rights and liberties, but it was not so clear that they were among the liberties protected by the Fourteenth Amendment from impairment by the states. Within a decade, the Court had looked both ways. It seemed to be waiting for a vigorous hand to turn the course of evolution in one direction or the other.

Hughes supplied this decisive influence. On three successive Mondays in the spring of 1931, he spoke fluently and inspiringly for free speech, free thought, and freedom of the press. *Stromberg* v. *California*[40] proclaimed the right of "free political discussion" and the privilege of a young woman to display the red flag in a Communist camp so long as she did not "incite to violence and crime and threaten the overthrow of organized government by unlawful means." *Near* v. *Minnesota*[41] struck down a state law that was designed to muzzle "malicious, scandalous and defamatory" newspapers and magazines by declaring them to be a public nuisance. Hughes found it "impossible to conclude" that freedom of the press "was left unprotected by the general guaranty of fundamental rights of persons and property." Here was a basic freedom that was inextricably woven into the fabric of American life. If public officials in the states could silence their journalistic critics by branding them as public nuisances, the right of the people to know the facts about their local governments would be dangerously compromised. Hughes was particularly exercised because the Minnesota statute had laid restraints on newspapers in advance of publication. For him there was no question that freedom from such arbitrary restraints was included in the liberty protected by the Due Process Clause of the Fourteenth Amendment. Nor was he shaken by the evidence indicating that the paper that had been suppressed was a miserable little scandal sheet. He spoke for a great principle, and that principle may now be regarded as firmly established in American law.

In his opinion on religious freedom,[42] Hughes spoke for only a minority of the court, but it was a powerful minority including also Holmes, Brandeis, and Stone. A majority of five Justices, with Sutherland writing the opinion, had denied citizenship to Douglas Clyde Macintosh, a Canadian-born professor of divinity at Yale University, because he would commit himself to fight in defense of the United States only if he thought the war to be morally justified. Hughes was in entire sympathy with Holmes's classic plea in the similar *Schwimmer* case[43] for "freedom for the thought that we hate." But in writing the *Macintosh* dissent he followed a very different line of reasoning, which was less philosophical and more judicial. Pushing aside the question of whether it was right to deny citizenship to persons who refuse to bear arms, he insisted that the real issue lay in what Congress had in fact required. Examining in detail the naturalization oath prescribed by Congress, he found no obligatory arms-bearing requirement. Indeed, the oath was substantially the same as that prescribed for civil officers. Since men with religious scruples against war were not deemed to be ineligible for public service because they would have to take an oath to support the Constitution, why should they be deemed ineligible for citizenship? He noted also that Congress had made a practice of excusing conscientious objectors from military service. Then the Chief Justice pressed home his central point that the requirement of the naturalization oath "should be read in the light of our regard from the beginning for freedom of conscience." Five years after Hughes had left the bench the Supreme Court, reversing the majority that had prevailed over him in 1931, made his opinion in the *Macintosh* case the law of the land.[44]

In 1933 Hughes extended the doctrine of *Near* v. *Minnesota* to handbills, circulars, and tracts, this time upsetting a city ordinance of Griffin, Georgia, at the behest of a Jehovah's Witness.[45] In another notable opinion by the Chief Justice the Court freed Dirk DeJonge from a seven-year sentence for helping to conduct a Communist party meeting in Portland, Oregon.[46] Freedom of assembly was thus added to the liberties that the states could not infringe. Always on guard against racial prejudices, Hughes wrote numerous opinions upsetting discriminatory practices. The Court overturned the convictions in the *Scottsboro* case because the defendants had not been given adequate counsel.[47] When the second case reached the Court, Hughes wrote the opinion rejecting the convictions because Negroes were systematically excluded from juries in the Alabama county where the trials had been held.[48] In 1938 he also spoke for the Court in a memorable decision compelling the University of Missouri to admit Lloyd Gaines, a Negro.[49] Scrupulous in not permitting anyone to abuse civil rights, Chief Justice Hughes always accorded a sympathetic hearing to the lowly citizen pleading for justice and equal standing before the law.

Turning now to the evolution of the Commerce Clause to which Chief Justice Hughes contributed, we must again begin with his opinions as an Associate Justice—opinions that were handed down more than forty years ago—the most notable opinion coming in the *Minnesota Rate* cases.[50] Government control over public service corporations was then in its infancy, and the regulation of railroad rates appeared to be near a breakdown. For one thing, powerful corporations were overwhelming the courts with a flood of complicated litigation. On the one hand, they insisted that Congress could not touch railroads operating wholly within a state, and, on the other hand, state regulation was challenged as an encroachment upon their property rights. There were grave questions of whether the courts could cope with the volume of these suits and of whether the rival claims of national and state regulatory power could be reconciled without doing violence to the federal system. All these problems seemed to be put before the Supreme Court at once in the *Minnesota Rate* cases.

The Court found the dilemma too baffling to dispose of by the usual procedures. After a discussion in conference, the brethren could agree on only one point: they were not ready to vote one way or the other. Some Justices expressed doubt whether it would be possible to write an opinion that would cut through the morass of precedents and bring order and system out of the existing regulatory chaos. Finally, Chief Justice White asked Hughes if he would take the case and see if he could work out a satisfactory solution that the majority would sustain. Hughes was especially qualified for this unique assignment by his experience with rate regulation in New York, where he was instrumental in creating the country's first full-fledged public service commission. Accepting the assignment, he toiled over the case for some months and produced a 100-page opinion that satisfied every member of the Court except Justice McKenna, who found it too long to read, although he concurred in the result.

Hughes's solution was a ringing affirmation of federal power to control commerce within the states whenever that appeared necessary to orderly and effective regulation of commerce among the states. "The authority of Congress," he wrote, "extends to every part of interstate commerce, and to every instrumentality or agency by which it is carried on; and the full control by Congress of the subjects committed to its regulation is not to be denied or thwarted by the commingling of interstate and intrastate operations."[51] Although the Court held that the states might impose regulations on local commerce so long as Congress had not occupied the field, the overriding power that it assigned to Congress is the source of much of the national regulatory legislation that has since come into being.

The doctrine of the *Minnesota Rate* cases was directly invoked in the *Shreveport* case[52] to strike down discriminatory state railway rates in Texas. Writing once more for the Court, Hughes declared: "By virtue of the comprehensive terms of the grant, the authority of Congress is at all times adequate to meet the varying exigencies that arise and to protect the national interest by securing the freedom of interstate commercial intercourse from local control." These decisions sustained in pointed form the doctrine that Congress could reach beyond interstate commerce itself to regulate any operations tending directly to injure or obstruct that commerce. Here was a formula that could readily be used to bring about federal control of the national economy.

As Chief Justice, Hughes did no more than further to expound, elaborate, and apply this doctrine. It is often said that in the so-called *"Hot Oil"* case[53] and the *NRA* case[54] Hughes turned his back upon this doctrine and took a narrower concept of the Commerce Clause. But that contention can be maintained, in my opinion, only by turning one's back upon what he said in those opinions. Anyone who takes the trouble to read them will note that he reiterated the broad scope of the commerce power. In the so-called "sick-chicken" case he was very pointed in this emphasis. "The power of Congress," he wrote, "extends not only to the regulation of transactions, which are part of interstate commerce, but to the protection of that commerce from injury. It matters not that the injury may be due to the conduct of those engaged in intrastate operations."[55] But in the case before him he could find no impact upon interstate commerce from the Schechters' chicken business. All their transactions were within the state of New York. No "flow of commerce" into or out of that state was involved in the Schechters' alleged offense. The "Live Poultry Code" which they had violated was a wholly local regulation that had no appreciable effect upon interstate commerce. Every member of the Court, including Justices Brandeis, Stone, and Cardozo, agreed that the NRA had extended its operations beyond the limits of federal power.

The other case in which Hughes is frequently said to have constricted the commerce power is *Carter* v. *Carter Coal Company*,[56] in which the Guffey Coal Act was held to be unconstitutional. It must be remembered, however, that Hughes dissented in part from the majority ruling in this case. He insisted that the price-fixing section of the law should have been permitted to stand. The labor provisions he regarded as invalid chiefly because of the broad delegation of legislative power, without standards or limitations, and the arrangement under which one group of producers and employees could impose rules governing hours and wages on other groups not parties to the agreement.

When the validity of the National Labor Relations Act was challenged before the Supreme Court in 1937,[57] different issues were presented. Here was a vast enterprise operating steel mills, steamships, railroads, and other industries in several states. Labor-management disputes in such an industrial empire would have immediate and far-reaching effects upon interstate commerce. In writing the opinion of the Court, Hughes did not suddenly abandon the obvious truth that industrial production is not commerce, but he concluded that "the fact that the employees here concerned were engaged in production is not determinative. The question remains as to the effect upon interstate commerce of the labor practice involved."[58]

The Chief Justice then went on to say: "Instead of being beyond the pale, we think that it presents in a most striking way the close and intimate relation which a manufacturing industry may have to interstate commerce and we have no doubt that Congress had constitutional authority to safeguard the right of respondent's employees to self-organization and freedom in the choice of representatives for collective bargaining."[59]

What we have in these opinions is a gradual unfolding of Hughes's concept of the breadth and amplitude of the commerce power. In the *NRA* case he and every other member of the Court felt that Congress had gone overboard in applying its power, and for this reason he led the Court in upsetting the venture. But Hughes was delighted to throw the emphasis once more upon the broad scope of the commerce power when *N.L.R.B.* v. *Jones & Laughlin* gave him that opportunity. Chief Justice Stone and several other notable authorities have recognized that in this momentous opinion Hughes merely projected the principles that he had enunciated twenty-four years before in the *Minnesota Rate* cases, and I know from many discussions with Chief Justice Hughes on this point that he regarded his Commerce Clause opinions as following a wholly consistent pattern.

It is too early, of course, to determine Hughes's ultimate standing among the great men of the Supreme Court, but he is rated highly by judges, lawyers, and students of the Court today.[60] He proved to be a presiding officer of unsurpassed skill, a judge of keen sensibilities, of profound knowledge of the law, and of sympathetic understanding of our political system. His life is a monumental challenge to students of the law and members of the bar.

Hughes presided over the Court during a period of great ferment. At a time when there was a tendency to dismiss constitutionalism as being old-fashioned and to strain the balance of power on which our political system as well as our freedom rests, his judicial-mindedness was a powerful restraint upon excesses. At the same time his sensitivity to the pulsing relationship between life and the law helped to save the country from economic and social atrophy. As Marshall in his day was the great expounder of the Constitution, Hughes in this century has been at once the great conservator of our political system and a tireless modernizer of outmoded judicial concepts. In my opinion, his genius in adapting the law to the requirements of our changing society, without impairment of its fundamental safeguards, will be increasingly recognized as we look back at his career through the perspective of history.

MERLO J. PUSEY *is associate editor of the* Washington Post– Times-Herald *and has been on the* Post's *editorial staff since 1928. He is a Pulitzer Prize winner and the holder of the Bancroft Prize and the Tamiment Institute Prize. In addition to his authorized biography of Charles Evans Hughes, which first appeared in 1951, his books include* The Supreme Court Crisis, 1937, Big Government: Can We Control It? *1945, and* Eisenhower the President, *1956.*

NOTES

1. *Taft and Roosevelt: The Intimate Letters of Archie Butt* (1924), I, 310.

2. Taft to Hughes, April 22, 1910.

3. Hughes to Taft, April 24, 1910.

4. Hughes's Biographical Notes, p. 42.

5. Letter from Representative Sam Hobbs, November 2, 1951.

6. Stephen Bonsal, in *New York Times,* January 16, 1921, §VII, p. 1, col. 7.

7. Hughes' Biographical Notes, p. 231.

8. *Ibid.*

9. Hughes to Joseph Buffington, July 24, 1916.

10. Interview with Henry P. Fletcher, August 10, 1946.

11. Taft to Hughes, July 8, 1921.

12. Hughes' Biographical Notes, p. 2.

13. *The Supreme Court of the United States* (1928), p. 57.

14. *"The Administrative Side"* of Chief Justice Hughes, 63 HARV. L. REV. 1, 4 (1949).

15. McElwain, *The Business of the Supreme Court as Conducted by Chief Justice Hughes,* 63 HARV L. REV. 5, 17 (1949).

16. *Ibid.,* p. 16.

17. Interview with Randolph Paul, February 9, 1950.

18. Roberts, Memorial Address before New York Bar Associations, December 12, 1948.

19. Interview with Hughes, May 15, 1946.

20. McElwain, *op. cit.,* p. 14.

21. Roberts, *op. cit.*

22. *Ibid.*

23. *Ibid.*

24. Interview with Justice Black, February 2, 1950.

25. *Ibid.*

26. *United States* v. *Butler,* 297 U.S. 1 (1936).

27. Hughes to Charles Evans Hughes, Jr., February 22, 1937.

28. Roberts, *op. cit.*

29. Hughes's Biographical Notes, p. 16.

30. Interview with Hughes, October 17, 1946.

31. *Norman* v. *B. & O. R.R.,* 294 U.S. 240 (1935); *Nortz* v. *United States,* 294 U.S. 317 (1935); *Perry* v. *United States,* 294 U.S. 330 (1935).

32. Interview with Hughes, May 28, 1947.

33. *Ibid.*

34. *Ibid.*

35. *Address to the Federal Judges of the Fourth Circuit at Asheville, N.C.* (1932).

36. 300 U.S. 379.

37. 298 U.S. 587.

38. *Stettler* v. *O'Hara*, 243 U.S. 629 (1917). This case was first argued in December, 1914, while Hughes was still on the Court. It was later reargued and decided after his resignation.

39. 219 U.S. 219 (1911).

40. 283 U.S. 359, 369 (1931).

41. 283 U.S. 697, 706–7 (1931).

42. *United States* v. *Macintosh*, 283 U.S. 605 (1931).

43. *United States* v. *Schwimmer*, 279 U.S. 644 (1929).

44. *Girouard* v. *United States*, 328 U.S. 61 (1946).

45. *Lovell* v. *Griffin*, 303 U.S. 444 (1938).

46. *DeJonge* v. *Oregon*, 299 U.S. 353 (1937).

47. *Powell* v. *Alabama*, 287 U.S. 45 (1932).

48. *Norris* v. *Alabama*, 294 U.S. 587 (1935).

49. *Missouri* ex rel. *Gaines* v. *Canada*, 305 U.S. 337.

50. 230 U.S. 352 (1913).

51. *Ibid.* at 399.

52. 234 U.S. 342, 350–51 (1914).

53. *Panama Refining Co.* v. *Ryan*, 293 U.S. 388 (1935).

54. *Schechter* v. *United States*, 295 U.S. 495 (1935).

55. *Ibid.* at 544.

56. 298 U.S. 238 (1936).

57. *N.L.R.B.* v. *Jones & Laughlin Steel Corp.*, 301 U.S. 1 (1937).

58. *Ibid.* at 40.

59. *Ibid.* at 43.

60. See, e.g., Hand, *The Spirit of Liberty* (2d ed., 1953), p. 220.

Courtesy of Harris & Ewing

MR. JUSTICE BRANDEIS

Mr. Justice Brandeis

By
PAUL A. FREUND

A critic as unperceptive as he was unfriendly once remarked that Charles Evans Hughes possessed one of the finest minds of the eighteenth century. A more plausible observer might maintain that Louis D. Brandeis had one of the finest minds of the nineteenth century. It is certain that most of the central features of the twentieth century were antipathetic to his view of man and man's potentialities.

The twentieth century is an era of mass movements; of the separation of ownership from control; of impersonal and anonymous corporate acts obscuring responsibility and shielding individuals from the consequences of their failings. With the enormous size of undertakings, mistakes become intolerable. It is possible to deal with them only by liquidating the wrongdoer (a phenomenon made familiar by twentieth-century totalitarianism) or in a more humane system by cushioning the effects of mistakes through insurance or public assistance or a rising price level. The problem of recognizing human fault and frailty, virtue and talent, in the context of giant enterprise is to be found in twentieth-century industry, in governmental undertakings, and in national structures themselves. This problem was, I believe, central in Brandeis' thinking. To him the rise of giantism and the moral dilemmas it has posed—the curse of bigness, as he was not ashamed to describe it[1]—was lamentable, corrupting man's character, and by no means so inevitable or irredressible as is commonly assumed.

In the 1930's, when it was fashionable to seek passage to the Soviet Union, Justice Brandeis asked, in the tone of Dr. Johnson speaking of travel to Scotland, "Why should anyone want to go to Russia when one can go to Denmark?" It is worth noting that for many years, with the aid of the Library of Congress, he kept up to date a bibliography on Denmark; and he was proud of the translation by his wife of a German volume on the Danish Folk Schools, published under the title *Democracy in Denmark*. He liked to quote Goethe: "Care is taken that the trees do not scrape the skies." For him the overriding challenge of the twentieth century was how to make the environment more hospitable to a reinvigoration of the moral sensibility and responsibility of the individual in the twentieth century.

Justice Brandeis would not have put it so sententiously. He refused to regard himself as a philosopher, insisting that he had always simply attacked problems that came to him and then moved on to another set of problems. Whether he was a philosopher is plainly a matter of definition. He was not, to be sure, interested in metaphysics and the questions which have been the staple topics for literary philosophers. But he had two requisites which some, at least, would be prepared to regard as the most important indicia of the philosopher. In the first place, he had a sense that speculative issues ought to be referable to human affairs, even as speculation itself is a human enterprise. He would not have disagreed, I think, with John Dewey's statement: "Philosophy recovers itself when it ceases to be a device for dealing with the problems of philosophers and becomes a method, cultivated by philosophers, for dealing with the problems of men."[2] Beyond this, he had an acute sense of the human comedy and the human tragedy in mortal striving. For the pretensions of those who prized prestige, his contempt was Swiftian in its irony. When it was reported to him in the spring of 1933 that the bankers were descending on Washington helpless, suppliant, and devoid of ideas, he remarked acidly, "Well, weren't they known as the Napoleons of finance?" The tragic mask in the human drama had been revealed to him unforgettably by the Homestead Strike of 1892, which caused him to reshape a course of lectures he was preparing on the subject of labor law and which led him to think hard and endlessly on the issues of freedom and responsibility, material provision and moral development, competition and the sense of community.

It is not difficult to document his passionate concern for enlarging the moral responsibility of the individual, a concern which drove him from one harsh contest to another, facing the inertia of friends and the bitter resistance of enemies, disciplining himself all the more severely as he sought ways to free men from the constraint of others in order to achieve the freedom of self-discipline. For each group in the community, he thought, the vital self-fulfilling role was to act responsibly, on the basis of an informed judgment, and thus to act wisely but with the risk that mistakes would carry their penalty. Corporate irresponsibility must be overcome. When it was objected that a drastic financial reorganization would injure "innocent" stockholders, Brandeis replied with austerity: "The idea of such persons being innocent in the sense of not letting them take the consequences of their acts is, to my mind, highly immoral."[3] In his view, no director should hold a directorship in more than one corporation. The responsibility of management should not be diluted through the device of insurance. To him fidelity insurance, covering the default of trusted employees, was an abomination. The insurance of public deposits in banks was likewise a vice, since it not only deferred the ordinary depositor in the event of the bank's insolvency but it weakened the motive of the public authorities to exercise constant vigilance over the condition of the bank. The consumer was no more spared from these stern judgments than the stockholder, director, and manager. In a letter written to

George Soule in 1923 on the lessening of labor's share in the national income, Brandeis wrote:

Distribution took, of course, the main increase—for a quarter of a century it has absorbed an ever-increasing percentage of the brains and the profits of business. It represents largely social waste. In distributors we have created a body of tax farmers more oppressive—because more efficient—than those of old. I guess the only remedy lies in educating the public. Here is the job for Stuart Chase. Teach the public—

1. To buy through consumers cooperatives.

2. To refuse to buy any nationally advertised brand and to look with suspicion on every advertised article.

3. Start a buyers' strike at any rise in price of any staple article of common consumption.

The consumer is servile, self-indulgent, indolent, ignorant. Let the buyer beware.

He could not be deterred from a course of action he believed right by an objection that it would entail some suffering. In the early days of the Hitler regime he urged an American consumers' boycott of German goods; it mattered not that some blameless Germans might suffer losses as a result. In comparing plans of unemployment compensation, he is known to have favored the Wisconsin, or plant reserve, system because of the correlation of reward and penalty for the employer with the record of regularity of employment which the plant was able to achieve, and this despite the strong opposition of professional social workers who pointed out that a plant reserve system afforded inadequate protection to employees and that the insurance fund must be pooled on a statewide basis to achieve true insurance protection. The opposition between the principle of insurance and the canons of responsibility was a pervasive theme in his thinking. He did not reject the device of insurance, of course. Indeed, he fathered the system of savings-bank life insurance in Massachusetts. But the system, it will be recalled, was designed not only to give more definite protection to wage earners at lower cost but also to provide a demonstration that the business of insurance could be carried on successfully by ordinary people without the prestige and power then attaching to the leaders of the insurance business.

In sum, his humanitarianism did not lead him to forget that the profit system is the profit-and-loss system. He was not a sentimentalist. "When you learn that this is a hard world," he reminded his daughter, "things will be so much easier for you." At the same time—and here he was marked off from the more doctrinaire among his contemporaries—he did not see freedom where there was no strength to make the choices that freedom implies. He pointed to the co-operative ventures of the old New England seafarers as the essence of freedom, courage, and responsibility; he did not romantically discern these qualities in the situation of the indentured seaman. Once a year he assembled a group of young people to take dinner at his house with Andrew Furuseth, the grand old man of the maritime labor movement, the begetter of seamen's legislation, whose noble bust sculptured by Jo Davidson stands fittingly in the rotunda of the Department of Labor building in Washington. On these occasions a certain ceremony was regularly performed. At a pause during the dinner the Justice would turn to Furuseth, white-haired, gaunt, and straight-backed, and ask, "Mr. Furuseth, will you tell these young people why it was that you went to sea as a boy?" The old Viking would take his cue and respond in the rich, slow Norseman's accent, with rising impassioned inflection, "I went to sea as a boy because I had the mad idea, the insane delusion, that a seaman was a free man!" The Justice would nod, smiling in gratitude, and the little ritual was ended. The young people would not forget the saga preserved in the seaman's log.

The social thought of Brandeis developed out of experience and observation. As a young lawyer he was brilliant, successful, and by the age of thirty financially independent. Improbable as it seems in retrospect, he was actually in his young manhood a player-member of the Dedham Polo Club, although in later years when this early association was recalled to him, he dismissed his role as that of a "supernumerary." Upon his marriage at the age of thirty-four the first visitor to pay a call to his wife, we are told by Brandeis' biographer, was Mrs. Higginson, the acknowledged leader of Boston society.[4] It was just a year after his marriage that the affair at Homestead occurred. The confrontation of personal security with the shock of a violent class war appears to have turned him resolutely to that grappling with social problems which in one form or another was to occupy the remainder of his life. Having begun his career without the youthful zeal of the reformer who in time becomes weary and discouraged or succumbs to the charms and comforts of the status quo, he never tired in the fight.

This is not the place to recite the story of his encounters at the bar. What is appropriate to recall is that in all these controversies, following hard upon each other year after year, he developed his larger conceptions from immersion in the facts of specific cases, in the best tradition of the common law. That tradition is not unlike the method of scientific discovery, which abstracts general truths through reflection on a mass of specific phenomena—a process which has been well described as "thinking on the side." Many a competent scientific investigator has missed being counted a discoverer of scientific truth because he has failed to detach himself from his immediate focus and to reflect on the data under a larger aspect. In the law, too, this capacity to discern, in Justice Holmes's phrase, the universal in the particular, marks off the competent practitioner from the architect of legal institutions.

No one has surpassed Brandeis in the capacity at once to master the facts under investigation and to draw from the whole experience ideas for constructive reform. As early as 1890, he wrote, with his partner Samuel Warren, a path-breaking article under the title "The Right to Privacy," which drew on the resources of the law, by analogy, to suggest a new category of protected legal interests.[5] The article was not the out-growth of closet speculation; it was the result of a disturbing experience which had befallen Warren when the latter's activities in Boston society were exploited for publication by a Boston gossip sheet. Later, out of his experience as arbitrator in the New York garment workers' strike, Brandeis drew up a so-called protocol for continuous collaboration between management and labor, a measure designed to avoid the kind of eruption that had brought him into the affairs of the industry. It is significant that in this industrial treaty of peace he rejected both the closed and the open shop, fixing instead upon a preferential union shop which was meant to promote the stability of the union without giving it a monopoly in the labor market. The protocol later foundered as the participants pressed with intransigence for their polar positions.

In Massachusetts, similarly, his contributions derived from specific responsibilities. His interest in the rates charged by gas utilities in the commonwealth stemmed from his role as counsel to the Massachusetts State Board of Trade. Out of this experience came the arrangement devised by him for a sliding scale, the permissible rate of return to stockholders varying inversely with the level of rates charged to the consumers. The familiar principle of incentive, of reward and penalty, was here neatly—some would say too neatly—applied to a vexing area of public control. His plan of savings-bank life insurance, which he regarded as the most significant of his achievements at the Bar, grew out of his experience as counsel to the New England policyholders of the Equitable Life Assurance company. The special merits of the system, already adverted to, provided more dependable protection at lower cost and under the management of ordinary men of business. It was meant to serve, in addition, as a yardstick for the more conventional systems. Once again there was an avoidance of reliance on complicated regulatory measures, and there was instead the creation of motivations that would carry inward compulsion.

The celebrated controversy over the New Haven monopoly was precipitated by Brandeis' responsibility as counsel for shareholders of the Boston and Maine. Out of this experience came firmly held convictions about bankers' control of industry. In the Ballinger investigation before a congressional committee Brandeis represented Norman Hapgood of *Collier's Weekly*, which had published articles undertaking to expose mismanagement in the Interior Department. In Brandeis' hands the affair dramatized the role of the junior departmental officer Glavis, who had been discharged for what was deemed by his superiors to be intermeddling, and thus the investigation was lifted to the level of the cause of the civil servant who finds misfeasance in high places. Other hearings in Washington took Brandeis before the Interstate Commerce Commission as counsel for shippers. Out of these responsibilities grew his arresting challenge to the railroads to save a million dollars a day through the introduction of scientific management. It was not enough that he present the case for his clients in its immediate aspect: his searching, probing, and constructive mind was satisfied only when it yielded a larger, more positive solution to a recurring problem. Characteristically, again, the solution did not depend on external regulation, which to be effective would require intimate knowledge on the part of the regulators exceeding that possessed by the regulated. Instead the solution rested on the principle that redemption comes from within.

Diverse as were these causes and complex as was each one of them, they reveal a striking symmetry in the approach which Brandeis made to them. He came to each with a prepared mind, like that of the best scientists, with simple basic ideas, with a determination to unearth and organize a vast disarray of unruly facts, and to impose some order on the disarray by contriving a solution which would be at once just, preventive, and self-motivating. This is the approach of the common law lawyer at his best. But while Brandeis came to these controversies as the representative of an interested party, his performance suggests unmistakably the mind not simply or primarily of an advocate but rather of a statesman or judge.

The judicial temperament, his possession of which was doubted by some critics at the time of his nomination to the Court, should have been evident enough in his career at the bar. Indeed, he was in the habit of lecturing his own clients on the need to recognize what was right in their adversaries' case. As counsel for employees, he urged upon them the cause of scientific management, which was strongly resisted by labor groups, and the incorporation of labor unions, which too was hardly a popular subject with a labor audience. As counsel to employers, he insisted upon the cause of collective bargaining and the merits of the Sherman Act. As counsel presenting the case for shippers before the Interstate Commerce Commission, on one occasion he agreed that a partial rate increase was justified—a position that cost him the lasting enmity of counsel representing midwestern shippers, who regarded Brandeis' judicial approach as little short of traitorous. It was perhaps these qualities of balance, of formidable advocacy lifted by wise detachment from the mere role of the mouthpiece that led Sidney Hillman, on a visit to Justice Brandeis in his later years, to part from the interview with the amiable remark, "Mr. Justice, I think you are a conservative." The Justice replied with equal affability, "I have always so regarded myself."

Brandeis brought to the Court a strong institutional sense that was quickly reflected in his opinions and in his relations with his associates. However sharply and often he disagreed with a majority of his colleagues, his opinions retained an impersonal tone. They were self-contained and did not rely on demeaning the opposition. His attack was upon problems and not upon personalities. Sometimes he withheld dissenting opinions on which considerable labor had been expended, for he believed that a more suitable occasion would present itself later or that still further work was needed to make the dissent as powerful as he wanted it. In the relations of the Court to outsiders, including committees or members of Congress, he stood aside so that the Chief Justice could serve as the spokesman for the Court.

His association with Holmes, which had begun years before in Boston, grew into a close and abiding relationship which called forth the best in each. Birthday greetings were regularly exchanged by note. The annual compliment of Brandeis to his friend was carried off with a lightness and charm of style that he did not often bestow upon his writing. It was a relationship, nonetheless, between men of markedly different temperament and faith. During Brandeis' first term on the bench, the draft of one of his opinions which had been circulated, as usual, among the Justices was returned by Holmes with the notation, "Yes, forcibly put—but I can't think it good form to treat an opinion as an essay and put in footnotes." Although the protest was subsequently renewed, the friendship was destined to endure the strain of thousands more of the disapproved annotations. A few years later Holmes, evidently reviving a subject that they had discussed, confessed poignantly to having been wounded: "Generally speaking I agree with you in liking to see social experiments tried but I do so without enthusiasm because I believe that it is merely shifting the pressure and that so long as we have free propagation Malthus is right in his general view. P.S. Your slight twit—that it is easy for those who don't suffer to philosophize—touched me. I have known some suffering in my day. . . ."

The Court to which Brandeis came was presided over by the ponderous figure of Chief Justice White. In addressing a draft opinion to White, Justice Brandeis used the inscription "Father Chief Justice." The designation derives no doubt from a conference between the two in the summer of 1916 when Brandeis, having just been appointed to the Court, was importuned by President Wilson to head a mission to Mexico. Brandeis sought out his prospective Chief in order to discuss the presidential request, and at this meeting, a record of which was made and preserved by Brandeis, White had proved to be in an expansive mood, insisting that Brandeis should look on him not as Chief Justice but as a father. In returning the draft opinion, White entered into the spirit of Brandeis' inscription, addressing his new colleague as "Grandfather Justice Brandeis." Another early opinion circulated in draft form drew from Justice McKenna the notation, "I was inclined to be the other way, but you cannot speak with reason to the Dane and lose your voice." Anyone who is able to make a McKenna regard himself as a Scandinavian is blessed, it is submitted, with supreme talents for conversion. With scarcely an exception—an exception reflected in an omission among the signatories of the Court's letter to Brandeis on his retirement[6]—his relations with his colleagues, however diverse their judicial outlook, continued to be marked by respect, courtesy, and appreciation. In 1935, when the division on the Court was as sharp as it has ever been, Brandeis' birthday on November 13 elicited from Justice Van Devanter, normally impassive and inarticulate, a note of cordial greeting and deep regard, concluding, "We are proud of you."

As a judge Brandeis exercised a degree of self-discipline in his daily schedule and in the realm of ideas to match that which his philosophy called for on the part of responsible citizens. His working day began in those pre-dawn hours of which his law clerk, burdened with the frailty of youth, had only circumstantial knowledge, as upon reaching the office the young man saw the volumes scattered on the floor of the study, the drafts of opinions already revised, and the frequent brief note on the law clerk's desk inviting him to a conference in the Justice's study upon the clerk's arrival. At night, however, a compensating schedule was maintained, under which the clerk, to the limit of his endurance, sought to carry forward his investigating and editorial tasks and embody the results in a memorandum or revision of a draft opinion to be placed stealthily under the outer door of the Justice's apartment. Since the Justice acted on the belief that judgments reached late at night when the mind was fatigued were unreliable—a rule akin to his principle that one can do a year's work in eleven months but not in twelve—the law clerk could not expect to find the Justice prepared to receive these nocturnal missiles. There is a well-authenticated legend, nevertheless, that on one occasion when the night was close to breaking into day, the law clerk carefully slipping his document under the door could feel it being retrieved on the other side.

What is more important is that the sense of self-discipline marked Brandeis' view of the judicial function itself. No one was more alert than he to the procedural and jurisdictional limitations on the business of the Court. To some observers for whom liberalism and conservatism are each a monochrome of preferences, the concern of Brandeis for apparently technical procedural niceties seemed incompatible with his largeness of outlook in deciding questions of public law. In fact there was no real inconsistency. If the Court was to exercise its grave function of reviewing the validity of acts of co-ordinate branches of government, the Court must be careful to keep within its appointed bounds as a condition of judging whether others had kept within theirs. Moreover, to one who, like Brandeis, regarded the Supreme Court as an educational institution that ought to set the highest standard of quality and power in its work, it was important that the Court decide no more than was necessary. This essentially common law tradition took on special importance in constitutional law, both in confining the decision to its narrowest terms and in rejecting for consideration, under the discretionary jurisdiction on certiorari, all those cases whose entitlement to Supreme Court review by virtue of their importance was not clearly manifest. Accordingly, Brandeis spent but little time in studying petitions for certiorari, nor did he employ his law clerks to any appreciable extent on that task. If a petition did not make out a clear case for review, it was to be denied. Individual injustices that may have survived review in the lower courts did not press on Brandeis with sufficient force to divert him from the principle that the energies of the Court must be conserved for their broader and essential tasks. Sentimentality can be an enemy of greatness of spirit; firmness and even hardness can be its friend.

Brandeis' masterful employment of procedural and jurisdictional rules was by no means simply a device for avoiding decisions by majority brethren who would have been opposed to his position on the merits. In the *Ashwander* case,[7] presenting certain aspects of the validity of the TVA program, a majority of the Court supported the government's case, a case wholly consistent with Brandeis' view on the constitutional merits. Nevertheless, he wrote a powerful and now classic separate opinion protesting that the case, a stockholder's suit in form, was not a proper vehicle for the determination of the important constitutional questions that had been argued.[8] Similarly, he was prepared to write massive opinions in support of the constitutionality of measures with which as a matter of legislative policy he had no sympathy. His dissent in the *Oklahoma ice* case,[9] in which the majority struck down a law requiring certificates of convenience and necessity for the ice business, was a resounding argument for the constitutional right of a state to experiment with economic measures for which there was some rational support, even though they seemed misguided and destined to failure.[10] He joined too, for example, in Justice Stone's dissent in the *Agricultural Adjustment Act* case,[11] although restriction of production, held invalid by the majority, was far from consistent with his notions of wise economic policy.

Believing as he did in the virtue of experiment, the danger of size, and the fruitfulness of diversity, it was natural that he labored greatly for the maintenance and wise administration of the federal balance. He was slow to conclude that the field left open for state action had been pre-empted by national legislation. The enactment by Congress of the Federal Employers Liability Act, providing for liability to railroad employees injured as a result of negligence, did not appear to him to foreclose a state from applying to railroad employees its workmen's compensation law allowing recovery irrespective of negligence.[12]

In the adjustment of interstate relations he sought resourcefully for a *via media* between centralization and Balkanization. He found in the Constitution a number of provisions which lent themselves to this kind of adjustment. One was the tax and credit device, employed in the federal estate tax and subsequently in the Federal Unemployment Insurance Act. While the opinion in the unemployment insurance case was not assigned to him, his intervention in the oral argument disclosed clearly the thrust of his thinking.[13] If in fact the federal government had shouldered, as a moral duty, the relief of unemployment through bounties and make-work programs, it was unthinkable to him that the federal government was powerless to act more constructively by inducing the states, through a credit against a federal tax, to establish unemployment compensation plans of their own. The federal government was utilizing its fiscal power by means of a credit that was germane to the fiscal function and that at the same time, by establishing minimum standards to qualify for the credit, ended the competition in laxity among the states which had largely blocked individual state experiments in social security. Another constitutional device which Brandeis took occasion to elaborate was the interstate compact, which provides a measure of regional uniformity and the safeguard of unitary interpretation through review in the Supreme Court.[14] Still another constitutional provision to which he endeavored to give greater vitality was the Full Faith and Credit Clause, which could serve to allay some of the friction and overlapping among state laws without resort to national legislation and administration. In a series of opinions for the Court, Brandeis gave uncommonly wide effect to this clause as a means of imposing a single regime of state law on the liability to pay workmen's compensation, the obligation to support a minor child, and the construction of a life insurance policy.[15] In each of these cases it so happened that under the decision of the Court as announced by Brandeis the claimant lost: a working man, a child, and a widow. Like the framers of the Constitution itself, he recognized that the important and relevant function of a constitutionalist was the allocation of public power.

His concern lest the states be emptied of power without necessity explains in part his dissent from the promulgation of the Federal Rules of Civil Procedure. Although hailed as a notable advance in simplifying and rationalizing the procedural steps in a lawsuit, the rules seemed to him needlessly to supplant local rules for the governance of trials in the federal district courts. He felt also that the Court, which was nominally promulgating the rules, ought not to take responsibility for them since the members had not been able to give them adequate consideration; and he feared that they would lead to the kind of frustrating complexities which marked the practice under the detailed Civil Practice Act in New York as compared to the relative simplicity of the common law system in his own Massachusetts. Quite of a piece with his opposition to the Federal Rules of Civil Procedure was his opinion for the Court in *Erie R.R.* v. *Tompkins*,[16] uprooting the landmark decision in *Swift* v. *Tyson*,[17] after ninety-five years of what Brandeis termed an unconstitutional course pursued by the federal courts in determining the common law independently of state decisions. The problem has, of course, its jurisprudential and practical aspects, but it may be enough to recall here that Brandeis' feeling for the reality of local law was deep-seated. Forty-five years before the opinion in *Erie* v. *Tompkins* he had written a letter to President Eliot, in 1893, urging that the

Harvard Law School offer a course on the "peculiarities of Massachusetts Law." The letter, foreshadowing strikingly the spirit of his opinion in *Erie* v. *Tompkins,* stated: "The school undertakes to teach in its other courses the general law, but the law of Massachusetts, while conforming in the main to the general law, has distinct individuality. Local customs, traditions and the peculiar habits of mind of its people have resulted in a spirit which is its own. This is manifested partly in its statutes, but even more largely in what may be termed its common law."

In one field, however, state experimentation was much less to be tolerated—the shutting-off by law of roads to knowledge. When the legislature of Nebraska, motivated no doubt by the presence of settlers speaking foreign tongues, forbade the teaching of modern foreign languages in the primary grades, a divided Supreme Court upset the statute as a deprivation of liberty without due process of law.[18] Justice Brandeis joined in the opinion of the Court, and Justice Holmes dissented. The issue in the case foreshadowed the recent perplexities over legislation subordinating freedom of expression and organization to the interest of unity and order. The cleavage between Brandeis and Holmes in the Nebraska case should be a sufficient reminder of the difficulty of the constitutional problem and of efforts to slip judicial votes into the tidy categories of liberal and conservative.

Refining on the standard of clear and present danger which Holmes had advanced for cases involving the dissemination of ideas, Brandeis elaborated the test in Anita Whitney's case.[19] The threatened evil that would justify suppression of the publication of ideas had to be a relatively serious one, in Brandeis' view, and proximate enough to warrant the conclusion that there was no time in which to counteract evil counsels with good ones. It is particularly regrettable that Justice Brandeis did not find occasion to formulate a rounded philosophy of judicial review in this area as compared with the function of the courts in reviewing other kinds of legislation. It is always dangerous, of course, to project the ideas of a thinker of another day into the specific controversies of our time. If it is asked what Jefferson would think about this or that law of the 1950's, it is not altogether unfair to answer that if Jefferson were alive today he would be too old to think clearly about anything. Nonetheless, the spirit pervading the opinion of Brandeis in the *Whitney* case strongly suggests that he would not defer to the judgment of the legislature embodied in a statute repressing the dissemination of ideas where the danger feared necessarily involved a speculation in historical futures. On quite a different footing would stand legislation that penalizes the teaching of espionage or sabotage or singles out clandestine activities for prohibition and punishment.

Brandeis' judicial technique comes into closer focus if one compares his opinions in two cases which bear a certain resemblance to each other, the *Associated Press* case and the *Olmstead* case.[20] In the first, the Associated Press was suing to enjoin the International News Service from "pirating" news reports of the AP and making them available to subscribers of the INS. The legal question was admittedly a rather novel one, in view of the special character of the legal interest in news. Three possible points of view could have been taken. First, it might have been decided that the AP should go without relief on the ground that there was no recognized "property interest" in news and, on the defendant's side, no wrong which could be categorized conventionally as a passing-off of one's own product as that of another. A second possibility was to maintain that the law keeps pace with the varieties of commercial interest, that the category of property is not a closed one, and that neither does the category of "passing-off" exhaust the class of business torts. In fact, this was the approach taken by a majority of the Court, in a decision that has generally been regarded as a high example of progressivism in the law. Justice Brandeis followed neither the first nor second view.[21] To him a larger and overriding consideration was involved, that of the public interest in the dissemination of news. He recognized the wrongful character of the defendant's conduct, but he pointed out that if a court of equity was to grant the extraordinary remedy of injunction it could not close its eyes to the position of the plaintiff as a purveyor of a necessity of modern life and as an organization dominant in its field, enjoying the benefits of restrictive by-laws which may have prevented the defendant's subscribers from sharing the plaintiff's services on a more orderly basis. In short, Justice Brandeis rejected the progressivism of the majority and did so by interpreting in the narrowest possible way the precedents and analogies which the Court relied upon. The so-called "ticker tape" cases, which were perhaps most closely in point, were distinguished by Brandeis as resting on a confidential relationship. In another sense, Brandeis was more progressive than his brethren, since he would have placed the news service in the class of public utilities bearing an obligation to serve all those offering to pay a reasonable charge. Since, however, such treatment could best be left to legislation, Brandeis concluded that the most just action for the Court was to take no action save to dismiss the bill of complaint.

The resemblance between the *Associated Press* case and the *Olmstead* case is evident on the surface. The latter presented the question whether wire tapping by federal officials, in violation of state law, constituted an unreasonable search and seizure in contravention of the Fourth Amendment of the Constitution. The classification of wire tapping within the categories of an eighteenth-century document confronted the Court with another opportunity to demonstrate the adaptability of the law to the advances in science and the practical arts. Here the roles were reversed. A majority of the Court refused to assimilate wire tapping to the search and seizure of premises or persons, while Brandeis' eloquent dissent is a *locus classicus* on the theme of the dynamism of law, including constitutional law.[22] In this case the responsibility of the Court was inescapable. The issue involved the basic processes of government as they impinge on the individual against whom the forces of the law are brought to bear. In the *Associated Press* case Brandeis had been willing, indeed insistent, that the inequities of the competitive struggle be left for resolution by the legislature, lest the Court do an ill-considered job. In the *Olmstead* case, where the processes of the criminal law had been applied to the individual, no agency of government more appropriate than the Court could be expected to resolve the contest between public power and personal immunity.

Even in the *Olmstead* case Brandeis did not come easily to the ultimate constitutional problem. Prior to the oral argument in the case he and his law clerk labored for several weeks in drafting an opinion resting on the doctrine of unclean hands, thus avoiding the Fourth Amendment and placing the case squarely on the irregularity of the conduct under state law. The statutes of all the states bearing on wire tapping were duly collected and abstracted, and several drafts of an opinion went through the printer's hands. After the oral argument, when it appeared that the Court's interest centered on the Fourth Amendment, the draft opinion was thoroughly reorganized. The constitutional issue was given first place, developed with a wealth of learning from English constitutional history and from the evolution of the law toward the protection of intangible interests against subtler interferences than those with which the more primitive law was concerned. Even after the opinion was thus reorganized, Brandeis did not give up hope of resolving the problem on a less heroic plane. He extracted from the revised draft the portion resting on the doctrine of unclean hands, had copies of this portion made by the printer, and circulated it to his brethren with the urgent suggestion that the case be disposed of on this ground. It was only after he met with rebuff in this endeavor that he pressed the constitutional dissent.

The evolution of this dissenting opinion illustrates the judicial methods of Brandeis. He drew on his own experience, on his legal learning and intensive study, on contemporary facts, and on his intuition verified by these personal and vicarious experiences and by the critical analysis of his law clerk. In the *Olmstead* dissent of 1928 the essay of 1890 on "The Right to Privacy" furnished useful and relevant matter. It may be of interest to set out in sequence excerpts from that article, then from a draft opinion of February 16, 1928, and finally from the opinion as it was delivered.

The essay of 1890 contained the following passages:

Recent inventions and business methods call attention to the next step which must be taken for the protection of the person, and for securing to the individual what Judge Cooley calls the right "to be let alone." Instantaneous photographs and newspaper enterprise have invaded the sacred precincts of private and domestic life; and numerous mechanical devices threaten to make good the prediction that "what is whispered in the closet shall be proclaimed from the house-tops." . . .

These considerations lead to the conclusion that the protection afforded to thoughts, sentiments, and emotions, expressed through the medium of writing or of the arts, so far as it consists in preventing publication, is merely an instance of the enforcement of the more general right of the individual to be let alone.[23]

The memorandum of February 16, 1928, held the following passage:

Since those days, subtler means of invading privacy and of curtailing personal liberty have been made available to the Government. The advances in science—discovery and invention—have made it possible for the Government to effect disclosure in court of "what is whispered in the closet"—by means far more effective than stretching the defendant upon the rack. By means of television, radium and photography, there may some day be developed ways by which the Government could, without removing papers from secret drawers, reproduce them in court and lay before the jury the most intimate occurrences of the home. It is conceivable, also, that advances in the psychic and related sciences may afford means of exploring a man's unexpressed beliefs, thoughts and emotions. Can it be that the constitution affords no protection against such invasion by the Government of personal liberty? As has been said of much lesser intrusions, that would "place the liberty of every man in the hands of every petty officer." It would "destroy all the comforts of society." And "no man could endure to live longer in this country."[24]

Finally, the opinion as delivered included these passages:

Discovery and invention have made it possible for the Government, by means far more effective than stretching upon the rack, to obtain disclosure in court of what is whispered in the closet.

Moreover, "in the application of a constitution, our contemplation cannot be only of what has been but of what may be." The progress of science in furnishing the Government with means of espionage is not likely to stop with wire-tapping. Ways may some day be developed by which the Government, without removing papers from secret drawers, can reproduce them in court, and by which it will be enabled to expose to a jury the most intimate occurrences of the home. Advances in the psychic and related sciences may bring means of exploring unexpressed beliefs, thoughts and emotions. "That places the liberty of every man in the hands of every petty officer" was said by James Otis of much lesser intrusions than these. To Lord Camden, a far slighter intrusion seemed "subversive of all the comforts of society." Can it be that the Constitution affords no protection against such invasions of individual security? . . .

. . . The makers of our Constitution undertook to secure conditions favorable to the pursuit of happiness. They recognized the significance of man's spiritual nature, of his feelings and of his intellect. They knew that only a part of the pain, pleasure and satisfactions of life are to be found in material things. They sought to protect Americans in their beliefs, their thoughts, their emotions and their sensations. They conferred, as against the Government, the right to be let alone—the most comprehensive of rights and the right most valued by civilized men.[25]

It is obvious that the opinion grew in strength and eloquence as it was hammered out and as it evolved, from a response to the unpleasantness in which Samuel Warren found himself, through the ethical principle of unclean hands to the ultimate philosophy of man's spiritual nature which Brandeis found embodied in our Constitution. The crescendo of feeling rises from stage to stage as Brandeis is driven to explore ever more deeply the foundations of individual security.

One distinction of the draft memorandum, it will be observed in passing, was lost in the final version. The reference to television would doubtless have been the first notice of that discovery in a judicial opinion, since the working papers of the Justice show that he was relying on a newspaper account of what was then a current experiment. Unhappily, the reference was deleted in deference to the scientific skepticism of his law clerk, who strongly doubted that the new device could be adapted to the uses of espionage.

A number of questions will inevitably be raised by this résumé of the thought of Justice Brandeis. Did he overrate the capacity of ordinary men for self-discipline and responsibility? Did he exaggerate the scope for diversity and local attachments in a country on wheels? Was his distrust of bigness and power justified? The answer to all these queries lies in the acceptance of a view of man's vocation which gave unity to the thought of Brandeis. For him achievement and destiny were not measured by size or power or comfort or safety but by character; and character was formed by the process of struggling against adversity, given a fair chance to succeed. The task must not be too easy, he thought, but it must be manageable, within the competence of the performer, be he citizen or judge. Perhaps it is all symbolized in Brandeis' respect for the art of sailing as the ideal form of recreation, since it pits the individual, relying on his own strength and skill and understanding, in a struggle for mastery against the force of the elements.

Is he, then, a voice from the nineteenth century? In truth, it is an ancestral voice coming from a far more distant time, where the wellsprings of Western thought are found. In him, as Justice Frankfurter has said, Hebraism and Hellenism were fused. There was the strain of Isaiah's stern reproach at want of wisdom and of the search for wisdom:

And I look, but there is no man,
Even among them, but there is no counsellor,
That, when I ask of them, can give an answer.
Behold, all of them,
Their works are vanity and nought;
Their molten images are wind and confusion.

And there was the spirit of striving as a civic duty praised by Pericles: "An Athenian spends himself in the service of the city as if his body were not his own, and counts his mind most his own when it is employed upon her business." Indeed, the reading Brandeis most often urged upon his visitors was Sir Alfred Zimmern's *Greek Commonwealth.* One of the eloquent passages in his opinion in the *Whitney* case was taken almost verbatim from the Zimmern translation of Pericles' Funeral Oration and applied to the founders of the American Republic: "They believed liberty to be the secret of happiness, and courage to be the secret of liberty."[26]

This tradition of seeking and striving has been kept alive in hundreds of pulpits and thousands of pages, by preachers and publicists and poets. The distinction of Brandeis is that he strove to domesticate this heritage in the institutions of twentieth-century America, with a resourcefulness gained from immersion in the complexities of our industrial civilization. As a judge he acted on the principle that knowledge must precede understanding, as understanding should precede judging, and to this end he committed himself to almost incredible labors of investigation and exposition, so that what he touched might be illuminated. Both as lawyer and as judge the necessity of working within the confines of specific controversies gave to his formulations strength, impact, and the quality of tested wisdom.

All of this is simply to say that the spirit and technique of the common law, when applied to the moral inheritance of the Western tradition, can give that tradition a reality, meaning, and immediacy that can hardly be matched by other disciplines. To have shown that with will and wisdom the law can redeem the ancient truths we profess and build them into the structure of our common life—to have shown this is to have pointed the way also to the redemption of the law itself.

PAUL A. FREUND *is Carl M. Loeb University Professor at Harvard. After receiving his S.J.D. from that institution, he served as law clerk to Justice Brandeis. He has held several posts of importance in the federal government, perhaps his most important being that of Special Assistant to the Attorney General in the Office of the Solicitor General from 1935 to 1939 and again from 1942 to 1946. He is the editor of the Supreme Court history being prepared under the Oliver Wendell Holmes bequest and the author of one of its volumes. Among his previous publications are three books:* On Understanding the Supreme Court, 1949; The Supreme Court of the United States, 1961; *and* Cases on Constitutional Law, 1952, *of which he was co-editor.*

NOTES

1. The phrase occurs in Brandeis' statement before the Interstate Commerce Commission in 1910, in opposition to an advance in railroad freight rates. *Hearings before the I.C.C.*, 61st Cong., 3d Sess., S. Doc. 725, IX, 5256. When the Viking Press was preparing to publish a selection of his papers in 1934, the editors suggested a number of titles for the book, including "Prophetic Powers," which the publisher favored, and "The Curse of Bigness." Brandeis preferred the latter, and the publisher acquiesced. The correspondence is preserved in the collection of Brandeis manuscript papers at the University of Louisville.

2. Dewey, *Creative Intelligence* (1917), p. 65; quoted in Morton White, *Social Thought in America* (1949), p. 128.

3. Testimony on competition and the trusts, in *Hearings before Senate Committee on Interstate Commerce*, S. Res. 98, 62d Cong., 1st sess., 1177 (1911). Brandeis drew a comparison with English absentee owners of Irish estates, who should have been held responsible for oppressive acts of the bailiffs.

4. Mason, *Brandeis: A Free Man's Life* (1946), p. 103.

5. 4 HARV. L. REV. 193 (1890).

6. 306 U.S. v–vi.

7. *Ashwander* v. *T.V.A.,* 297 U.S. 288 (1936).

8. *Ibid.* at 341.

9. *New State Ice Co.* v. *Liebmann,* 285 U.S. 262 (1932).

10. *Ibid.* at 280.

11. *United States* v. *Butler,* 297 U.S. 1, 78 (1936).

12. *New York Cent. R.R.* v. *Winfield,* 244 U.S. 147, 154 (1917).

13. The oral arguments are printed in S. Doc. 53, 75th Cong., 1st sess. (1937). See especially pp. 70–71.

14. See, e.g., *Hinderlider* v. *La Plata River Co.,* 304 U.S. 92 (1938).

15. *Bradford Electric Light Co.* v. *Clapper,* 284 U.S. 221 (1931); *Yarborough* v. *Yarborough,* 290 U.S. 202 (1933); *John Hancock Mut. Life Ins. Co.* v. *Yates,* 299 U.S. 178 (1936).

16. 304 U.S. 64 (1938).

17. 16 Pet. 1 (1842).

18. *Meyer* v. *Nebraska,* 262 U.S. 390 (1923).

19. *Whitney* v. *California,* 274 U.S. 357 (1927).

20. *International News Service* v. *Associated Press,* 248 U.S. 215 (1918); *Olmstead* v. *United States,* 277 U.S. 438 (1928).

21. 248 U.S. at 248.

22. 277 U.S. at 471.

23. 4 Harv. L. Rev. at 195, 205 (1890).

24. MS in the Harvard Law School Library.

25. 277 U.S. at 473–74, 478.

26. The passage in Zimmern, *The Greek Commonwealth* (1924), p. 207, reads, "knowing the secret of happiness to be freedom and the secret of freedom a brave heart. . . ."

Courtesy of Harris & Ewing

MR. JUSTICE SUTHERLAND

Mr. Justice Sutherland

By

J. FRANCIS PASCHAL

For most of us, I suppose, there is a certain ambivalence in George Sutherland. On the one hand, he represents a way of thinking about political and constitutional problems that we have long since discarded. Indeed, Sutherland wrote more opinions that have been specifically overruled than any other Justice in the history of the Supreme Court. Of those opinions repudiated by name since the reconstruction of the Court in the late thirties, Sutherland was the author of more than 20 per cent.[1] And, of course, his obsolescence is not confined to those of his cases formally consigned to the rubbish heap. Some of his most elaborate productions have so far decomposed that a ceremonial interment is unnecessary.[2] But the failure reflected here is not merely Sutherland's failure. If that were all, we could forget him. It is the failure of American conservative thought since the Civil War. One of Sutherland's claims on our attention, therefore, is as a representative of the conservative tradition. No Justice of the twentieth century, certainly none of Sutherland's conservative colleagues during his tenure on the Court, so well fits this role.

On the other hand, Sutherland is important in a more immediate way. As notable as was his devotion to the idea of laissez faire, he was the author of some of the most significant power-producing decisions of our time. He was, moreover, the author of opinions distributing power among the three departments that continue to have vitality. He had also a decisive contribution to make in respect to civil liberties. In each of these particulars, Sutherland stands apart from the Justices with whom he was most often aligned. Van Devanter, Mc-Reynolds, and Butler, with the same general outlook as Sutherland, have left little, if anything, for us. Why Sutherland, alone of the four, was capable of an enduring achievement is a question to which I shall return.

First, however, I should like briefly to consider Sutherland in his representative aspect. He was a child of the last half of the nineteenth century. Brought up in Utah while it was still a territory, serving his apprenticeship there as a young lawyer, he was cast on the national scene in 1900 as a Republican Representative from Utah. From 1905 to 1917 he was in the Senate. On leaving public office, he practiced law in Washington until his appointment to the Court in 1922, taking time off to serve as President of the American Bar Association in 1917 and as Warren G. Harding's principal adviser in the campaign of 1920. Through all the struggles of the Progressive era, he was closely identified with the Old Guard of the Republican party, recoiling with it at Theodore Roosevelt's proposal for the recall of judicial decisions and Woodrow Wilson's nomination of Brandeis to the Court. His appointment and unanimous confirmation in 1922 signaled, as well as anything could, the return to normalcy.

Once on the Court, Sutherland joined with Van Devanter, McReynolds, and Butler in a virtually unbreakable coalition which for fifteen years was able to win sufficient additional support on important issues to form a majority and bring the Court to the crisis of 1937. The history of the Court in these years is well known, and I shall not attempt to review it in any detail. Suffice it to say that the record, and Sutherland's record in particular, is one of judicial aggrandizement and the negation of the validity of what is today the most commonplace sort of governmental action, both state and national. As a practical matter, the power of the states to regulate economic affairs was confined within the limits of previously sanctioned legislation. Under various guises, statutes were overthrown which attempted to regulate trucking in California,[3] the cotton-ginning and ice businesses in Oklahoma,[4] meat packing in Kansas,[5] and drugstores in Pennsylvania.[6] A general prohibition on price-fixing was imposed, whether it involved the price of labor,[7] or of theater tickets in the hands of a broker,[8] or gasoline,[9] or the price charged by an employment agency for its services.[10]

In the tax field, Sutherland was particularly active, leading the Court in its ill-conceived drive on what it considered to be double taxation[11] and further leading in the unfortunate expansion of the reciprocal immunity doctrine.[12] He resisted a graduated tax on chain stores[13] and exhibited a willingness to find loopholes in the Internal Revenue Code.[14] And when Congress became aware of a loophole and attempted to say, for example, that gifts made within three years of death were irrebuttably presumed to have been made in contemplation of death, Sutherland was ready to say that this was beyond the legislative power.[15]

Sutherland was, of course, a leader in the Court's fight on the New Deal. He resisted the outlawing of the gold clause[16] and concurred in the opinions destroying the NRA, the AAA, and the Railroad Retirement Act.[17] He wrote the opinion in the *Carter* case holding that coal mining was a local operation beyond the control of Congress,[18] and when the inevitable retreat of the Court from these exposed positions came, Sutherland preferred to remain behind, insisting to the end that the National Labor Relations Act and the Social Security Act were also invalid.[19]

Sutherland's is not a happy record, but it merits attention because its underlying ideas once came pretty close to being the creed of American conservatism and because some would have us believe that they have vitality even today. It is plain from the record alone that Sutherland had no very great respect for the idea of majority rule. Indeed, I would suppose that he is one of the last men ever to hold high office in the government of the United States to leave behind public expressions of distrust and suspicion of majority rule. As a young man, in speaking of how a legislator should discharge his duties, Sutherland said that the legislator had only to consult his own conscience and his own intelligence and that when he had done this, the "stiff-necked and unappreciative public,"[20] to use his words, could be profanely dismissed, just as Commodore Vanderbilt had dismissed it. Years later we find him inveighing against the notion that "there is some mysterious virtue in mere numbers."[21] We hear him remarking that "there could be no greater delusion than to suppose that by putting a ballot into the hands of a voter you thereby put wisdom into his head."[22] And we have his conclusion that, after all, democracy is "but a form" of government, that "the errors of a democracy and the errors of an autocracy will be followed by similar consequences."[23]

Here is a suggestion that Sutherland's quarrel with majority rule was really a quarrel with government of any kind. We can understand this quarrel only if we recall that Sutherland matured in the last quarter of the nineteenth century when Herbert Spencer's Social Darwinism swept like wildfire across America. Over 400,000 volumes of the philospher's works were sold in the United States alone, and Henry Holt was on the mark when he declared: "Probably no other philosopher ever had such a vogue as Spencer had from about 1870 to 1890."[24] Sutherland felt Spencer's influence in a special way— through a forceful teacher at Brigham Young. And in the area of constitutional law, the Spencerian prescriptions were reinforced for him by his experience as a student of Thomas M. Cooley at the University of Michigan Law School. Moreover, his companions at the Bar were also bearers of the word, and, finally, the Supreme Court itself apparently adopted the philosopher's creed as its own.[25]

Spencer was thus a powerful and continuing influence on

Sutherland—the source, I believe, of the Justice's ideas on the limits of political authority. In Spencer's view, and in that of his American followers, state intervention in economic affairs was neither right nor desirable. His reliance was the principle of adaptation, the compelling urge of an organism to establish harmony with its environment. "Whatever possesses vitality," he argued, "from the elementary . . . up to man himself, obeys this law." Given free rein, man's adaptive faculties would eventually produce utopia, he thought.

. . . progress, therefore, is not an accident, but a necessity. Instead of civilization being artificial, it is a part of nature; all of a piece with the development of the embryo or the unfolding of a flower. The modifications mankind have undergone, and are still undergoing, result from a law underlying the whole organic creation; . . . . As surely as the tree becomes bulky when it stands alone, and slender if one of a group; as surely as the same creature assumes the different forms of cart-horse and race-horse, according as its habits demand strength or speed; as surely as a blacksmith's arm grows large and the skin of a labourer's hand thick; as surely as the eye tends to become long-sighted in the sailor, and short-sighted in the student; . . . as surely as the musician learns to detect an error of a semitone amidst what seems to others a very babel of sounds; as surely as a passion grows by indulgence and diminishes when restrained; . . . as surely as there is any efficacy in educational culture, or any meaning in such terms as habit, custom, practice; so surely must the human faculties be moulded into complete fitness for the social state; so surely must the things we call evil and immorality disappear; so surely must man become perfect.[26]

With utopia thus guaranteed, Spencer had little need for the compulsive power of the state. It was, in his view, a temporary institution, its mission being to hold man in some sort of equilibrium during the transition from solitude to society. This period would of course be unhappy.

. . . Humanity is being pressed against the inexorable necessities of its new position—is being moulded into harmony with them, and has to bear the resulting unhappiness as best it can. The process must be undergone, and the sufferings must be endured. No power on earth, no cunningly-devised laws of statesmen, no world-rectifying schemes of the humane, no communist panaceas, no reforms that men ever did broach or ever will broach, can diminish them one jot. . . .[27]

With all its restrictions on state power, the Spencerian theory recognized the state's duty to provide a defense to external aggression. A basic condition for the operation of the adaptive process was security from attack. Accordingly, in this area the liberty of the individual was not to be considered. This exception to the general rule had, as we shall see, important results for Sutherland, as indeed did the whole Spencerian scheme. Sutherland was certain that "there is at the very heart of things some mighty power which silently and surely, if slowly, works for the exaltation and uplifting of all mankind."[28] His hope of social improvement lay in the "unpleasant consequences" that automatically follow bad conduct. There were, he believed, "certain fundamental social and economic laws which are beyond the power, and certain underlying governmental principles, which are beyond the right of official control, and any attempt to interfere with their operation inevitably ends in confusion, if not disaster." Government must therefore confine its activities, "as a general rule, to preserving a free market and preventing fraud."[29] It is not surprising that Sutherland, holding such convictions, could say to the wage earner that his salvation lay not in a minimum wage but in freedom of contract; or to the debtor that he must be relieved by his own devices; or to the job-seeker that he must learn from his predicament not to repeat the errors that led him to his present plight; or to the state of Oklahoma that a statute that eliminated the competitive struggle from the ice business was unconstitutional.

Even so, Sutherland had the problem of adjusting constitutional theory to the demands of his laissez faire ideology. In some cases, the doctrine of dual federalism would suffice. In others, resort could be had to the idea of separation of powers. In still other cases, the concept of equality was available, and, on occasion, there was an appeal to history with the argument that the intent of the framers must govern constitutional interpretation. For the difficult cases when none of these doctrines produced wholly satisfactory results, Sutherland was equal to the challenge and ready to respond with judicial fiat if nothing else was at hand. He could do this, I think, only because of his deep-seated conviction that popular government, unrestrained by judges, was an impossibility. "The forward march of democracy," he remarked in 1911, "will be of little avail if in the end it rescues us from the absolutism of the king only to hand us over to the absolutism of the majority."[30] To avoid this result was, to him, the special function of the courts. Some agency must have a supervising power, and the constitution had not left its identity in doubt.[31]

When one turns to consider Sutherland's influence on the law of today, it is not surprising, in view of his repeated expressions of concern, to find that he contributed significantly to the protection of the liberty of the individual. What is surprising is that he was on several notable occasions indifferent to the claims of the individual. In *Moore* v. *Dempsey*,[32] he was for affirming a murder conviction secured in a clearly prejudiced atmosphere. He alone joined with Holmes to approve a Nebraska law prohibiting the teaching of the German language.[33] He was unwilling to espouse free speech in either the *Gitlow* or the *Near* case,[34] and he wrote a distressingly technical opinion for the Court in sanctioning the conviction of a Georgia Negro for attempting to incite insurrection.[35] The defendant's lawyers were guilty of the error of failing at the trial to anticipate what the Georgia Supreme Court would later have to say concerning the standard by which his utterances were to be judged. In Sutherland's view, even though at the trial the judge gave the defendant all he asked, the defendant should have then lodged his protest in anticipation of what the appellate court might say.

On other occasions, however, Sutherland wrote in the finest tradition of the Court. The Sutherland opinion in *Berger* v.

United States[36] is a leading one on the right to a fair trial. There the government prosecutor had resorted to obviously improper tactics. He had misstated facts in his questions; he had put into the mouths of witnesses words they never uttered; he had suggested personal knowledge of facts on which he offered no proof; and in general he had attempted to bully and browbeat all opposing witnesses. In spite of all this, the Court of Appeals for the Second Circuit had been unable to find reversible error. But Sutherland, in reversing the conviction, set a standard for prosecutions which endures to this day. The United States Attorney, he declared,

is the representative not of an ordinary party to a controversy, but of a sovereignty whose obligation to govern impartially is as compelling as its obligation to govern at all, and whose interest, therefore in a criminal prosecution is not that it shall win a case, but that justice shall be done. . . . He may prosecute with earnestness and vigor—indeed he should do so. But, while he may strike hard blows, he is not at liberty to strike foul ones. It is as much his duty to refrain from improper methods calculated to produce a wrongful conviction as it is to use every legitimate means to bring about a just one.[37]

Sutherland also figured decisively in the notable series of opinions that converted the liberties protected by the Fourteenth Amendment into a national bill of rights against state action. He wrote the opinion bringing within this protection the freedom of the press from discriminatory taxation.[38] And it was his opinion in *Powell* v. *Alabama*[39] that recognized for the first time the right to counsel as a part of due process. What is today so obviously proper a result was not so obvious in 1932 when the *Powell* case was decided. At common law there had been no such right, and there were, moreover, the difficulties posed by the *Hurtado*[40] decision. But Sutherland brushed them aside to reach the real issues of the case. The first was the adequacy of the trial court's appointment of counsel. No definite appointment was made until the morning of the trial and the counsel then appointed entered a merely

routine appearance. Sutherland refused to accept this as sufficient. It is not enough, he declared,

> to assume that counsel thus precipitated into the case thought
> there was no defense, and exercised their best judgment in proceed-
> ing to trial without preparation. Neither they nor the court could
> say what a prompt and thorough-going investigation might dis-
> close as to the facts. No attempt was made to investigate. No op-
> portunity to do so was given. Defendants were immediately hur-
> ried to trial. . . . Under the circumstances disclosed, we hold that
> defendants were not accorded the right of counsel in any sub-
> stantial sense. To decide otherwise, would simply be to ignore
> actualities.[41]

Sutherland's opinion deals not only with the necessity of
appointing counsel in certain circumstances; rather it goes
further and, as was recently demonstrated,[42] secures absolutely
the right to employ counsel of one's own choice. The opinion
is also important in a more general way. Its healthy realism
stands as a reminder that a merely formal compliance with
the demands of due process will not suffice. Indeed, in the
continuing struggle for more just results in criminal prosecutions, *Powell* v. *Alabama* can fairly be said to be one of the
most influential decisions in the history of the Court.

A second area where Sutherland's work is important today
might be called the "structural constitution." His contribution
to the definition of the place within the American federal judicial system of the courts of the District of Columbia and the
Court of Claims was long-lived.[43] And he is the author of a
number of opinions of continuing vitality on the relationship of
the federal courts to those of the states.[44] But his great opinion
in respect to the distribution of power undoubtedly is *Massachusetts* v. *Mellon* and its companion, *Frothingham* v. *Mellon*.[45]
In the first, Massachusetts, moving to protect what it deemed
to be its sovereign political rights, sought to enjoin a federal
grant to the states under the Maternity Act of 1921. In the second, a taxpayer sought the same result, arguing that he had an

interest as a taxpayer that federal moneys should be spent only for purposes sanctioned by the Constitution. But the Court denied that either the state or the taxpayer had standing to raise the question. So far as the state was concerned, Sutherland wrote, "we are called upon to adjudicate not rights of person or property, not rights of dominion over physical domain, not quasi-sovereign rights actually invaded or threatened but abstract questions of political power, of sovereignty, of government."[46] As for the taxpayer, he was dismissed with the assertion that his interest, shared with millions of others, was not sufficient to give him standing to sue. This decision, liberating as it does the spending power of Congress from the threat of judicial attack, is surely one of the most significant in the Court's history. Whatever might be accomplished by the spending of money was brought within the unchallengeable power of the national government. The vast grant-in-aid program was rendered constitutionally secure. The old notion of competing sovereignties was replaced by that of a cooperative federalism. A citizen of Illinois may now be sure that his concern with the problems of education in North Carolina will not be dismissed as unconstitutional.

Massachusetts v. *Mellon* also had an effect on the Court itself—two effects, I should say. First, coming at the beginning of an era of judicial aggrandizement, it might have been all that saved the Court from destroying itself. For had the Court employed a check on spending along with its other weapons of control in the years that led to the crisis of 1937, it is not unreasonable to think that the Court would have succeeded in its effort at self-destruction.[47] Second, I should say that the decision undoubtedly contributed to the great reversal of 1937 when the Court decided to surrender control of the economy to the people. It must finally have been realized that the effort was a futile one, that a tool indispensable to the task had been surrendered by unanimous vote fourteen years previously.

Again, so far as the structural constitution is concerned,

Sutherland had significant things to say and a highly personal contribution to make in respect to the division of authority between President and Congress. Passing, for the moment, the *Curtiss-Wright* and *Belmont* cases, dealing with the foreign affairs field, I think a word should be said about the *Rathbun* case.[48] It concerned the controversy that has been with America intermittently since 1789 relative to the extent of the President's power of removal. May the President remove a person from office though Congress has said that such officer shall serve a stipulated term? The Court had first met this question in 1927 and had responded in sweeping terms that the President rather than Congress should control. But the officer involved there had been only a postmaster. In 1935 President Roosevelt went after a member of the Federal Trade Commission for a reason that seemed quite compelling to him—the commissioner's mind and his, as he put it, "did not go along" together. Sutherland, speaking for a unanimous Court, held that there must be some retreat from the broad language of the earlier case when the officer involved exercised judicial and legislative authority. Whether or not the limitation on the President to discharge officials appointed for a term of years with the advice and consent of the Senate makes for efficient administration is debatable; but wise or not, the decision continues to have strength as an important organizational factor in the government.

Thus far in speaking of Sutherland's achievement that has a validity for us today, I have adverted first to his part in checking power and then to his part in distributing power. Surprisingly, he also contributed significantly to the expansion of power. He was the author, over the opposition of his conservative colleagues, of the Court's first indorsement of a zoning statute,[49] and he liberally construed the bankruptcy grant to bring within its orbit direct reorganizations.[50] Even more important is his role in the development of the foreign affairs power. In this connection, Sutherland wrote what may

be the most significant power-producing opinions of this century. At any rate, the American Bar Association and Senator
Bricker apparently so regarded them. The scheme of Bricker
and the Bar Association, simply stated, was the repudiation of
the theory of the foreign relations power articulated by Sutherland in the *Curtiss-Wright* case. In that case, Sutherland
won his brethren to the view that the power of the United
States in the field of foreign relations is not attributable to the
Constitution but rather to the nation's status as a member of
the international community. This decision has been protested
as being revolutionary, and in a sense it is. The *Curtiss-Wright*
case itself sanctioned a criminal conviction for the violation
of an embargo imposed, not by Congress, but by the President.
It is true that Congress had authorized the President to act,
but the final decision was left with the President. In other
words, the President could make or unmake the criminal law
in this area when so authorized by Congress, without regard
to the traditional notions limiting the transfer of power. Constitutional limitations, other than express prohibitions, in the
field of foreign affairs were thus destroyed. With them, in this
area went the notion that the federal government is depend-
ent on some specific grant of authority or that the rights of the
states are to be considered in assessing the competence of
the nation.

In addition to this sweeping assertion of power, Sutherland
in the *Belmont* case put on a firm legal footing the President's
authority to conclude executive agreements. The opinion
secures for these agreements recognition as the law of the
land to which the policy of a state, however it might commend
itself, must yield. We can see this opinion's importance more
clearly if we look at the factual situation involved. When
finally the United States recognized Russia in 1933, certain
claims the Russians held to property in this country were assigned to the national government. One such claim was a

confiscated bank deposit in New York which formerly belonged to Russian nationals. When collection was attempted, the United States was resisted on the ground that the state of New York did not approve of expropriation and could not be forced by this Presidential agreement to abandon this policy. The answer given by Sutherland was that the policy of New York was irrelevant, that for the purposes of American dealings with other nations the state of New York did not exist.

In these two cases Sutherland has, since the American Bar Association and Senator Bricker could not take it away, a sure claim on future generations. The cases assure us that national policy in foreign affairs may not be frustrated or limited by state power. Moreover, they weaken a senatorial minority's anachronistic power of obstruction by furnishing judicial approval of two devices for evading it. Under the *Belmont* decision the President may, on occasion, gain for his actions in the international field the standing of the "supreme law of the land," even though he has not consulted the Senate. The *Curtiss-Wright* case, in addition to recognizing a vast authority in the President, clearly implies an indefinite congressional, not merely senatorial, power in foreign affairs. As Professor Corwin has said: "This, in principle, must be as great as the external requirements of the nation itself, provided only that the power does not in its exercise run counter to some specific limitation of the Constitution; and the prerogative of the Senate in the making of treaties does not . . . comprise such a limitation."[51] Professor Corwin further points out that the use of the legislative power of Congress as a substitute for the treaty power is by no means a novel idea. It was so used to annex Texas and Hawaii; it was used to end the first World War; and, more recently, to enable the United States to join the International Labor Office.[52] The *Curtiss-Wright* case now furnishes a solid legal sanction for such procedures. It also guarantees us that whatever our responsibilities, in the UN or in some stronger world organization, we have authority adequate for the job. There are, thanks to George Sutherland, no constitutional obstacles.

Enough has been said to show that Sutherland's performance on the Court was a highly uneven one. Indeed, he emerges as a man of puzzling contrasts. Suspicious of all power and continually opposing its exertion, still he could write the *Curtiss-Wright* opinion destroying constitutional limitations in one of the most important fields of governmental activity. Alert always to the claims of the states and regarding them as the original source of political power, still he could assert in the *Belmont* case that for certain purposes the state of New York did not exist. Keenly sensitive to judicial prerogative, he nevertheless authored perhaps the most notable surrender of judicial power in the Court's history. He believed in the strict separation of powers, that the doctrine was "basic and vital—not merely a matter of governmental mechanism," but he was willing to abandon it on occasion. He was, as we have seen, ambivalent in his attitude toward civil liberties.

This by no means exhausts the difficulties. In regard to statutory interpretation, he could tell us that a statute must be interpreted as written, that "hard and objectionable," even absurd, consequences of a statute were to be corrected only by the legislature.[53] Yet in other cases, especially where seamen were involved, he did not feel bound to a literal reading.[54] He rejected the doctrine of *additur* because it was unknown to the common law,[55] but with as liberal opinion as any ever written in the law of evidence, he abrogated the common law disability of a wife to testify for her husband in a criminal proceeding.[56]

Obviously reflected here is a compartmentalized mind. It is as if Sutherland stored each problem away in a separate portion of the brain and permitted only that portion to function when the problem was being considered. The result is that we have a man necessarily deprived of the large view, unable to see a problem in its relationship to other problems, and thus unable to make the generalizations on which the law relies. Therefore, if the question was one of a woman's minimum-wage law geared to what is necessary to protect health and morals, Sutherland was ready to retort that the inquiry presents an individual, not a composite, question and must be answered "for each individual considered by herself and not by a general formula. . . ."[57] A progressive tax on chain stores, increasing with the number of stores on the theory that such stores have thereby an economic advantage, was bad because some single store may be conceivably have the same advantage.[58] Again, if it was a question of limiting to a stipulated amount the quantity of beverage alcohol that may be prescribed by a physician, that too involved an unallowable generalization, for some people may manifestly need more.[59] And an irrebuttable presumption that gifts made within three years of death were made in contemplation of that event must be disallowed because of the odd case that would do violence to the presumption.[60]

Despite his partial viewpoint, Sutherland did manage a considerable achievement. He towers over Van Devanter, McReynolds, and Butler, with whom he was so often associated. These last three are gone, influencing little for good or evil. Why this difference?

The answer lies first, I think, in Sutherland's penchant for legal and political theory. It is true that his theory was an inadequate one and largely irrelevant to the problems of our day. It is also true that Sutherland at times forgot his theory, so much so that he may be suspected of opportunism, of being concerned merely with the protection of an economic interest. But, paradoxically, it is his theory that saves him from the charge of opportunism. The *Adkins* opinion, far from being the reflex of an economic royalist, is based on the notion that to sustain freedom of contract "is not to strike down the common good but to exalt it. . . ."[61] Moreover, the fact that Sutherland was in the habit of deciding cases from the viewpoint of a rounded theory stood him in good stead when he came to issues unrelated to the theory. This habit kept him from becoming a conservative by instinct or out of mere perversity, and it resulted in his being free to make a contribution when his theory was not called in question.

Again, theory was helpful to Sutherland in winning a place in history in that it made him an extremist. We may not care for the extremists of our day, but we do honor those of other days. We tend to forget the moderate approach of Lincoln to the slavery question and remember him as the Great Emancipator. The historical images of Jefferson and Hamilton also illustrate the point. The moderates of their day, however indispensable they then were, are left behind, caught in the equivocation that practical adjustments require. Sutherland could not equivocate. He saw no neutral colors, It is not surprising that Holmes had to tell him that the great ordinances of the Constitution do not divide fields of black and white, that even the most specific terminate in a penumbra.[62] Sutherland was unimpressed, however. The sanctity of contracts bordered on the absolute. The fact that chaos might be the result of their enforcement was to him an altogther insufficient excuse for refusing a constitutional protection. It is the theorist who has such a power of commitment. It may be, as in the contract cases, that Sutherland's commitments were unwise, but they did succeed in establishing him as the authentic representative of a point of view. Happier results obtain where the commitment had a solid base in fact as well as in theory—results presently useful and which history delights to honor.

It should be noted also that Sutherland's theory helped him reach the *Curtiss-Wright* and *Belmont* decisions. The whole Spencerian philosophy placed a premium on defense from external attack. Security from invasion was an indispensable condition for the waging of the evolutionary struggle. There could be no question, therefore, of measures directed toward

achieving that security. Deceptive as this idea is, it undoubtedly conditioned Sutherland's thinking about governmental
power in foreign affairs and gives some explanation of Sutherland's espousal of the *Curtiss-Wright* idea.

A second reason for Sutherland's superiority to his conservative colleagues is his formal education. It was his good
fortune to have as a teacher Thomas M. Cooley, who was
certainly one of the most stimulating law professors active in
America in the nineteenth century. Another instructor was
Judge James V. Campbell of the Michigan Supreme Court.
Both men were zealots, men with obsessions from which they
did not spare their students. Campbell's obsession was the basic
idea of the *Curtiss-Wright* case, the underlying theory of
which he outlined in full in his lectures. That he made a convert of Sutherland is certain, Sutherland explicitly acknowledging his debt on occasion.[63] Sutherland's debt to Cooley is
equally obvious. Besides the general correspondence of their
views, there is the frequent citation of Cooley throughout the
Sutherland opinions. In the *Powell* case, for example, Cooley
is cited at four crucial points.

Sutherland got more than doctrine from Campbell and
Cooley. He also got from them the notion that law is subject
to change if properly approached. We are so accustomed to
thinking of the exponents of an extreme laissez faire as conservative that we sometimes forget that these men were in a
very real sense revolutionaries. In their fear of majorities,
they abandoned the traditional conservative virtues. Their
denial of the community, their embrace of rugged individualism, represents a direct contradiction of earlier conservative
thought. Sutherland's teachers, and later Sutherland himself,
had these essentially revolutionary notions. And, as I have
said, they fixed also on the idea that law had no claim to immunity from the forces of changes swirling about in their
world. When Cooley taught law to Sutherland the student at
the University of Michigan, Cooley had no warrant for believ-

ing that the Fourteenth Amendment had enacted Herbert
Spencer's *Social Statics*. Even so, Cooley refused to take the
world as he found it and left with Sutherland the idea that he
too could so refuse. It was this, I think, that enabled Sutherland
to win for himself greatness in his role as mouthpiece for the
conservatism of his day. It was the reason he was able to resur-
rect in the *Adkins* opinion the *Lochner* case,[64] which even Taft
supposed had been overruled *sub silentio;* or why in *Colgate*
v. *Harvey*[65] he could invoke the Privileges and Immunities
Clause in spite of the Court's having declined to use it on at
least forty-four previous occasions; or why he dared in the
Carter Coal opinion to treat the *E C. Knight* case[66] as if it
still were entitled to respect. These performances and others
like them won for Sutherland no more than a claim to a place
in a historical museum, representative of a point of view once
dominant but now gone forever. But on other occasions his
conviction that law was subject to influence, that it could be
directed toward desired ends, had happier results, results
which are presently relevant.

Finally, Sutherland's escape from oblivion may be attributed
to his experience before going on the Court. He alone among
the conservative Justices had pursued a political career of
any consequence before taking his seat. Butler had been for
almost his entire adult life a lawyer in Minnesota. McReynolds
had been a lawyer and then, of all things, a professor of law,
although he did later enjoy a year's tenure as Attorney-General.
Van Devanter's career somewhat paralleled that of McReynolds in that he too was a professor who served McKinley
as Assistant Attorney-General. But he was also Chief Justice
of Wyoming for two years and a Court of Appeals judge for
eight.

I do not wish to be understood as saying that the practice
of law, or previous judicial experience, or even service on a
law faculty disqualifies one from serving significantly on the
Supreme Court. Great names crowd in to refute instantly

any such nonsense. But I am willing to assert that an exclusive preoccupation with law in all but the most spacious sense is bound to prove inadequate. The consequence of such a preoccupation is that a premium is put on order within the law and none at all on a result acceptable alike to the litigant and to society. Moreover, the man of the law, unless he is the occasional genius who secures one for himself, has no measuring stick outside the law with which to test his conclusions. Conversely, a wide experience in the world of affairs, a practical knowledge of men, can liberate the prisoner of the most hopeless theory for a career of achievement.

I suggest that this is what happened, to a degree, in Sutherland's case, but first I suggest that this is what happened at Philadelphia in 1787. The significant thing at the Constitutional Convention was not the anti-democratic bias of the framers but rather that men staunchly holding that bias, could say, as Madison said, that government must rest "on the solid foundation of the people," and that the people must provide the chief defense against tyranny. There were many lawyers at Philadelphia, but they were lawyers in a tradition radically different from that of our day. Law was merely a branch of politics, and the lawyers knew it. They therefore had the habit of referring matters to a larger context and from this habit gained a knowledge of the world at large. Accordingly, they knew something of the strength of democracy and had the wisdom to draw the proper conclusion. Here, they said of democracy, was a force that must be consulted.

In Sutherland's case I should say that his great achievements, and some of his lesser ones, are partly attributable to his political career. He served in the Senate from 1905 to 1917. Before that, he was a member of the House of Representatives. Before he ever came to Congress, he had a fully developed philosophy of government, a theory that denied the state any creative role in society. Nevertheless, under the compulsion of bearing the responsibility of governing he frequently abandoned his irrelevant theories to support measures directed at solving the pressing problems of the day. Even as a young legislator in Utah he had supported the eight-hour day upheld in *Holden* v. *Hardy*.[67] As a member of the Senate he supported the Employer's Liability Act, the Pure Food and Drugs Act, the Hepburn Rate Bill, the eight-hour day for laborers employed by the United States, Postal Savings Banks, workmen's compensation, and the Seamen's Bill of 1915. Nor was his support of these measures merely perfunctory. In the case of workmen's compensation, Sutherland was a pioneer, heading the special commission which prepared the bill, and he was its most articulate advocate. In the course of this advocacy, he was even brought to declare that "the individualistic theory has been pushed with too much stress upon the dry logic of its doctrines and too little regard for their practical operation from the humanitarian point of view. We are discovering," he continued, "that we cannot always regulate our economic and social relations by scientific formulae, because a good many people perversely insist upon being fed and clothed and comforted by the practical rule of thumb rather than by the exact rules of logic."[68] Here was wisdom plainly the result of being forced by position to consider the needs of ordinary men and women in an industrial society and to consider them in a way not usually found in the courts of his day. Or we may take the case of Sutherland's support of legislation to benefit seamen. He happened, as a Senator, to meet the head of the seamen's union, Andrew Furuseth. Furuseth proceeded to give Sutherland an education on conditions of life in the merchant marine. The result was that Sutherland became, in Furuseth's words, "an earnest champion of legislation which would restore to us our rights as men and to the travelling public such increased safety as the law could provide."[69] But the result was something more, for his experience in this matter taught Sutherland as a Justice even how to interpret a statute, at least when seamen were involved.[70]

When we come to a larger matter like that involved in *Massachusetts* v. *Mellon,* again I think it may be said that Sutherland's experience served him well. He knew that the Supreme Court was really not a fit substitute for the Appropriations Committees of Congress. Likewise, his experience must have contributed to the *Curtiss-Wright* decision. He had been a member of the Foreign Relations Committee. He had served as an adviser to the American delegation at the Washington conference. He had therefore a firsthand knowledge of the realities of the struggles between the great powers and a grasp of the difficulties that a sterile legalism could pose to our policy-makers. When he tackled this problem as a Justice, he was therefore armed with something more than a lawyer's conceptions. To the American Bar Association and Senator Bricker the result may have been anathema. Their reaction involves a note of irony, for Sutherland is the only man besides Taft ever to serve as president of the Bar Association before coming to the Court.

To sum up, Sutherland had a remarkably useful career, especially when we remember that he was a heretic in two important respects. He had no faith in majority rule or in the efficacy of government. The judgment of the twentieth century is against him on both counts. Therefore, his record is for us today largely irrelevant. But his career demonstrates that even the heretic has his uses. We forget this at our peril.

J. FRANCIS PASCHAL *is a professor of law at Duke University School of Law. Before turning to the law, he acquired a Doctor of Philosophy degree at Princeton, where his interest in the subject of this biographical sketch was stimulated by Professors Mason and Corwin. He is the author of a full-length biography of Justice Sutherland, which was published in 1951.*

NOTES

1. See Pritchett, *The Roosevelt Court* (1948), p. 300, for a list of the cases specifically overruled from 1937 to 1947. Of the thirty-two cases listed by Pritchett, Sutherland wrote the opinion in seven. They are, together with the overruling decisions: (1) *Brush* v. *Commissioner*, 300 U.S. 352 (1937); *Helvering* v. *Gerhardt*, 304 U.S. 405 (1938); (2) *Colgate* v. *Harvey*, 296 U.S. 404 (1935); *Madden* v. *Kentucky*, 309 U.S. 83 (1940); (3) *Ribnik* v. *McBride*, 277 U.S. 350 (1928); *Olsen* v. *Nebraska*, 313 U.S. 236 (1941); (4) *First National Bank* v. *Maine*, 284 U.S. 312 (1932); *State Tax Comm.* v. *Aldrich*, 316 U.S. 174 (1942); (5) *New York ex rel. Rogers* v. *Graves*, 299 U.S. 401 (1937); *Graves* v. *New York*, 306 U.S. 466 (1939); (6) and (7) *United States* v. *Macintosh*, 283 U.S. 605 (1931) and *United States* v. *Bland*, 283 U.S. 636 (1931); both overruled by *Girouard* v. *United States*, 328 U.S. 61 (1946). *Adkins* v. *Children's Hospital*, 261 U.S. 525 (1923), overruled in *West Coast Hotel Co.* v. *Parrish*, 300 U.S. 379 (1937), may be added to this list, although its destruction was accomplished before there were any additions to the Court.

2. A notable example is *Carter* v. *Carter Coal Co.*, 298 U.S. 238 (1936). For a detailed account of Sutherland's obsolescence see Frank, Book Review, 61 YALE L. J. 598 (1952).

3. *Frost & Frost Trucking Company* v. *Railroad Commission*, 271 U.S. 583 (1926).

4. *Frost* v. *Corporation Commission*, 278 U.S. 515 (1929); *New State Ice Company* v. *Liebmann*, 285 U.S. 262 (1932).

5. *Wolff Packing Company* v. *Industrial Court*, 262 U.S. 522 (1923).

6. *Liggett Company* v. *Baldridge*, 278 U.S. 105 (1928).

7. *Adkins* v. *Children's Hospital*, 261 U.S. 525 (1923).

8. *Tyson* v. *Banton*, 273 U.S. 418 (1927).

9. *Williams* v. *Standard Oil Co.*, 278 U.S. 235 (1929).

10. *Ribnik* v. *McBride*, 277 U.S. 350 (1928).

11. *First National Bank* v. *Maine*, 284 U.S. 312 (1932).

12. *Macallen Company* v. *Massachusetts*, 279 U.S. 620 (1929).

13. *State Board of Tax Commissioners* v. *Jackson*, 283 U.S. 527 (1931).

14. *Crooks* v. *Harrelson*, 282 U.S. 55 (1930).

15. *Heiner* v. *Donnan*, 285 U.S. 312 (1932).

16. *Norman* v. *Baltimore & Ohio Railroad*, 294 U.S. 240 (1935); *Perry* v. *United States*, 294 U.S. 330 (1935).

17. *Schecter Poultry Corp.* v. *United States*, 295 U.S. 495 (1935); *United States* v. *Butler*, 297 U.S. 1 (1936); *Railroad Retirement Board* v. *Alton Railroad Company*, 295 U.S. 330 (1935).

18. *Carter* v. *Carter Coal Company,* 298 U.S. 238 (1936).

19. *Associated Press* v. *N.L.R.B.,* 301 U.S. 103 (1937); *Carmichael* v. *Southern Coal & Coke Co.,* 301 U.S. 495 (1937); *Steward Ice Machine Co.* v. *Davis,* 301 U.S. 548 (1937).

20. *Territorial Inquirer* (Provo, Utah), Dec. 10, 1886.

21. 47 CONG. REC. 2795–96 (1911).

22. *The Courts and the Constitution,* S. Doc. 970, 62d Cong., 3d sess., 11 (1912). This was an address before the American Bar Association.

23. *Private Rights and Government Control,* 42 A.B.A. REP. 197, 203 (1917).

24. Quoted in Goldman, *Rendezvous with Destiny* (1953), p. 91.

25. See generally my *The Education of a Justice,* 1 J. LEGAL EDUC. 333 (1949).

26. *Social Statics* (1883), p. 80.

27. *Ibid.* at 356.

28. 41 CONG. REC. 1499 (1907).

29. *Principle or Expedient,* 44 N.Y. STATE BAR ASS'N REP. 263, 264 (1921). This address by Sutherland to the New York State Bar Association is perhaps the fullest single statement by him of his philosophy.

30. 47 CONG. REC. 2800 (1911).

31. Cf. *West Coast Hotel Co.,* v. *Parrish,* 300 U.S. 379, 401 (1937).

32. 261 U.S. 86 (1923).

33. *Meyer* v. *Nebraska,* 262 U.S. 390 (1923).

34. *Gitlow* v. *New York,* 268 U.S. 652 (1925); *Near* v. *Minnesota,* 283 U.S. 697 (1931).

35. *Herndon* v. *Georgia,* 295 U.S. 441 (1935).

36. 295 U.S. 78 (1935).

37. *Ibid.* at 88.

38. *Grosjean* v. *American Press Co.,* 297 U.S. 233 (1936).

39. 287 U.S. 45 (1932).

40. *Hurtado* v. *California,* 110 U.S. 516 (1884).

41. 287 U.S. at 58.

42. *Chandler* v. *Fretag,* 348 U.S. 3 (1954).

43. *O'Donoghue* v. *United States,* 289 U.S. 516 (1933); *Williams* v. *United States,* 289 U.S. 553 (1933).

44. E.g., *Kline* v. *Burke Construction Co.,* 260 U.S. 226 (1922).

45. 262 U.S. 447 (1923).

46. *Ibid.* at 484–85.

47. *United States* v. *Butler,* 297 U.S. 1 (1936), sufficiently reveals the possibilities.

48. *United States* v. *Curtiss-Wright Export Corp.,* 299 U.S. 304

(1936); *United States* v. *Belmont,* 301 U.S. 324 (1937); *Rathbun* v. *United States,* 295 U.S. 602 (1935).

49. *Euclid* v. *Ambler,* 272 U.S. 365 (1926).

50. *Continental Ill. Bank* v. *Chicago, R. I. & P. R. Co.,* 294 U.S. 648 (1935).

51. Corwin, *The Constitution and World Organization* (1944), pp. 46–47.

52. *Ibid.,* p. 46.

53. *Crooks* v. *Harrelson,* 282 U.S. 55, 60 (1930).

54. See *O'Hara* v. *Luckenbach Steamship Co.,* 269 U.S. 364 (1926).

55. *Dimick* v. *Schiedt,* 293 U.S. 474 (1935).

56. *Funk* v. *United States,* 290 U.S. 371 (1933).

57. *Adkins* v. *Children's Hospital,* 261 U.S. 525, 556 (1923).

58. *State Board of Tax Commissioners* v. *Jackson,* 283 U.S. 527 (1931) (dissenting).

59. *Lambert* v. *Yellowly,* 272 U.S. 581 (1926) (dissenting).

60. *Heiner* v. *Donnan,* 285 U.S. 312 (1932).

61. *Adkins* v. *Children's Hospital,* 261 U.S. 525, 561 (1923) (dissenting).

62. *Springer* v. *Government of the Philippine Islands,* 277 U.S. 189, 209–10 (1928) (dissenting).

63. See Sutherland, *Internal and External Powers of the National Government,* 191 NORTH AMERICAN REVIEW 373 (March, 1910).

64. *Lochner* v. *New York,* 198 U.S. 45 (1905).

65. 296 U.S. 404 (1935).

66. *United States* v. *E. C. Knight Co.,* 156 U.S. 1 (1895).

67. 169 U.S. 366 (1898). See 48 CONG. REC. 6797 (1912) for Sutherland's account of his support of this statute.

68. *Compulsory Workmen's Compensation Law,* S. Doc. 131, 63d Cong., 1st sess., 11 (1913).

69. *Utah Labor News,* August 5, 1916.

70. See *O'Hara* v. *Luckenbach Steamship Co.,* 269 U.S. 364 (1926); for Sutherland's handling of a compensation case, see *Bountiful Brick Co.* v. *Giles,* 276 U.S. 154 (1928).

MR. CHIEF JUSTICE STONE

Mr. Chief Justice Stone

By
ALLISON DUNHAM

In May, 1931, the United States Supreme Court held that unwillingness to bear arms because of pacifist religious belief was a bar to naturalization under the applicable act of Congress.[1] Justice Harlan F. Stone joined with Holmes and Brandeis in the dissent of Chief Justice Hughes. Fifteen years later, on April 22, 1946, Justice Douglas, speaking for a new Court, declared that the earlier dissenters had been right.[2] Stone, Chief Justice by then, read a dissent from this new position of the Court, declaring that the subsequent legislative consideration of the problem had served to confirm the interpretation of the language of the statute that earlier he had thought to be an erroneous one. As Stone saw the problem anew, it was the duty of the Court to abide by the congressional will. The Chief Justice had barely concluded his statement when his speech faltered and he had to be helped from the bench. He died later that day. Thus after Stone had served a little more than twenty-one years as a Justice and Chief Justice,[3] the judicial career of the man who saw more of his dissenting opinions and positions become the law of the Court than any other Justice in history[4] ended almost in the act of dissenting from the adoption by the Court of his earlier minority position.

I begin with this incident not to suggest that time and events had first caught up with Stone and then passed him by, leaving him again a dissenter; for such was not the case. Rather I use this event as a vivid illustration of two significant aspects of the judicial philosophy of the twelfth Chief Justice of the United States. For his last dissent illustrates his independence in performance of his judicial duty of decision without regard to his personal preferences or reputation. It illustrates, too, one facet of his conception of the judicial function—deference to the legislative branch of government when it is acting in its appropriate sphere. In this essay, I would like to dwell briefly on his judicial disinterestedness and to consider in some detail his conception of the role of the Supreme Court in constitutional controversy.

During his twenty-one years on the bench, from 1925 to 1946, the contentious areas of constitutional theory shifted. Through at least the first half of his tenure the great constitutional controversy was state experimentation—the power of a state to make changes in its economic or legal order by regulations, prohibitions, or taxes deemed by the legislative majority of the moment to promote the general welfare. Almost before this debate was resolved, the problem changed into a controversy over the power of the national government to make changes in the economic or legal order of the nation. This was the period of the New Deal legislation of the early thirties and of the great fight over President Roosevelt's "Court-packing plan." Throughout both these periods and, indeed, until the untimely termination of Stone's career, the Court was faced with a perennial constitutional controversy—the problem of policing our federalism, that is, assessing the authority of some one state to regulate or tax persons or institutions for transactions connected in some way with several states. Hardly had the battles concerning national power ended when a new constitutional dispute struck the Court: the contenders argued differences between the power of the popular majority to control man's economic activity and its power to control matters touching affairs of conscience and expression.

In each of these great controversies Justice Stone, as occasion offered, brought to bear his great creative power to make new law or to give sensible arrangement to old constitutional doctrines.[5]

Many who are accustomed to assume that all men, including those in positions of public trust, make decisions in terms of personal economic predilection or advantage, will find it hard to understand Justice Stone's great self-subordination and absolute disinterest. Not only his craftsmanship and intellectual talents but even his passion often was given to sustaining legislation which, if he had been a legislator, he would have denounced just as passionately. Thus in his famous dissent in *United States* v. *Butler*,[6] involving the constitutionality of the first Agricultural Adjustment Act, Stone bitterly accused his brethren of lack of self-restraint and sought to demonstrate that the Court was striking this law down only because of its belief in the badness of the law. Yet Stone regarded this legislative act as so bad that, even four years later when I first came to know him, he would talk about it in scathing terms. Another illustration of Stone's restraint may be found in his attitude toward the Gold Clause cases,[7] involving the power of Congress to refuse to pay government bonds in gold as had been promised. Stone, it is reported by Gardner, his clerk at the time,[8] was so incensed at this "welshing," as his New England conscience told him it was, that he proposed never again to purchase government bonds (a proposal from which he relented); yet he alone of the Justices was willing to concede that the constitutional power to regulate money might affect government bonds even to this extent.[9]

Even when Stone thought the Constitution required a value judgment by the Court, he was willing to stand alone to protect men or doctrines or activities of which he disapproved. Thus in June, 1940, when the clouds of war were gathering over his country, he, an intensely patriotic man, stood alone even against the conclusions of men so sensitive to personal liberties as Chief Justice Hughes and Justices Black, Frankfurter, Douglas, and Murphy to say, in another passionate dissent, that a compulsory flag salute violated the religious freedom of a minority that conceived the flag salute to be idolatry.[10]

As a final illustration I mention again Stone's response to *Girouard* v. *United States*, the instance which I described at the beginning of this essay. If the legislative decision had been his in this case, he undoubtedly would not have barred naturalization to religious pacifists. Moreover, he could expect his "reputation" to be tarnished among those inclined to classify Justices as civil libertarians and liberals according to whether the result of a Justice's decision supports or opposes a particular proposition. Although it must have hurt him to do so, he was prepared to adhere to his customary deference to the legislative judgment to which his conception of his judicial duty led him, even though this would make him appear in the eyes of the less discerning to dissent from his own dissent.

At a time when so many tend to particularize what they are for or against in terms of specific issues and particular persons, we can well afford to take a new look at this great judge and his capacity for disinterested judging. For his was a canon of adjudication that applied equally to government officials or victims of government officials and was constant in application whatever might be politically acceptable for the time. His was a principle which produced an acceptance for unpopular decisions, a principle engendered by a confidence that the power of the Court could not depend on the popularity or unpopularity of particular issues or parties.

When one talks of a Justice's contributions to, or influence on, judicial doctrine, it is always a little unreal to attribute to one of nine the source of the doctrine appearing in a common product. We do not know the extent to which a Justice's views have been sharpened, borrowed from, or even changed by, the Saturday (now Friday) conference with his brethren of the Court. Moreover, ever since Marshall abandoned the practice of seriatim opinions and introduced the concept of "the opinion of the Court," the concept itself has influenced Justices, we know not how much, to temper an opinion of the Court so as to accommodate the varying views of the brethren for whom he is speaking. Stone's sense of his duty to the Court in this respect contained a strong obligation to seek the concurrence of his brethren if possible. Upon returning from conference and reporting that tentative disagreement (all votes at the first conference are tentative) had been recorded by some to the decision reached in the case assigned to him to write for the Court, he would frequently add: "I think I can write the opinion so as to get the concurrence of the dissenters." More often than not he succeeded.

United States v. *Classic*[11] in the 1940 term is an illustration. Previously, as a result of *Newberry* v. *United States,* decided in 1921,[12] it had been thought that Congress had no power to reach abuses in primary elections conducted to determine a nomination for Congress. In *Grovey* v. *Townsend,* decided in 1935,[13] a unanimous Court including Stone had held (Justice Roberts speaking for the Court) that the Fourteenth and Fifteenth Amendments were inapplicable to racial disqualification for voting in a primary when the primary was conducted by a political party without explicit authority from the state. Some of the Justices were concerned about whether these cases controlled *United States* v. *Classic,* which involved an indictment under the rarely used Civil Rights Acts[14] of two election commissioners in Louisiana for injuring citizens in the exercise and enjoyment of rights guaranteed by the Constitution, rights allegedly violated by a false count of votes in a primary election conducted to determine a party nomination for Congress.

The judicial method of Stone is fully revealed in this case. He first examined the Louisiana statutes and concluded that the right to vote for a representative to Congress was restricted by law to a vote for a successful party candidate at the pri-

mary. Thus, without even mentioning *Grovey* v. *Townsend*, he
disposed of the argument that a Louisiana party primary was
nothing more than the nomination of officers of a voluntary
private association, as the Court had considered the Texas
political parties to be in the *Grovey* case. He then found that
even if, as the defendants had argued, nominees could be
selected by another method, the practical operation of the
primary system was to the same end: a nomination in the
primary was in practical effect a condition precedent to being
a candidate for Congress. This was a point ignored or not considered by the Court in *Grovey* v. *Townsend* which could later
serve as a basis for distinguishing or overruling that case.[15]
Having concluded that interference with the right to vote in a
primary was in law and in fact an interference with the right
to vote for Congress, he addressed himself to the question
whether the right to vote in a primary for a nominee to Congress was a right protected by the Constitution. He eliminated
Newberry v. *United States* as a barrier by pointing out that it
really decided nothing on the point because the Court had
split four-to-four on this issue with the odd judge deciding on
another ground. Not being bound by precedent, he addressed
himself to first principles. The defendants had, of course,
argued that a primary was unknown by the framers of the
Constitution and that therefore a primary election could not
be within the word "election" as used in the Constitution.
Stone agreed that the framers had not thought of a primary
and in the circumstances of 1787 could not have expected
"election" to include a primary. But he said the absence of
judgment by the framers was irrelevant: "For in setting up an
enduring framework of government they undertook to carry
out for the indefinite future . . . those fundamental purposes
which the instrument itself discloses. Hence we read its
words, not as we read legislative codes which are subject to
continuous revision with the changing course of events, but as

the revelation of the great purposes which were intended to be achieved by the Constitution as a continuing instrument of government."[16] In light of the spirit and purpose of the Constitution, he concluded that the right to choose a member of Congress, admittedly protected by the Constitution, embraced the right to vote in a primary which in law and in practical effect was to determine the selection of a member of Congress. By thus disposing of the earlier case law he was able to obtain the concurrence of some would-be dissenters. Only Justices Black and Douglas, who were joined by Justice Murphy, were unconverted.

It cannot be maintained that this method was used because he was hesitant to overrule an earlier decision of the Court, for three years later, in *Smith* v. *Allwright*,[17] he was with the majority that overruled *Grovey* v. *Townsend*. Indeed, it would appear that his technique in *Classic* was directed to that end, for the opinion was written so that the Court in *Smith* v. *Allwright* could say that the reasoning of *Classic* was inconsistent with that of *Grovey* v. *Townsend*. Neither can it be maintained that insufficient support among his brethren prevented him from overruling the *Grovey* case: the change in personnel between *Classic* and *Smith* could not have affected the result.[18] Rather it was enough for Stone that he could obtain the greatest concurrence to a narrower revision and that he could support the narrower revision by reasons which disclosed an acceptable principle on which the Court could approach future cases. He would leave it to later argument before the Court to point out that the principle accepted in this case made the earlier case untenable.

This strong loyalty to the concept of the opinion of the Court and its attendant obligation on the Justice writing the opinion was compatible with, and supported by, another of Stone's views. In his address at the tercentennial of Harvard on "The Common Law in the United States," he likened the judicial process in constitutional cases to the judicial process in common-law cases. He said:

> ... While these are variations in the nature of the subject matter of judicial inquiry, they involve no necessary variation of the methods by which the common law has been accustomed to solve its problems. Its method of marking out, as cases arise, step by step, the line between the permitted and the forbidden, by the process of appraisal and comparison of the experiences of the past and of the present, is as applicable to the field of public law as of private. Courts called upon to rule on questions of constitutional power have thus found ready at hand a common law technique suitable to the occasion.[19]

Thus Stone seldom found it necessary to support an answer to one problem by an appeal to reasons which might decide all constitutional questions or even all of the questions arising under the same clause of the Constitution. It was enough to answer the question at hand and support it with reasons sufficient for the purpose.

A narrow statement of issue and reasons may result from the common-law judging tradition or from an obligation arising from the concept of the opinion of the Court, and such narrowing need not suggest that a Justice has been defeated in a doctrinal controversy. Neither should this practice suggest that Justice Stone felt narrowly bound by precedent. He was one of the great creative Justices of the Supreme Court. Nothing delighted him more than to examine a subject or body of law in which there was a morass of decisions with conflicting or untenable reasons and then to restate the rule with reasons having real substance.

Nevertheless, with respect to a Justice's views on the function of the judiciary in constitutional controversy, it is easier to assume that a Justice's opinions reflect his basic beliefs uninfluenced by his colleagues' reasoning than is the case of his views on some substantive legal problem. Although Court opinions generally do not concern themselves with a philosophy of judicial review, Chief Justice Stone's opinions reflect a rather unique awareness of, and concern with, the nature of judicial review in constitutional controversy. His writings and his opin-

ions reflect a sureness that it was the Court's duty to participate in constitutional debate;[20] and he was not concerned with
the ancient debate about whether the Court should resolve
such controversy or about whether the framers intended that it
do so. But participation was to Stone something other than
using formulae or a literal reading of words to answer a constitutional problem. Although, even during Stone's term on the
Court, it was asserted that answers could be found by laying a
statute alongside the Constitution and comparing the language
of each,[21] Stone knew that this could not be done.

His opinions reflected a constant drive to show that the Constitution had few absolutes to limit democratic action,[22] that
the conflicts involved were practical problems of the relation
of authority to individuals, and that accommodations of these
competing interests must be made in practical terms. The
Court, as he understood it, must always address itself to the
actualities of the situation. Much of the first half of his tenure
was spent in sweeping away meaningless formulae and trying
to get his brethren and advocates to address themselves to
realities. Thus, within two years after he came to the bench,
he attacked in a dissent a venerable formula by which the
Court had sought to test the validity of state taxation and
regulation under the Commerce Clause. The test was said to
be whether the state action directly or indirectly interfered
with commerce. If directly, the state action was bad; if indirectly, the state action was valid. Stone said of this formula:

. . . [T]he traditional test . . . seems to me too mechanical, too uncertain in its application, and too remote from actualities, to be of
value. In thus making use of the expressions, "direct" and "indirect
interference" with commerce, we are doing little more than using
labels to describe a result rather than any trustworthy formula by
which it is reached.[23]

He then went on to describe what he thought the Court should
do and how it should approach this problem.

. . . [I]t seems clear that those interferences not deemed forbidden
are to be sustained . . . because a consideration of all of the facts
and circumstances, such as the nature of the regulation, its function,

the character of the business involved and the actual effect on the flow of commerce, lead to the conclusion that the regulation concerns interests peculiarly local and does not infringe the national interest in maintaining the freedom of commerce across state lines.

Even where the labels used came from analytical articles by Dean Stone of Columbia Law School, he attacked their use. Thus, in a case where some of the dean's articles were referred to in argument and by the majority to help the Court attach a label to an interest in order to determine its taxability under the Due Process Clause, Justice Stone's dissent dismissed the theories of Dean Stone and of the Court as irrelevant:

> It is unimportant what labels writers on legal theory, the courts of Ohio, or this Court may place upon this interest. . . . In applying the Fourteenth amendment we may recognize . . . that whether [interests] are rightly subjected to state taxing power must be determined by recourse to the principles upon which taxes have universally been laid and collected, rather than by the choice of a label which, by definition previously agreed upon, will infallibly mark the interest as non-taxable.[24]

Justice Stone's main contribution to the philosophy of the judicial function in constitutional controversy came, however, when he was called upon to cope with a doctrine of which he was only a junior architect but which he was called upon to mold and to fit into new areas of controversy when it came to be an accepted doctrine. The question was whether the same deference to legislative judgment should be given by the Court in all constitutional cases.

When Justice Stone came to the bench in 1925, the dominant constitutional problem was, as I have said, that of the power of the states to regulate economic enterprise. Since the 1890's the Due Process Clause and the Equal Protection Clause of the Fourteenth Amendment had been used to restrict the power of the states to regulate property. The majority of the Supreme Court had conceived the judicial function to be that of determining almost as a third legislature whether state action was, in the judgment of the Court, a valid regulation. Issue with this position had been framed first by Holmes and later reinforced by Brandeis. Almost immediately on taking his seat on the bench, Stone accepted the canon of adjudication advanced by Holmes. These dissenters had argued that state statutes were to be upheld by the Supreme Court so long as anyone could find a reasonable basis for supporting them. Since it was nearly always possible to find a plausible justification for any measure that had commanded enough support to pass a legislature and a governor, little, if anything, would be declared unconstitutional under this test. It was this test and the failure of the majority to apply it that produced the great line of dissents of Holmes, Brandeis, Stone, and later Cardozo.[25]

By 1937 the dissenting position had become the majority position. However, the subject of constitutional debate had begun to change to that of personal liberties, and it fell to Stone, the only remaining architect of the canon of adjudication, to consider the doctrine in light of this new problem. In reality the position of both the old dissent and the new majority had some embarrassing inconsistencies. The old majority that had found so much of the regulation of economic activity "unreasonable" and therefore a denial of Due Process could find much less to review when the guarantees of the First Amendment were under consideration. On the other hand, Holmes and Brandeis, the architects of the new doctrine of giving deference to the judgment embodied in legislation, seemed to demand of the judiciary, when governmental action limiting freedom of speech was involved, a much more extended evaluation by the Court of the competing values than they did when economic regulation was involved.[26] Furthermore, as Stone himself knew, there were other areas in the constitutional framework where the Court, including Brandeis and Holmes felt compelled to weigh competing values and decide for or against some state legislation on the basis of this judgment rather than to defer without question to the legislative determination. Thus under the Commerce Clause, unless one was prepared to accept the position that the states could regulate anything however it affected interstate commerce until Congress prohibited such state action, it was clear that the Court was making value judgments very much like a legislature. Why should not this doctrine of extreme deference to the legislative judgment apply here as well as under the Due Process Clause? Was the Court really making this distinction in terms of some predilection concerning the particular matter in dispute?

It is not surprising that a Justice who had so passionately challenged his brethren about reading their own predilections into the Constitution, and who had followed so faithfully a canon of adjudication that avoided personal preferences, should address himself to establishing a standard that would try to maintain an even-handed approach to similar problems. Neither Holmes nor Brandeis had had to address themselves specifically to this problem.

Stone rejected avenues of solution based on magical formulae or a rhetoric which appeared to deny judges the power of judging. It did not seem to him to help matters, for example, to make personal liberty questions a matter of Privileges and Immunities under the Fourteenth Amendment to which a standard of review could be applied differing from that used in Due Process questions.[27] Nor did it seem to him to help matters to use different rhetoric. To him the Court was judging competing values whether, for example, it stated the question to be: "Does the statutory authority for martial law include the power to deny access to the civil courts?" or "Is the martial law decree denying access to the civil courts a reasonable exercise of the statutory power?"[28] When judging called for making value judgments, he saw no reason to conceal that he was doing just that.

Stone characteristically then sought to classify constitutional cases into those in which he thought the Court should assess the situation, if necessary making a political judgment, and those in which it should defer to legislative judgment. Significantly, he sought not only to state a suggested classification but to give reasons which he hoped would so disclose the basis of classification that personal predilections in making the classification could be held to a minimum.

His first attempt at this came in a footnote to a case involving the power of South Carolina to limit the weight and width of trucks passing through the state while engaged in commerce among the states. On occasion it has been suggested that in Commerce Clause cases as in Due Process cases involving economic matters the same standard of deference to the legislative judgment should be applied.[29] This view was not acceptable to Stone, who had no doubt that in the absence of congressional action the Court could perform an important function in representing the national interest. In the footnote to *South Carolina Highway Department* v. *Barnwell Bros.*,[30] in 1938, he suggested a tentative reason why complete deference should not be given to the legislative judgment. After referring to the rule whereby the Court struck down state legislation concerning interstate commerce, he said: "Underlying the stated rule has been the thought, often expressed in judicial opinion, that when the regulation is of such a character that its burden falls principally upon those without the state, legislative action is not likely to be subjected to those political restraints which are normally exerted on legislation where it affects adversely some interest within the state." In substance, the Court should review the legislative judgment where political restraints could not be expected to stay the hand of the legislature. Thus in an interstate commerce case the Court would not accept at face value (as it would in a Due Process case) a determination by a state legislature that a matter was of local concern. Rather it would look to all of the facts and circumstances to determine for itself whether such was the case, and, in addition to that, it would determine for itself whether the regulation unduly imperiled the national interest in the free flow of commerce.[31]

This idea of the absence of political restraint as the basis for the Court making a value judgment appears to be first introduced in this case. Stone stated it again in a footnote some two months later in a case where the Court had under consideration a traditional Due Process question.[32] In the course of the case, it was asked whether a federal act regulating interstate shipment of filled milk products was a violation of the Due Process Clause of the Fifth Amendment. Stone answered this question in the negative, using the Brandeis-Holmes canon of adjudication. He said: "Regulatory legislation affecting ordinary commercial transactions is not to be pronounced unconstitutional unless in the light of the facts made known or generally assumed it is of such a character as to preclude the assumption that it rests upon some rational basis within the knowledge and experience of legislators."[33]

To this customary statement of the judicial function in Due Process cases generally, he appended a footnote in which he said:

There may be narrower scope for operation of the presumption of constitutionality when legislation appears on its face to be within a specific prohibition of the Constitution, such as those of the first ten amendments, which are deemed equally specific when held to be embraced within the Fourteenth. It is unnecessary to consider now whether legislation which restricts those political processes which can ordinarily be expected to bring about repeal of undesirable legislation, is to be subjected to more exacting judicial scrutiny under the general prohibitions of the Fourteenth Amendment than are most other types of legislation. . . . Nor need we enquire whether similar considerations enter into the review of statutes directed at particular religious . . . or national . . . or racial minorities . . . may be a special condition, which tends seriously to curtail the operation of those political processes ordinarily to be relied upon to protect minorities, and which may call for a correspondingly more searching judicial inquiry.[34]

Six weeks later he again mentioned the idea of absence of political restraint as a basis for close judicial review, and this time in the text of his opinion. In a case considering reciprocal immunity of the nation and its instrumentalities and the state and its instrumentalities from taxation by the other sovereign,[35] the Justice greatly narrowed the immunity of the states and their instrumentalities from federal taxation while adhering to a more stringent rule for state taxation of federal instrumentalities. The reason advanced for the distinction in judicial treatment was that national taxation of the states was subject to political restraints but state taxation of national instrumentalities was subject to no such restraint inasmuch as the people outside the state had no representatives participating in that state's legislative process.[36]

But the suggestion in the *Carolene Products* case that under the Due Process Clause there were two different standards of judicial review remained in the realm of theory until 1940, when the issue was squarely presented. The Board of Education of Minersville, Pennsylvania, had expelled two children from school for refusing to accompany teachers and schoolmates in the salute to the flag as required by board rule. The refusal was based on religious grounds: the tenets of Jehovah's Witnesses to which sect these children belonged characterized this ceremony as idolatry. In a suit by the father to enjoin the board from continuing this rule, the Court held that the father had no case.[37] It said: "To stigmatize legislative judgment in providing for [the flag salute] . . . as a lawless inroad on that freedom of conscience which the Constitution protects, would amount to no less that the pronouncement of . . . dogma in a field where courts possess no marked and certainly no controlling competence." Justice Frankfurter in applying the customary canon of deference to the legislative judgment wrote for everyone but Stone. In one of his more passionate dissents Stone conceded that the constitutional guarantees of personal liberty are not absolutes and that "where there are competing demands of the interests of government and liberty . . . there must . . . be reasonable accommodation between them," but he also said, "it is the function of courts to determine whether such accommodation is reasonably possible." He continued, that to defer to legislative judgment here is

no less than the surrender of the constitutional protection of the liberty of small minorities to the popular will. . . . Here we have such a small minority entertaining in good faith a religious belief, which is such a departure from the usual course of human conduct, that most persons are disposed to regard it with little toleration or concern. In such circumstances careful scrutiny of legislative efforts to secure conformity of belief and opinion by a compulsory affirmation of the desired belief, is especially needful if civil rights are to receive any protection.[38]

What happened in the particular controversy is well known. Three years later the judgment of Justice Stone on the flag salute had been adopted by a majority of the Court,[39] a situation made possible only by a change of position of three judges who had stood with the majority in the *Minersville* case. Although the transformation of dissent to judgment was by this time familiar to the Chief Justice, this was the first time that such had occurred by a change of position of Justices who participated in both cases. What is more striking is that the same thing happened again when Justices of the new Court were persuaded by a dissent of Stone to change the majority position again. This time the question was the validity of municipal license taxes imposed upon sale by solicitation of pamphlets and books by members of the Jehovah's Witnesses sect.[40] Perhaps we get some indication of the man from the fact that Stone as Chief Justice controlling the assignment of cases gave others the opportunity to state the position of the Court when vindication of his dissent came.

The idea of a difference between civil liberty cases and other Due Process cases attracted some supporters from other members of the Court, but the untimely death of Stone before full development of the theory has put the testing and refining of the political restraint idea in the hands of others. Whether these ideas will ultimately triumph as did so many of the ideas developed by his creative approach to the judicial process we do not now know. Their significance then as now, a decade after his death, lies, I believe, in four points. First, Stone was unwilling to use absolutes where he knew no absolutes existed or could exist in interpreting a document that was stated in terms of great purposes. Second, Stone was trying for an approach which would minimize both the appearance and practice of deciding cases on the predilection of the Justices of the moment. He sought to state the purposes of close judicial review and of judicial self-denial in such terms that the Justices could allocate a specific controversy to its appropriate place without passing judgment on the petty details of the controversy. Third, Stone, by recognizing categories of constitutional controversy where the Court makes avowedly political judgments, was indicating that the justification for the detached view of Brandeis and Holmes was neither indifference to the effect of a decision nor unwillingness to judge. He clearly indicated that where tough-minded inquiry and weighing of competing values were required, he had no fear of the decision-making process or of the consequences of his decision. Fourth, deference to legislative judgment was an approach which applied in statutory as well as in constitutional cases—if normal political processes were available to check the legislative judgment.

I close with a word about the Justice himself. Unlike Holmes, Brandeis, and Cardozo, with whom Stone was so often associated in legal views, Stone was not apart from the ordinary run of man. His law clerks were relieved, I think, to find that he behaved as an ordinary man with no pride in position or native aloofness. He startled his clerks and Washington hostesses by whistling shrilly with two fingers, like a boy, to call his chauffeur, preferring that to the aid of doormen and their mechanical devices.

One of his most appealing qualities was his boylike enthusiasm for his work, his pleasure in his own accomplishments and at being told of his accomplishments. He was sometimes impatient with those who did not readily accept his views and yet he had respect and consideration for them. He enjoyed discussing with his law clerks the merits of cases, even to the extent of letting us forget in the excitement of discussion that he was the man the President and Senate had chosen.

While Justice Stone had great devotion to his daily task and would let nothing interfere with the prompt dispatch of his business, the clerks soon saw that here was a man whose satisfactions came also from things apart from his job. Pleasure came to him in many ways. He enjoyed reading in a wide range of subjects; music and the arts, including not undistinguished collecting; wine from a well-selected cellar; and fine things for his home, preferably if he could obtain them after a bit of Yankee bargaining. He found pleasure in his participation in the affairs of philanthropic institutions, Amherst College, the Folger Shakespeare Library, the Smithsonian Institute, and the National Gallery. He enjoyed long and brisk walks each day, as heedless of the weather as a mailman but preferring a companion who had sufficient breath during the rapid walk to engage in talk of many things. Indeed, he enjoyed companionship and talk whether with a person of grand position or of none at all.

In short, to borrow the words spoken by Professor Herbert Wechsler at the memorial service in the Supreme Court, "He loved the things that in the end we have law for."

ALLISON DUNHAM *is professor of law at the Law School of the University of Chicago. He was law clerk to Justice Stone during the 1939 and 1940 terms. Before going to Washington he practiced law in New York. He has been a member of the faculties of Indiana University, Columbia University, and the University of New Zealand. Among his writings is a book on* Modern Real Estate Transactions.

NOTES

1. *United States* v. *Macintosh,* 283 U.S. 605 (1931). See also *United States* v. *Schwimmer,* 279 U.S. 644 (1929).

2. *Girouard* v. *United States,* 328 U.S. 61 (1946).

3. Stone was nominated as an Associate Justice by President Coolidge on January 5, 1925. After some opposition the Senate confirmed the appointment, and he took his seat on March 2, 1925. He was appointed Chief Justice by President Roosevelt, taking the oath of office on July 3, 1941.

4. The following is only a partial list: *Tyson & Bro.* v. *Banton,* 273 U.S. 418 (1927), and *Ribnick* v. *McBride,* 277 U.S. 350 (1928), have been replaced by *Nebbia* v. *New York,* 291 U.S. 502 (1934); *DiSanto* v. *Pennsylvania,* 273 U.S. 34 (1927), by *California* v. *Thompson,* 313 U.S. 109 (1941); *Macallen Co.* v. *Massachusetts,* 279 U.S. 620 (1929), by *Pacific Co.* v. *Johnson,* 285 U.S. 480 (1932); *Indian Motocycle Co.* v. *United States,* 283 U.S. 570 (1931), by *James* v. *Dravo Contracting Co.,* 302 U.S. 134 (1937); *United States* v. *Chicago, M. St. P. & P. R.R.,* 282 U.S. 311 (1931), by *United States* v. *Lowden,* 308 U.S. 225 (1939); *Burnet* v. *Coronado Oil & Gas Co.,* 285 U.S. 393 (1932), by *Helvering* v. *Mountain Producers Co.,* 303 U.S. 376 (1938); *Senior* v. *Braden,* 295 U.S. 422 (1935), by *New York* ex rel. *Cohn* v. *Graves,* 300 U.S. 308 (1937), *Curry* v. *McCanless,* 307 U.S. 357 (1939), and *State Tax Commission* v. *Aldrich,* 316 U.S. 174 (1942); *West* v. *Chesapeake & Potomac Tel. Co.,* 295 U.S. 662 (1935), by *Railroad Comm'n* v. *Pacific Gas Co.,* 302 U.S. 388 (1938); *Colgate* v. *Harvey,* 296 U.S. 404 (1935), by *Madden* v. *Kentucky,* 309 U.S. 83 (1940); *United States* v. *Butler,* 297 U.S. 1 (1936), by *Mulford* v. *Smith,* 307 U.S. 38 (1939); *Morehead* v. *New York* ex rel. *Tipaldo,* 298 U.S. 587 (1936), by *West Coast Hotel Co.* v. *Parrish,* 300 U.S. 379 (1937); *Carter* v. *Carter Coal Co.,* 298 U.S. 238 (1936), by *Sunshine Coal Co.* v. *Adkins,* 310 U.S. 381 (1940); *Minersville School District* v. *Gobitis,* 310 U.S. 586 (1940), by *West Virginia State Board of Education* v. *Barnette,* 319 U.S. 624 (1943); *Jones* v. *Opelika,* 316 U.S. 584 (1942), by *Murdock* v. *Pennsylvania,* 319 U.S. 105 (1943). See also *United States* v. *Macintosh,* 283 U.S. 605 (1931), replaced by *Girouard* v. *United States,* 328 U.S. 61 (1946).

5. In this process he was able to overrule old landmark cases such as *Collector* v. *Day,* 11 Wall. 113 (1870), overruled by *Graves* v. *New York* ex rel. *O'Keefe,* 306 U.S. 466 (1939); *Hammer* v. *Dagenhart,* 247 U.S. 251 (1918) (the child labor case), by *United States* v. *Darby Lumber Co.,* 312 U.S. 100 (1941).

For descriptions of his contribution to substantive doctrine see

46 Col. L. Rev. 693–800 (1946); and Konefsky, *Chief Justice Stone and the Supreme Court* (1945).

6. 297 U.S. 1 (1936).

7. *Perry v. United States,* 294 U.S. 330 (1935).

8. See Gardner, *Mr. Chief Justice Stone,* 59 Harv. L. Rev. 1203, at 1204 (1946).

9. See 294 U.S. at 359.

10. See *Minersville School District* v. *Gobitis,* 310 U.S. 586 (1940).

11. 313 U.S. 299 (1941).

12. 256 U.S. 232.

13. 295 U.S. 45.

14. Now 18 U.S.C. §§ 241 and 242, originally enacted in 1870, 16 Stat. 40.

15. This was an approach which Stone frequently used. See *Group No. 1 Oil Corp.* v. *Bass,* 283 U.S. 279 (1931), where he ignored *Gillespie* v. *Oklahoma,* 257 U.S. 501 (1922), and *Burnet* v. *Coronado Oil Co.,* 285 U.S. 393 (1932).

16. 313 U.S. at 316.

17. 321 U.S. 649 (1944).

18. Jackson and Rutledge had replaced Hughes and McReynolds while Black, Douglas, and Murphy, dissenters in *Classic* on another ground, had indicated in *Classic* disagreement with the *Grovey* doctrine.

19. See Stone, *The Common Law in the United States,* 50 Harv. L. Rev. 4, 23 (1936).

20. See, e.g., Stone, *Law and Its Administration* (1915); and *Fifty Years Work of the United States Supreme Court,* 53 A.B.A. Rept. 259, 8 Ore. L. Rev. 248 (1929).

21. See Roberts, in *United States* v. *Butler,* 297 U.S. 1, 62 (1936).

22. See, e.g., his treatment of the Full Faith and Credit Clause in *Alaska Packers Assn.* v. *Industrial Accident Commission,* 294 U.S. 532, 547 (1935): "A rigid and literal enforcement of the full faith and credit clause, without regard to the statute of the forum, would lead to the absurd result that, wherever the conflict arises, the statute of each state must be enforced in the courts of the other, but cannot be in its own. . . . It follows that not every statute of another state will override a conflicting statute of the forum by virtue of the full faith and credit clause; . . . ."

23. *DiSanto* v. *Pennsylvania,* 273 U.S. 34, 44 (1927).

24. *Senior* v. *Braden,* 295 U.S. 422, 438 (1935).

25. From 1925 to 1935 Justice Stone recorded 140 dissenting votes, dissenting more frequently than any of his brethren, and during this period he wrote 42 dissenting opinions. See Dowling, Cheat-

ham, and Hale, *Mr. Justice Stone and the Constitution,* 36 COL. L. REV. 351, 352 (1936).

26. For an analysis of the implications of the clear and present danger test, see Wechsler, *Symposium on Civil Liberties,* 9 AM. L. SCH. REV. 881, 887 (1941).

27. This was attempted by Roberts and Black in *Hague* v. *C.I.O.,* 307 U.S. 496 (1938). Stone concurred in a separate opinion.

28. Compare the opinions of Stone and Black in *Duncan* v. *Kahanamoku,* 327 U.S. 304 (1946).

29. See, e.g., dissenting opinion of Black in *Adams Mfg. Co.* v. *Storen,* 304 U.S. 307, 316 (1938); *Gwin, White & Prince* v. *Henneford,* 305 U.S. 434 (1939).

30. 303 U.S. 177, 185.

31. For an application of this principle see *Southern Pacific Co.* v. *Arizona,* 325 U.S. 761 (1945).

32. *United States* v. *Carolene Products Co.,* 304 U.S. 144 (1938).

33. *Ibid.,* at 152.

34. *Ibid.,* at 152 and 153, note 4.

35. *Helvering* v. *Gerhardt,* 304 U.S. 405 (1938).

36. See particularly *ibid.,* at 412:
"In sustaining the immunity from state taxation [in *McCulloch* v. *Maryland,* 4 Wheat. 316], the opinion of the Court, by Chief Justice Marshall, recognized a clear distinction between the extent of the power of a state to tax national banks and that of the national government to tax state instrumentalities. He was careful to point out not only that the taxing power of the national government is supreme, by reason of the constitutional grant but that in laying a federal tax on state instrumentalities the people of the states, acting through their representatives, are laying a tax on their own institutions and consequently are subject to political restraints which can be counted on to prevent abuse. State taxation of national instrumentalities is subject to no such restraint, for the people outside the state have no representatives who participate in the legislation; and in a real sense, as to them, the taxation is without representation. The exercise of the national taxing power is thus subject to a safeguard which does not operate when a state undertakes to tax a national instrumentality."

37. *Minersville School District* v. *Gobitis,* 310 U.S. 586 (1940).

38. *Ibid.,* at 599, 603, and 606.

39. *West Virginia Board of Education* v. *Barnette,* 319 U.S. 624 (1943).

40. *Jones* v. *Opelika,* 316 U.S. 584 (1942); overruled by *Murdock* v. *Pennsylvania,* 319 U.S. 105 (1943).

Courtesy of Harris & Ewing

MR. JUSTICE CARDOZO

Mr. Justice Cardozo

By

ANDREW L. KAUFMAN

On January 12, 1932, at the age of ninety, Oliver Wendell Holmes, Jr., probably the outstanding and most revered judge our country has known, sent his resignation as Justice of the Supreme Court of the United States to President Hoover. There followed the usual speculation about a successor, but with a difference. Throughout the country leading newspapers, political leaders, spokesmen for the bar, deans and professors at law schools, virtually all were in accord that Holmes required a worthy successor, and that Benjamin Nathan Cardozo, then Chief Judge of the New York Court of Appeals, was the man most fitted to take his place. This near unanimity of opinion was not merely surprising. It was unparalleled in the history of the country. President Hoover deliberated for a month. Then, despite the fact that the Court already included two Justices from New York City, Hughes and Stone, and one Jew, Brandeis, Hoover nominated Cardozo.

Cardozo did not become a great judge on the United States Supreme Court. He was a great judge when he arrived there, having made significant contributions to the law of his state and of the nation both as a judge and as a jurist. As Associate Judge of the New York Court of Appeals for thirteen years and Chief Judge for five years, Cardozo was the most distinguished judge of the most distinguished state court in the country. In addition, he had contributed a unique volume to the study of jurisprudence, *The Nature of the Judicial Process*, and was active in several movements for law reform.

Except for his obvious talents, nothing in the first forty-three years of Cardozo's life hinted at the prominence he was to attain so rapidly thereafter. His whole life theretofore had been characterized by devotion to his family and to his work and by an avoidance of the outside world. He was born in 1870 and was a descendant of a prominent family of Sephardic Jews, both branches of which had lived in this country since the middle of the eighteenth century and had contributed men and women of talent to the American scene: a courageous Rabbi during the Revolutionary War, who was one of the first trustees of Columbia College; prominent businessmen; the author of the immortal words inscribed on the base of the Statue of Liberty. Closer to home and of vital and indeterminable effect on Benjamin Cardozo's life was the specter of his father's career—a religious man and a judge first of the Court of Common Pleas and then of the Supreme Court of New York who became heavily involved in the judicial machinations of Tammany Hall and the Tweed Ring and resigned just in time to avoid impeachment.

Benjamin Cardozo's childhood was lived in the aftermath of these events. His schooling consisted of home tutoring, one tutor being Horatio Alger; Columbia College, which he entered at the age of fifteen and from which he graduated at the top of his class; and Columbia Law School, leaving, as was not uncommon in those days, before his third year to enter practice with his older brother's firm. Cardozo never married, and he lived with his older, unmarried sister Ellen until her death in 1929. They were extremely close, both intellectually and emotionally, and this relationship was the most important in each of their lives.

Cardozo became known at the bar early and before too long other lawyers were referring important cases to him, especially at the appellate level. By the time he went on the bench, he had already presented some seventy-five cases in the New York Court of Appeals. Unlike Brandeis, however, Cardozo's career at the bar is not linked with vital litigation affecting the organization of society or with any important reform movements. His counsel was sought primarily in corporate and commercial litigation or in litigation involving the disposition of property. The common law and statutes dealing with common-law subjects were his bailiwick.

As an advocate, Cardozo must have been deceptive. Quiet, mild-mannered, an almost feminine softness, gentle, shy, courteous, courtly, lonely, ascetic, saintly—these are the descriptive words most often associated with what John Lord O'Brian has called "the strangely compelling power of that reticent, sensitive and almost mystical personality."[1] Such a personality is not usually associated with the successful advocate. However, when combined with intellectual curiosity, perseverance, persuasiveness, great ability and learning, these qualities became assets.

There was also another, a less well-known, side to Cardozo's personality. Learned Hand once said: "Very few have ever known what went on behind those blue eyes." The calm, courteous exterior concealed a detached, observing outlook on life and on people. As life and people are not always kindly, so his view of them was not always kindly. Cardozo did not like to cause hurt, however, and he usually kept his views to himself. It required an unusual occasion or an unusually close friend, of whom there were few, for him to speak his mind. More often, he erred on the side of fulsome praise, which he both gave to others and enjoyed himself.

All these unusual qualities combined to make an attractive figure and, despite the fact that Cardozo took very little part in the extracurricular life of the bar and none at all in politics, he was known to the leading lawyers of New York City, who put forth his name as a judicial candidate on the Fusion ticket that wrested control of the city government from Tammany Hall in 1913. The story is told that Cardozo would not campaign for himself and that his campaign was run by others.

Cardozo's letters reveal, however, that he kept abreast of events and he made several suggestions that dispel any aura of political naïveté. In any event, he won a narrow victory, and at the age of forty-three, he began his public career as a Justice of the New York Supreme Court. After one month he was assigned by Governor Glynn to the Court of Appeals to help it clear its calendar and, thereafter, he became a permanent member of that Court.

To attempt to summarize in a few pages Cardozo's contribution to the law during his eighteen years on the Court of Appeals is a virtual impossibility. Unlike Marshall, who laid the foundations of national power, Story and Kent, who gave substance to the primitive state of law in the new United States, Holmes, who rethought basic principles of the common law and expressed dynamically basic principles of constitutional adjudication, Cardozo's contributions, though numerous and important, are more elusive. It is possible in this essay only to suggest briefly and without detailed examination some of the more important aspects.

Let us turn first to Cardozo's opinions. In a joint memorial issue to Justice Cardozo published shortly after his death by the law reviews of Harvard, Yale, and Columbia, Professor Seavey set forth his analysis of Cardozo's contribution to the law of torts, those civil cases dealing with injury to the person or property, such as negligence, assault, and defamation cases:

> Cardozo was a progressive judge but not primarily a reforming judge. He did not remake the law of torts. On the contrary, by and large, he accepted the common law as he found it, merely choosing between precedents where choice was possible, and choosing the best. His power lay in his ability to see the plan and pattern underlying the law and to make clear the paths which had been obscured by the undergrowth of illogical reasoning.[2]

Writing in the same issue, Professor Corbin used similar language in dealing with Cardozo's contribution to the law of contracts:

It cannot be said that he made any extensive changes in the existing law of contract. To state the facts of the cases, the decision, and the reasoning of his opinion will not show the overthrow of old doctrine or the establishment of new. Instead, it will show the application of existing doctrines with wisdom and discretion; an application that does not leave those doctrines wholly unaffected, but one that carries on their evolution as is reasonably required by the new facts before the court. When Cardozo is through, the law is not exactly as it was before; but there has been no sudden shift or revolutionary change.[3]

It is true that Cardozo was not a Lord Mansfield. The common law and, in particular, commercial law, was in a formative state in the eighteenth century; thus Mansfield had, comparatively, a free hand. By the twentieth century, the generalized rules in all branches of the common law were fairly well settled and no court could have attempted a large-scale revision. In addition, many of the great problems facing the common law in our modern complex industrial society implicate a myriad of competing economic and social interests far beyond the ability or power of courts to deal with in a case-by-case approach. Grandiose solutions are for the legislature. The system of workmen's compensation legislation, for example, could only have been a legislative solution. The ultimate disposition of the ever-increasing automobile accident cases may eventually require similar action. Not that courts have not often been forced to deal with large social and economic problems because of legislative inaction. But the solutions reached, of necessity, have been piecemeal and unsatisfactory, as may be seen from the unhappy history of labor law in the courts in the nineteenth and early twentieth centuries.

This is not to disparage the role of the courts. They have a vital role to play in the fields of both private and public law. It is, however, not the same free-wheeling role that existed two hundred years ago, when society was less complicated and the adjustment of competing interests in the courts was practicable. Such adjustment still goes on today, but in a narrower field. It is with this understanding that Cardozo's work must be studied and appreciated.

In the usual case he was merely applying "existing doctrines." Occasionally, existing doctrine would be applied to new instances, and by such application the general principle, in that subtle, evolutionary manner of the common law, would itself be transformed. Occasionally, it was a question of resisting a new application. Most often, however, it was a matter of assimilating a particular set of facts to one or another of two lines of precedents, neither of which directly controlled the case at hand. The Cardozo court did not, because it could not, uproot established doctrine to any great extent, partly because the areas where uprooting was needed were beyond its ability to effect a solution, and partly because such drastic action is not the method of the common law. As Cardozo himself stated, with a characteristic quotation from Holmes, "Mr. Justice Holmes has summed it up in one of his flashing epigrams: 'I recognize without hesitation that judges must and do legislate, but they do so only interstitially; they are confined from molar to molecular motions. A common-law judge could not say, I think the doctrine of consideration a bit of historical nonsense and shall not enforce it in my court.' "[4]

Cardozo himself summarized the work of the Court of Appeals and its function as follows:

Of the cases that come before the court in which I sit, a majority, I think, could not, with semblance of reason, be decided in any way but one. . . . In another and considerable percentage, the rule of law is certain, and the application alone doubtful. . . . Finally there remains a percentage, not large indeed, and yet not so small as to be negligible, where a decision one way or the other, will count for the future . . . . These are the cases where the creative element in the judicial process finds its opportunity and power. . . . In a sense it is true of many of them that they might be decided either way. By that I mean that reasons plausible and fairly persuasive might be found for one conclusion as for another. Here come into play . . . balancing of judgment . . . testing and sorting of considerations of analogy and logic and utility and fairness . . . . Here it is that the judge assumes the function of a lawgiver. . . . I have grown to see that the process in its highest reaches is not discovery, but creation . . . .[5]

This approach was by no means obvious in Cardozo's time; it is not universally accepted today. The notion that law is a "brooding omnipresence in the sky"[6] still has its adherents in theory—and even more so in practical application.

What were some of these cases? A railroad guard jostled a passenger, who dropped his package under a moving train. It contained fireworks, and the resulting explosion caused some scales to fall, thus injuring Mrs. Palsgraf some distance away on the platform. Does the railroad have to pay for her injuries?[7] Mr. Wagner's cousin was thrown from a street railway car, through the railway's negligence, while the car was passing over a trestle. The car was stopped and Mr. Wagner was injured when he slipped from the trestle while searching for his cousin. Should the railroad have to pay for his injury?[8] Mary Johnston pledged $5000 to a college, payable after her death, the purposes of the gift to be restricted and the fund to bear her name. While alive she made, and the college accepted, a part payment, but she later revoked the balance of the pledge. Can the college nevertheless enforce it?[9]

A telegraph company failed to send a coded radiogram and thereby caused great loss to the sender. Is it liable for the loss? Does it make any difference that the code was a standard code contained in a book in the telegraph office? Does it make any difference that even if decoded the meaning of the radiogram was obscure? Should a court be influenced by the fact that the telegraph company if held liable could be exposed to a very great judgment whereas it may have received only a few dollars? Should a court take account of the fact that the company could obtain insurance against that risk? And if it does, should it also consider that the undefined amount of the loss and the experience of insurance companies might lead to very high premiums, raising the cost of service to all? What about the availability of insurance to the sender?[10]

Questions of the extent of common-law liability in tort and contract have traditionally been decided by the courts, and the legislature has up to now played a relatively small role in the evolution of the various doctrines. Yet, as the above summary of issues indicates, problems today can involve some issues that are beyond the court's power to resolve effectively. In this respect, the problem is not unlike that delineated by Professor Freund in his discussion of Justice Brandeis' opinion in the *Associated Press* case.[11] When the legislature has not dealt with the problem, the court must nonetheless assess the factors it deems relevant and decide the case. Occasionally however, the competing considerations may be so complex that the court will not reassess them, but will simply reiterate the old rule and state that any change must come from the legislature. Such a case was that involving the radiogram that was never sent, and a generous extract from Cardozo's opinion may give some small hint of how he approached the issues of a case.

Referring to the general rule that the telegraph company is liable only if the general nature of the transaction is disclosed to it, he stated:

> We are not unmindful of the force of the plaintiff's assault upon the rule . . . in its application to the relation between telegraph carrier and customer. The truth seems to be that neither the clerk who receives the message over the counter nor the operator who transmits it nor any other employee gives or is expected to give any thought to the sense of what he is receiving or transmitting. This imparts to the whole doctrine as to the need for notice an air of unreality. The doctrine, however, has prevailed for years, so many that it is tantamount to a rule of property. The companies have regulated their rates upon the basis of its continuance. They have omitted precautions that they might have thought it necessary to adopt if the hazard of the business was to be indefinitely increased. Nor is the doctrine without other foundation in utility and justice. Much may be said in favor of the social policy of a rule whereby

the companies have been relieved of liability that might otherwise be crushing. The sender can protect himself by insurance in one form or another if the risk of nondelivery or error appears to be too great. The total burden is not heavy since it is distributed among many, and can be proportioned in any instance to the loss likely to ensue. The company, if it takes out insurance for itself, can do no more than guess at the loss to be avoided. To pay for this unknown risk, it will be driven to increase the rates payable by all, though the increase is likely to result in the protection of a few. We are not concerned to balance the considerations of policy that give support to the existing rule against others that weigh against it. Enough for present purposes that there are weights in either scale. Telegraph companies in interstate and foreign commerce are subject to the power of Congress. . . . If the rule of damages long recognized by state and federal decision is to give way to another, the change should come through legislation.[12]

This is not the place to assess the decision in this case. The considerations are many and varied, and the question whether and when an issue "should be left to the legislature" is one of the more difficult that a court must decide. This case, like the others mentioned above, is of the type in which, as Cardozo stated, reasonable men could reach different results. The fact that a judge reached one conclusion instead of another does not rank him as a "great" judge. The greatness of a judge, the greatness of Cardozo was that he was able to perceive in the particular facts of cases the principles that were contending for recognition, realizing that there is "many a common law-suit, which can be lifted from meanness up to dignity if the great judge is by to see what is within."[13] Recognizing the issue, he did not reach a conclusion merely by stating it, or by the route of the familiar cliché. "The repetition of a catch-word," as he put it, "can hold analysis in fetters for fifty years or more."[14] He would expose the issue, marshal the arguments, and logically and persuasively reach a result, usually in language calculated to decide only the case before him. Finally, he announced the result in an opinion marked by his own distinct style of writing. No matter that in one case the injured party or the person whose contract was broken was victorious, and in the other he was not. Unlike so many opinions which read as if the judge first decided who wins and then why, the nature of the winning party was not a consideration for Cardozo. Not that he was not properly sensitive to the human factor, but basic principles of law demanded even-handed justice:

> Our jurisprudence has held fast to Kant's categorical imperative, "Act on a maxim which thou canst will to be law universal." It has refused to sacrifice the larger and more inclusive good to the narrower and smaller. A contract is made. Performance is burdensome and perhaps oppressive. If we were to consider only the individual instance, we might be ready to release the promisor. We look beyond the particular to the universal, and shape our judgment in obedience to the fundamental interest of society that contracts shall be fulfilled. There is a wide gap between the use of the individual sentiment of justice as a substitute for law, and its use as one of the tests and touchstones in construing or extending law.[15]

Cardozo's approach to the process of decision was exemplified in his opinions, spelled out explicitly in his lectures printed under the title, *The Nature of the Judicial Process,* and further refined in two subsequent series of lectures printed as *The Growth of the Law*[16] and *The Paradoxes of Legal Science.*[17] A large part of the debt that law owes to Cardozo results from the fact that not only was Cardozo, drawing on and adding to the work of Holmes before him, able to make the legal profession, bar and judiciary, think and re-think the nature of the function of the judge, but he was able to explain these very difficult and elusive ideas to laymen as well. *The Nature of the Judicial Process,* although perhaps somewhat marred by a tendency to indiscriminate and excessive quotation, is cast in terms that make it valuable for lawyer and layman alike. One of the very first efforts by a judge to articulate his function, it still possesses the same validity and vitality today as it did when published more than forty years ago.

One final word should be said about Cardozo and the Court of Appeals. This brief summary of Cardozo's labors during his New York judicial career does not give any hint of the extraordinary influence that he had on his fellow judges. The Court of Appeals in Cardozo's time was an unusual collection of good judges. Two of Cardozo's colleagues, Andrews and Pound, would have distinguished any court in the country. Many of the others with whom he sat during his long tenure were more than ordinarily able. That Cardozo's influence could pervade such a court attests the combination of gentle persuasiveness and intellectual power that was his. Judge Irving Lehman, his colleague and perhaps his closest friend in his later years, may have understated the power of Cardozo's opinions, but he expressed his appreciation of the power of Cardozo's oral advocacy, when he said: "Those who sat with Judge Cardozo in the Court of Appeals will, I am sure, agree with me that Judge Cardozo made his greatest contribution to the development of the common law, not in his written words —though they will long be read—but in the words spoken in the conference room, heard by few and soon forgotten, yet forgotten only after they had clarified each problem and had served to guide a great court along the road to sound development of the common law. I cannot bring back the spoken word, but I can record here its enduring influence."[18]

This was, in brief, the extraordinary man who, at the age of sixty-two, was transported from the very pleasant and congenial surroundings of a Chief Judge in Albany to "homesick exile," as he called it, as junior Justice in Washington. Gone was the easy companionship of the Court of Appeals. In its place was the more solitary work that characterized the Supreme Court in those days. Social intercourse, even with Justice Stone with whom he was closest on the Court, was infrequent. Intellectual exchange about the Court's work was largely limited to the Saturday conferences and to discussions with his law clerks with whom he had a very friendly, if slightly formal, relationship. Only in the last years did he regularly meet with Justices Stone and Brandeis for thirty minutes to an hour on Friday nights before the Saturday conference of the Court, and this only as a defensive reflex to the regular caucuses of Justices McReynolds, Sutherland, Van Devanter, and Butler.

The change was not only one of scene. A new type of labor was also involved. Cardozo's preoccupation was now to be primarily the field of public law, statutory and constitutional, instead of the common law. His tenure on the Court was only five and one-half Terms, normally insufficient for any Justice to make an imprint. But Cardozo was not "any Justice" and these were not "normal" times. For almost three decades Holmes, joined in 1916 by Brandeis and in 1930 by Stone, had conducted the fight against the restrictive constitutional principles that had held unconstitutional much legislation, primarily state legislation, designed to mitigate the rigors and sufferings created by the workings of nineteenth-century capitalism. Cardozo's appointment in 1932 was followed by Franklin Roosevelt's election, and attention largely shifted from sporadic state legislation to the extensive New Deal program that poured out of Congress. This new intensified struggle, for struggle it was, was carried out in an atmosphere of deep public concern, reached one climax in the court-packing plan, and another climax and conclusion in the startling series of decisions by the Court in the 1936 term—all this within Cardozo's brief period on the Court.

Mere presence on the Court at that time would give interest to Cardozo's work, but he also made a definite contribution to the Court despite the fact that as junior Justice the more important opinions were not often assigned to him. Holmes' successor had long been devoted to Holmes, whom he referred to as "The Master." In his writings before his appointment to the Supreme Court, Cardozo had deplored the restrictive decisions of the Supreme Court and had indicated his complete sympathy with Holmes' constitutional philosophy:

"The movement from individualistic liberalism to unsystematic collectivism" [in England] had brought changes in the social order which carried with them the need of a new formulation of fundamental rights and duties. In our country, the need did not assert itself so soon. Courts still spoke in the phrases of a philosophy that had served its day. Gradually, however, though not without frequent protest and intermittent movements backward, a new conception of the significance of constitutional limitations in the domain of individual liberty, emerged to recognition and to dominance.[19]

Cardozo's optimism was somewhat premature, as his long series of dissents indicates, but his role, mostly as dissenter in the important cases but eventually as one of the majority, is as successor to Holmes. Cardozo and his colleagues, Brandeis and Stone, believed that the legislature had broad power to experiment in dealing with the problems before it, and that the courts should not be inquiring expressly or implicitly into the wisdom of particular legislation. "It is not the function of a court to make itself the arbiter between competing economic theories professed by honest men on grounds not wholly frivolous."[20] This was the philosophy with which Cardozo approached such legislation. It was a judicial, not a political or economic philosophy. That is what set him apart from Justice Brandeis. Commentators who speak of Holmes and Brandeis, or Cardozo and Brandeis, in one breath as if they shared a common outlook on the cases they judged are greatly in error. Their judicial philosophy was similar, but Brandeis had a well-developed social and economic philosophy that affected his approach to particular cases.[21]

The difference in view may best be perceived in a case in which both dissented. *Liggett* v. *Lee*[22] involved the validity of Florida's chain-store legislation. The Florida statute set a different rate of taxation based on the number of Florida stores owned, either by an individual or a corporation, and then set a higher rate for all stores if the chain operated in more than one county. The majority of the Court declared the statute unconstitutional, holding that there was no reasonable basis for a classification based on whether the stores were located in one, or more than one, county.

Justice Brandeis, dissenting, first stated that there was nothing in the record to show that the tax might not be reasonable in view of the Florida conditions. He then proceeded to broader grounds. Noting that only corporations were plaintiffs, he considered the case as if the statute were directed only at corporations. He saw no reason why the tax could not be regarded as a charge for doing business in the corporate form and that since operation in more than one county was a greater privilege than operation in a single county, a larger fee could be charged. Finally, he delivered what was in effect an economics treatise on the danger of the chain store, especially the giant chain store, and justified the tax as socially and economically desirable to preserve the competition of independent stores with chain stores or even to eliminate chain stores.[23]

Cardozo, also dissenting, did not join Brandeis' opinion, but prepared a dissent along more conventional lines. His initial draft relied heavily on the fact that the county was the historical unit of government in the South. Further research disclosed statistics indicating that chain stores were often classified as local, sectional, and national, and that the transition from local to either sectional or national tended to come when the chain store crossed the county line. With these two bulwarks, the case was decided. "The question is how it [a business] *does* develop in normal or average conditions, and the answer to that question is to be found in life and history. When the problem is thus approached, the movement from one county to another becomes in a very definite sense the crossing of a frontier, a change as marked as the difference between wholesale trade and retail. . . . So at least the Legislature might not unreasonably believe, and act on that belief in the formulation of the law."[24] And he continued, in lines reminiscent of Holmes' classic statement in *The Common Law*,[25] "In discarding as arbitrary symbols the lines that it has chosen, there is danger of forgetting that in social and economic life the grooves of thought and action are not always those of logic, and that symbols may mean as much as conduct has put into them."[26]

Having formulated a rational basis for the Florida legislation, Cardozo's function as a judge was ended. He would certainly not follow the Brandeis course. Not that he did not recognize the purpose of the statute. Indeed he found in it another basis on which the statute could be supported:

It will not do to shut one's eyes to the motive that has led so many Legislatures to lay hold of this difference and turn it into a basis for a new system of taxation. The system has had its origin in the belief that the social utility or inutility of one group is less or greater than that of others, and that the choice of subjects to be taxed should be adjusted to social gains and losses. Courts would be lacking in candor if they were not to concede the presence of such a motive behind this chain store legislation. . . . The concept may be right or wrong. At least it corresponds to an intelligible belief, and one widely prevalent to-day among honest men and women. . . . With that our function ends.[27]

This was a very different approach from the Brandeis opinion which set forth his personal, social, and economic views approving the statute in a powerful opinion that Professor Freund has described as a "labor of love."[28] It seems fairly certain that Cardozo did not have any such comparably developed social or economic philosophy. It is even more certain that he did not believe that a judicial opinion was the proper forum for its exposition. His job was "judging" and only judging. Indeed he even, in uncharacteristic fashion, chided Justice Brandeis, albeit somewhat obliquely:

Holding these views, I find it unnecessary to consider whether the statute may be upheld for the additional reasons that have been stated by Mr. Justice Brandeis with such a wealth of learning. They present considerations that were not laid before us by counsel either in the briefs or in the oral argument, and a determination of their validity and weight may be reserved with propriety until the necessity emerges.[29]

The same deference was due to the legislation that poured forth from Congress, and to a lesser extent from the state legislatures, to meet the vast economic dislocation caused by the great depression. That deference was not given by the Court majority, and the history of the Court in the early 1930's is a long series of cases holding such legislation invalid, generally on the basis of the Commerce Clause, the Tenth Amendment, or the Fourteenth Amendment, and generally also with Justices Cardozo, Brandeis, Stone, and occasionally Chief Justice Hughes, dissenting. Enough has been said of Cardozo's views on the Fourteenth Amendment. The Commerce Clause presented different problems. Ever since the decision of the Marshall Court in *Gibbons* v. *Ogden*,[30] subsequent Courts struggled with a proper formulation of the extent of congressional power over intrastate transactions having more or less effect on the interstate problem sought to be regulated. One formulation of the test expressed the distinction in terms of "direct" and "indirect" effect on interstate commerce. Cardozo, dissenting in *Carter* v. *Carter Coal Co.*,[31] which struck down the Guffey Coal Act because coal mining had only an "indirect effect" on interstate commerce, sought to remove some of the barnacles that had become encrusted on the Commerce Clause by use of that test. At the same time he demonstrated the same distrust of labels that had characterized his opinions on the Courts of Appeals.

Sometimes it is said that the relation must be "direct" to bring that power [of regulation] into play. In many circumstances such a description will be sufficiently precise to meet the needs of the occasion. But a great principle of constitutional law is not susceptible of comprehensive statement in an adjective. The underlying thought is merely this, that "the law is not indifferent to considerations of degree." . . . Perhaps, if one group of adjectives is to be chosen in preference to another, "intimate" and "remote" will be found to be as good as any. At all event, "direct" and "indirect," even if accepted as sufficient, must not be read too narrowly. . . .[32]

That Cardozo believed, as he wrote, that these questions were indeed questions of degree may be seen from his concurring opinion in the *Schecter* case,[33] holding the NRA's Live Poultry

Code of Fair Competition unconstitutional as involving an excessive delegation of legislative power to the executive and, as applied to the particular wholesale poultry slaughterhouses who were defendants, an unconstitutional exercise of the commerce power. Previously Cardozo had been the lone dissenter in the "*Hot Oil*" case[34] where a separate section of the National Industrial Recovery Act had been held to involve an unconstitutional delegation of legislative power to the President. In *Schecter,* however, on both questions, Cardozo believed that Congress had gone too far—too much undefined power delegated to the President and over a field of activity too remote from interstate activity. The case troubled Cardozo—troubled him even in the opinion-writing stage, which was unusual. He produced draft after draft, first deciding the case on the delegation issue by holding the code, but not the statute, unconstitutional, then deciding the case only on the Commerce Clause question, and finally discussing both issues and holding the statute as well as the code unconstitutional on both grounds. There is evidence that he felt uncertain about his opinion even after the case came down, which for Cardozo was unusual in the extreme. As he often said, his job was judging and once an opinion came down, he turned his mind to the next case.

Near the end of Cardozo's career on the Court came a dramatic change. As the 1935 term ended, Justice Stone wrote to a friend, "We finished the term of Court yesterday, I think in many ways one of the most disastrous in its history."[35] The public clamor against the Court is difficult to reproduce, but it equalled the rage of the Jeffersonians over Marshall's decisions, that of the North over *Dred Scott,*[36] and that of the South over the *School Segregation Cases.*[37] The following autumn came the Roosevelt landslide; in February, 1937, the Court-packing plan; and, finally, in April, 1937, the beginning of a whole series of decisions eventually undoing virtually all the restrictive constitutional law of a half century. There has been a great deal of discussion about the "switch in time," as to whether there actually was a "switch" by Chief Justice Hughes and Justice Roberts, and what cases demonstrate it. Cardozo, however, believed that there had been a change of views. Having unsuccessfully attempted to distinguish to his own satisfaction *Jones & Laughlin*[38] (upholding the Wagner Act) from *Carter*, he was amazed at the vote in conference in the latter case and in many of the cases that followed. Eventually Cardozo even had a chance in the *Social Security Cases*[39] to express his views speaking for the Court in upholding an important piece of New Deal legislation.

Cardozo's views as to the deference owed legislative action had one limitation:

Only in one field is compromise to be excluded, or kept within the narrowest limits. There shall be no compromise of the freedom to think one's thoughts and speak them, except at those extreme borders where thought merges into action. There is to be no compromise here, for thought freely communicated, if I may borrow my own words, is the indispensable condition of intelligent experimentation, the one test of its validity. There is no freedom without choice, and there is no choice without knowledge—or none that is not illusory. Here are goods to be conserved, however great the seeming sacrifice. We may not squander the thought that will be the inheritance of the ages.[40]

The Cardozo years on the Court mark the beginning of the present Court's strong interest in what is called "civil liberties," although as has been pointed out so often, it is not always so easy to decide when a question is one of "economics" or is one of "civil liberties." It is particularly interesting to see how judges whose constitutional views had been moulded in the conflict over "economic" regulatory legislation reacted to action by the state affecting "civil liberties." The study also provides an amusing commentary on the labels of "liberal" and "conservative" that were so readily applied to the members of the Cardozo Court, for not only were some of the so-called "conservatives" often found proclaiming the cause of individual rights, but some of the so-called "liberals," Brandeis,

Cardozo, and Stone, were often found giving recognition in the same cases to the state's interest.

For Cardozo, the problem was an especially difficult one. He was widely read in literature and philosophy and interested in the political developments of the day. Although he had initially been elected to the New York judiciary as an independent reform Democrat on the Fusion ticket and was friendly to both Franklin Roosevelt and his program, his temperament was not passionate; it was dispassionate. He had no such burning sense of the right as did Justice Brandeis. While he could occasionally feel a sense of outrage when something touched him personally, the problems of the world did not generally touch his emotions deeply, if at all. He read the commands of the Fourteenth Amendment and the Bill of Rights in the context of the whole Constitution and excepting only perhaps the protection of freedom of speech, thought, and the press, he approached each case with a strong awareness of the claims both of society and of the individual.

In the field of criminal law, Cardozo came to constitutional law through long experience reviewing criminal trials in the New York Court of Appeals. In that court too, he had shown a strong awareness of the interests of society in effective law enforcement. While he examined the cases on their individual merits, an impressive showing of prejudice had to be made out before error in the trial led to reversal of a conviction. Cardozo also wrote the opinion for the New York court in the important case of *People* v. *Defore*,[41] holding that evidence obtained through an illegal search and seizure was nevertheless admissible in a criminal proceeding. When, however, the New York Criminal Anarchy Act was applied to convict Benjamin Gitlow for his publication of the Left Wing Manifesto, Cardozo joined Judge Pound's dissent that the utterance was not within the prohibitions of a statute that was aimed at anarchism and not communism, which is something quite different.[42]

Cardozo's views on the Supreme Court evolved from previously expressed views, judicial and extrajudicial. Thus in *Snyder* v. *Massachusetts*,[43] Cardozo wrote for a majority of five, with Justices Roberts, Brandeis, Sutherland, and Stone dissenting, in upholding a state court murder conviction where defendant's counsel, but not defendant, was permitted to be present when the jury was taken to view the scene of the crime. Although he had originally voted to reverse the conviction, and was assigned to write the opinion, Cardozo found that such a view just "wouldn't write." Relying heavily on the common law precedents that a "view" is something different from the "trial" itself, where defendant's presence was required, and finding no prejudice to the defendant, Cardozo concluded that the trial judge's action did not deny the defendant due process of law:

The law . . . is sedulous in maintaining for a defendant charged with crime whatever forms of procedure are of the essence of an opportunity to defend. Privileges so fundamental as to be inherent in every concept of a fair trial that could be acceptable to the thought of reasonable men will be kept inviolate and inviolable, however crushing may be the pressure of incriminating proof. But justice, though due to the accused, is due to the accuser also. The concept of fairness must not be strained till it is narrowed to a filament. We are to keep the balance true.[44]

Beyond the questions of fair procedure, the Court was also faced with a series of important Fourteenth Amendment cases dealing with the applicability of certain provisions of the Bill of Rights to governmental action by the states. In *Grosjean* v. *American Press Co.*,[45] a Louisiana gross advertising receipts tax against newspapers with greater than 20,000 circulation was attacked as being violative of the Equal Protection Clause and of the freedom of the press. Justice Sutherland at first wrote an opinion holding the statute unconstitutional on the first ground. Cardozo, with strong views about the power of the legislature to adopt reasonable classifications in exercise of its taxing power, could not agree. He wrote a concurring opinion, disagreeing on the equal protection point but, after reviewing the history of such legislation in this country and in England, he found the statute unconstitutional as a discriminatory tax on freedom of the press. Justice Sutherland then rewrote his opinion, adopting the position and much of the thought of the Cardozo opinion, which was then withdrawn, and Sutherland spoke for a unanimous Court, without passing on the "equal protection" issue.

The important question of how much of the Bill of Rights was incorporated into the Fourteenth Amendment was presented to the Court in the form of a Connecticut statute giving the state, with permission of the presiding judge, a right of appeal on questions of law in a criminal case. Cardozo's formulation of the answer has been much quoted and is still law today, though not without dissent. In holding that the double jeopardy provisions of the Fifth Amendment were not binding on the states, Cardozo stated that only those provisions of the Bill of Rights were incorporated into the Fourteenth Amendment that were "of the very essence of a scheme of ordered liberty." Justice could be done without jury trial, the privilege against self-incrimination, indictments.

We reach a different plane of social and moral values when we pass to the privileges and immunities that have been taken over from the earlier articles of the Federal Bill of Rights and brought within the Fourteenth Amendment by a process of absorption. . . . If the Fourteenth Amendment has absorbed them, the process of absorption has had its source in the belief that neither liberty nor justice would exist if they were sacrificed. . . . That is true, for illustration, of freedom of thought and speech. Of that freedom one may say that it is the matrix, the indispensable condition, of nearly every other form of freedom.[46]

It is ironic that the sole Justice who would have held the statute unconstitutional was Justice Butler. It is even more ironic that the majority included Justice Black, then in his first Term on the Court, who has long since repudiated his concurrence in *Palko.*

One can see from Cardozo's language in *Palko* that he had

a deep commitment to freedom of thought and speech. Thus he joined in, and made substantial literary contribution to, Justice Roberts' opinion for the bare majority of the Court that reversed the conviction of Angelo Herndon by a Georgia court for attempted insurrection, holding that the application of the statute to the particular facts of that case was an unreasonable infringement of freedom of speech and assembly.[47] But when the University of California required all students to take military science courses and refused to exempt conscientious objectors, Cardozo voted to uphold the regulation, although besides joining the majority opinion, he also wrote separately.[48] One cannot avoid the impression in reading his opinion that he was carefully spelling out his reasons for upholding the regulation because he desired to make them public in a case that evidently troubled his conscience. But troubled as he may have been about the wisdom of the policy, he did not let his sympathies shape his constitutional views. There was a toughness to Cardozo the judge and he took pride in his ability to put aside his personal feelings, sympathies, and prejudices, as far as humanly possible, when he put on his judicial robes. This was the philosophy he had expressed in his extrajudicial writings and he adhered to it as a judge.

How does one assess Cardozo's performance on the Supreme Court, or rather that portion of the Court's work that we have discussed here? It must be done in the context of the problems of the 1930's and not of the 1960's. On the other hand, since in those words of John Marshall that Cardozo was fond of quoting, "it is *a constitution* we are expounding,"[49] it is not unfair to assess generally the constitutional principles, the theory of constitutional adjudication that he enunciated.

The most important issues faced by the Court during Cardozo's tenure were the New Deal regulatory cases which involved principally an interpretation of the extent of the taxing and commerce power of Congress and the deterrent effect of the Fourteenth Amendment on the states. Of growing but subordinate interest were the so-called "civil liberties" cases. It was apparent in the 1930's, and it is apparent in today's assessments of that period, that virtually all the leading legal commentators were in accord that the McReynolds foursome interpreted the commerce and taxing power too narrowly. On the other hand, although Justices Cardozo, Brandeis, and Stone set forth a broader view with respect to the Commerce Clause, which, nevertheless, left a certain area to state power, they never formulated successfully the limits on congressional power that they believed to exist. The result was that after 1937 case after case pushed congressional power further and further so that there is not any significant area today that seems beyond the potential reach of the congressional power. Perhaps that was inevitable, but Cardozo did not seem to think so. His *Schecter* opinion, which he might have used to develop his theories, is in this respect a failure since, unusually for Cardozo, it deals in generalities only.

Likewise, as one reads the decisions of the Supreme Court today, the constitutional principles with regard to "substantive due process" enunciated by Holmes, Brandeis, and Cardozo seem somewhat remote, at least in the "economic" sphere. This may be partly because the problems those principles were designed to meet are no longer problems today. But perhaps it may be partly because of the very formulation of the test that they applied: except where speech and thought were involved, legislative action was to be upheld once shown to be not unreasonable or "not wholly frivolous."

The cases that Cardozo was dealing with did not seem to him and his dissenting colleagues to raise difficult questions of competing rights. Perhaps if the cases had, they would have stated differently the test to be applied. But they had before them the example of how a so-called right (for example, the "right" of a man to contract to work for as many hours and as little money as he wanted, no matter that this contract was imposed upon him because of a crushing disparity of economic bargaining power) could be erected into a constitutional principle to thwart maximum-hour and minimum-wage legislation. It was doubtless this example that led to the formulation of a doctrine that would minimize the Court's role except where thought and speech were involved. This differentiation between the nature of the "rights" involved led to the subsequent formulation by Chief Justice Stone of the theory of the "preferred position" of certain individual rights and the more extreme formulation by Justice Black of the "absoluteness" of the specific provisions of the Bill of Rights.

It certainly is possible to regard legislation involving a regulation of business as involving different considerations from legislation affecting civil liberties and to apply a different test to each. Yet a great deal of legislation has a way of defying neat categorization. Is restriction of picketing one or the other? How about Sunday closing laws? Or closed-shop legislation? Or fair trade laws?[50] Or a law collectivizing farms? Justice Frankfurter has said:

> Yesterday the active area in this field was concerned with "property." Today it is "civil liberties." Tomorrow it may again be "property." Who can say that in a society with a mixed economy, like ours, these two areas are sharply separated, and that certain freedoms in relation to property may not again be deemed, as they were in the past, aspects of individual freedom?
>
> The Due Process Clauses extend to triune interests—life, liberty, and property—and "property" cannot be deleted by judicial fiat rendering it nugatory regarding legislation touching property. Moreover, protection of property interests may, as already indicated, quite fairly be deemed, in appropriate circumstances, an aspect of liberty. Regulation of property may be struck down on assumptions or beliefs other than narrow economic views. . . .[51]

To this it might be added that in the history of man's strivings, the "right" to eat and to make a living, an "economic" right, has probably agitated man at least as much as the right to speak his mind and practice his religion freely. Somehow the "simple" constitutional principles enunciated by Cardozo in the 1930's do not seem completely satisfactory in dealing with some of the more subtle and complex problems of the 1950's and 1960's.

It is therefore not surprising that although the three current interpretations of the Due Process Clauses all derive from the heritage of Holmes, Brandeis, Stone, and Cardozo, they represent three very different views, different both from one another and, to a greater or lesser degree, from that which prevailed in the late 1930's. Judge Learned Hand believed that the Holmes-Cardozo view of the danger of the Court's involvement in questions of wisdom should be rigorously applied to all "substantive due process" cases and that this is a subject that the Court should abjure.[52] Justice Frankfurter believes that although the Court has a duty to apply the Due Process Clauses, it must be wary in these cases. Although heavily influenced by Holmes, and also by Brandeis and Cardozo, he has evolved a somewhat different statement of the test to be applied: all "substantive due process" cases, whether involving "economic" or "civil liberties" regulation or a mixture of the two, require consideration not merely of the rationality of the governmental action but also of the nature of the interest being affected and of the extent of that effect, and then require a weighing of the competing interests. This puts the Court into, or rather back into, the very difficult situation in which McReynolds & Co. dabbled so disastrously, but he has wielded the power with a completely different set of judicial values from McReynolds & Co.[53]

Justice Black regards questions of economic regulation with a similar formulation to that of Justice Frankfurter, but as to the Bill of Rights and especially with respect to those liberties dealt with by the First Amendment, his views would keep Government from taking any action touching the subjects of that Amendment.[54] This is not the place to assess the merits of these three current views of constitutional principles, but their emergence demonstrates the durable qualities of the Constitution whose generality permits constant reformulation even of those principles that seemed in their day to express immutable truth.

This discussion of one phase of the work of Cardozo and his dissenting colleagues should not obscure the proper estimate of their work. The principle task of judges is to decide the particular cases presented to them, not cases that may be presented in the future, although one may hope that present statements will not embarrass future decision. This task Cardozo and his colleagues accomplished in eloquent fashion for themselves and eventually for the Court. In the great constitutional struggle of the first part of the twentieth century, theirs was the voice of the present and of the future, and they finally prevailed. This essay has attempted to summarize Justice Cardozo's contributions to common law, to constitutional law, and to law itself. The work as we have seen was not his alone, and we have noted the special influence of Justice Holmes. The result of Cardozo's twenty-five years as judge and jurist was elucidation for judges, lawyers, and laymen of the proper function of the courts in our twentieth-century society.

ANDREW L. KAUFMAN *is a member of the Newark, New Jersey, law firm of Kaufman, Kaufman & Kaufman. He is currently engaged in the preparation of a biography of Mr. Justice Cardozo, to be published by the Harvard University Press. During the 1955 and 1956 Terms of Court, he was law clerk to Mr. Justice Felix Frankfurter.*

NOTES

1. Proceedings of the Bar and Officers of the Supreme Court of the United States, November 26, 1938, 305 U.S. ix (1938).
2. *Mr. Justice Cardozo and the Law of Torts*, 52 HARV. L. REV. 372 (1939).
3. *Mr. Justice Cardozo and the Law of Contracts*, 52 HARV. L. REV. 408, 408–9 (1939).
4. *The Nature of the Judicial Process* (1921), p. 69.
5. *Ibid.* at 164–66.
6. To borrow the expression of Holmes, J., dissenting, in *Southern*

Pacific Co. v. *Jensen,* 244 U.S. 205, 222 (1917), where he rejected that concept.

7. See *Palsgraf* v. *Long Island Railroad Co.,* 248 N.Y. 339, 162 N.E. 99 (1928).

8. See *Wagner* v. *International Railway Co.,* 232 N.Y. 176, 133 N.E. 437 (1921).

9. See *Allegheny College* v. *National Chautauqua Bank,* 246 N.Y. 369, 159 N.E. 173 (1927).

10. See *Kerr S.S. Co.* v. *Radio Corporation of America,* 245 N.Y. 284, 157 N.E. 140 (1927).

11. See pp. 193–95 *supra.*

12. 245 N.Y. at 291–292, 157 N.E. at 142.

13. Cardozo, *Mr. Justice Holmes,* 44 HARV. L. REV. 682, 685 (1931).

14. *Ibid.* at 689.

15. *The Nature of the Judicial Process,* pp. 139–40.

16. Cardozo, *The Growth of the Law* (1924).

17. Cardozo, *The Paradoxes of Legal Science* (1928).

18. *Judge Cardozo in the Court of Appeals,* 52 HARV. L. REV. 364, 371 (1939).

19. *The Nature of the Judicial Process,* p. 78 (footnote omitted).

20. *Stewart Dry Goods Co.* v. *Lewis,* 294 U.S. 550, 566, 569 (1935).

21. See Freund, *Mr. Justice Brandeis, supra* at 177.

22. 288 U.S. 517 (1933).

23. *Ibid.* at 541 *et seq.*

24. *Ibid.* at 583.

25. "The life of the law has not been logic: it has been experience. The felt necessities of the time, the prevalent moral and political theories, intuitions of public policy, avowed or unconscious, even the prejudices which judges share with their fellow-men, have had a good deal more to do than the syllogism in determining the rules by which men should be governed." Holmes, *The Common Law* (Howe ed. 1963), p. 3.

26. 288 U.S. at 586.

27. *Ibid.* at 585–86.

28. Freund, *The Supreme Court of the United States* (1961), p. 124.

29. 288 U.S. at 586.

30. 9 Wheat. 1 (1824).

31. 298 U.S. 238, 324 (1936).

32. *Ibid.* at 327–28.

33. *Schecter Poultry Corp.* v. *United States,* 295 U.S. 495, 551 (1935).

34. *Panama Refining Co.* v. *Ryan,* 293 U.S. 388, 433 (1935).

35. Quoted in Mason, *Harlan Fiske Stone* (1956), p. 425.

36. *Scott* v. *Sandford,* 19 How. 393 (1857).

37. *Brown* v. *Board of Education,* 347 U.S. 483 (1954).

38. *N.L.R.B.* v. *Jones & Laughlin Steel Corp.,* 301 U.S. 1 (1937).

39. *Steward Machine Co.* v. *Davis,* 301 U.S. 548 (1937); *Helvering* v. *Davis,* 301 U.S. 619 (1937).

40. Cardozo, *Mr. Justice Holmes,* 44 Harv. L. Rev. 682, 688 (1931).

41. 242 N.Y. 13, 150 N.E. 585 (1926).

42. *People* v. *Gitlow,* 234 N.Y. 132, 154, 136 N.E. 317, 326 (1922), *aff'd,* 268 U.S. 652 (1925).

43. 291 U.S. 97 (1934).

44. *Ibid.* at 122.

45. 297 U.S. 233 (1936).

46. *Palko* v. *Connecticut,* 302 U.S. 319, 326–27 (1937).

47. *Herndon* v. *Lowry,* 301 U.S. 242 (1937). See also *De Jonge* v. *Oregon,* 299 U.S. 353 (1937).

48. *Hamilton* v. *Regents of University of California,* 293 U.S. 245, 265 (1934).

49. *McCulloch* v. *Maryland,* 4 Wheat. 316, 407 (1819).

50. Since 1950, more than a dozen states have, on state constitutional grounds, declared their fair trade laws unconstitutional. See also *Morey* v. *Doud,* 354 U.S. 457 (1957), where the Supreme Court, in fact if not in theory, applied a test to state legislation that was incompatible with the "rational basis" or "not wholly frivolous" test.

51. *John Marshall and the Judicial Function,* 69 Harv. L. Rev. 217, 230 (1955).

52. Learned Hand, *The Bill of Rights* (1958).

53. The fact that all interests are considered does not mean that all interests are to be regarded equally. See Frankfurter, J., in *Kovacs* v. *Cooper,* 336 U.S. 77, 95 (1949) (concurring opinion), for a statement regarding the claims of freedom of thought and speech that is reminiscent of Cardozo's statement in *Palko.* The most thoughtful study of the standards to be applied by the Court in Fourteenth Amendment cases is to be found in Freund, *The Supreme Court of the United States* (1961), *passim.*

54. It is impossible to set forth briefly the views of Mr. Justice Black as they must be pieced out from his numerous opinions and occasional writings. The best exposition of these views is to be found in Reich, *Mr. Justice Black and the Living Constitution,* 76 Harv. L. Rev. 673 (1963).

Courtesy of Harris & Ewing

MR. JUSTICE MURPHY

Mr. Justice Murphy

By

JOHN P. ROCHE

THE CONFRONTATION

"It is disheartening to find so much that is right in an opinion which seems to me so fundamentally wrong." Mr. Justice Murphy's last dissent, *Wolf* v. *Colorado*, 338 U.S. 25, 41 (1949).

"To rely on a tidy formula for the easy determination of what is a fundamental right [search and seizure] for purposes of legal enforcement may satisfy a longing for certainty but ignores the movements of a free society." Mr. Justice Frankfurter, for the Court, *Wolf* v. *Colorado*, 338 U.S. 25, 27 (1949).

On July 19, 1949, Frank Murphy, Associate Justice of the Supreme Court of the United States, died in Detroit. The liberal press mourned the passing of a mighty warrior for civil liberty. Other journals observed the protocol of the occasion by politely deploring his death: the University of Michigan Law School prepared a memorial issue of the *Michigan Law Review*[1] in honor of its distinguished alumnus, a few encomiums appeared in the law journals,[2] then silence set in. This silence has been broken only by occasional slighting references to Murphy's talents, and by a word-of-mouth tradition in law-school circles that the Justice was a legal illiterate, a New Deal political hack who approached the sacred arcana of the Law with a disrespect that verged on blasphemy, who looked upon hallowed juridical traditions as a drunk views a lamppost—as a means of support rather than a source of light.

Murphy was indeed a strange phenomenon and, given the political developments of the past generation, it seems probable that we shall not see his likes again. An Irish-American, Roman Catholic, Frank Murphy was also a militant, dedicated liberal. Probably one of the best-hated figures of the New Deal period for his uncompromising refusal to employ martial law against sit-down strikers, he also collected enemies among the followers of President Roosevelt for his unswerving defense of civil liberties against even the "enlightened" administration. In addition, because of his thoroughly instrumental approach to law and to legal traditions, he incurred the enmity of all legal scholars in the apostolic succession from Mr. Justice Felix Frankfurter. An ideological, even ritualistic liberal, he brought upon himself the scorn of the tough-minded "realists" such as Justice Jackson. While Jackson fulfilled Holmes' dictum that a judge must have in him something of Mephistopheles—in fact, sometimes making Holmes himself, by comparison, appear angelic—Murphy lacked this quality completely. In a real sense, I suggest, Mr. Justice Frank Murphy was a utopian pilgrim in this vale of tears, a man with a deep-rooted, religious commitment to the building of a new society in which men would be both free and prosperous. Thus when Murphy died, the Court lost more than its leading civil libertarian; it lost a Justice who was the living incarnation of the militant liberal myth of the New Deal.

The criticisms of Justice Murphy are themselves interesting for the light they throw on his symbolic stature. The mildest critics, such as Herman Pritchett, suggest that the Justice's "hyperactive concern for individual rights" led him "into ventures little short of quixotic."[3] This is gentle, indeed, when compared with the strictures of Philip B. Kurland. Comparing Murphy to Chief Justice Vinson, Kurland observed:

> Neither had any great intellectual capacity. Both were absolutely dependent upon their law clerks for the production of their opinions. Both were very much concerned with their place in history, though neither had any feeling for the history of the Court as an institution. . . . Neither dealt with the cases presented as complex problems;

for each there was one issue which forced decision. Each felt a very special loyalty to the President who had appointed him.[4]

Chief Justice Stone apparently shared this view. From Alpheus Mason's biography of the Chief Justice we learn that Stone considered Murphy, along with Rutledge, a "weak sister." Consequently Stone refused to give Murphy important decisions:

"The job of the Court," [Stone] said of one of [Murphy's] opinions "is to resolve doubts, not create them." The Chief Justice was well aware that he slighted Murphy; he often agreed to give him a "break," but in the end Murphy would be nosed out partly because Stone disliked leaving a fine case to the rumination of a law clerk.[5]

The essential difference between Murphy's judicial attitude and that of his more conservative brethren was brought out in 1944 by an exchange of compliments between Murphy and Roberts. Writing for the Court in *Tennessee Coal, Iron & R.R. Co.* v. *Muscoda Local 123*,[6] the Justice observed in passing:

Such an issue [portal to portal pay] can be resolved only by discarding formalities and adopting a realistic attitude, recognizing that we are dealing with human beings and with a statute that is intended to secure to them the fruits of their toil and exertion.[7]

Dissenting, Mr. Justice Roberts crystallized his opposition to Murphy's approach:

The question for decision in this case should be approached not on the basis of any broad humanitarian prepossessions we may all entertain, not with desire to construe legislation so as to accomplish what we deem worthy objects, but in the traditional and, if we are to have a government of laws, the essential attitude of ascertaining what Congress has enacted rather than what we wish it had enacted.[8]

We shall subsequently examine Murphy's judicial attitude and technique in detail; suffice it here to note the standard counts of the indictment that has been drawn up against him and examine it briefly. Murphy, it is alleged, was a New Deal politician disguised as a Justice of the Court, and not a very bright politician at that. He was legally a creature of his law clerks, excessively loyal to President Roosevelt, simplistic in his approach to complex legal problems, and bereft of any historical appreciation of the role of the Supreme Court.

Now, as will appear later, I do not look upon my function in this essay as one of glorification, or even rehabilitation—I come neither to praise nor to bury. However, I do feel compelled to demur at the outset to the terms of this indictment. In the first place, since the days when John Marshall filled the office of Secretary of State in the morning and Chief Justice of the United States in the afternoon, we have had a high incidence of politicians concealed beneath the judicial robes of the high Court. Indeed, I have suggested elsewhere[9] that, given the policy functions of the Supreme Court, this is both inevitable and wise: to paraphrase Clemenceau, the meaning of the Constitution is far too important to be left in the hands of legal experts. Thus the complaint against Murphy, to stand up, must be reformulated to assert that he was a "bad" political justice, and this accusation must rest upon more than a subjective dislike of the politics with which he suffused his opinions. This charge must, in other words, rest upon some empirical evidence that his decisions were technically incompetent, and none of his critics have appeared with any documentation of this point, or even with any criteria by which an evaluation can be made.

So here the argument shifts: *Enter* the ubiquitous law clerks who seemingly saved Murphy from his stupidity. Without the kind of information that could supply substance to this accusation one way or the other, I can enter no judgment on the merits of Murphy's legal knowledge and intelligence. However, I suggest that the law clerk gambit is one best left unexplored, since who can tell how many judicial reputations may be destroyed by candid revelation of what occurs in the chambers? Mr. Justice Frankfurter seems to have implied to Professor Mason that Mr. Justice Stone's dissent in the *Gobitis* case[10] was a consequence of fervent advocacy of the Jehovah's Witness position by his clerk, Allison Dunham.[11] Elsewhere in the biography of the Chief Justice it appears that his famous footnote 4 in the *Carolene Products* case was the handiwork of his clerk, Louis Lusky,[12] as was the rationale of the *Gerhardt* case.[13] Obviously we are here in dangerous territory. Yet in a fundamental casting up of accounts, is this law clerk proposition relevant? Why should a Justice not have the right to assimilate the talents of his apprentices? And, if he takes on brilliant young men and gives them leeway, is it not evidence of his own judgment and intellectual capacity?[14]

The other points in the indictment seem to rest on equally flimsy factual assumptions. The charge that Murphy was overly loyal to President Roosevelt flies in the face of the facts: what Justice asserted more vigorously the rights of the individual, even of individuals who happened to be Nazis, Communists, or Japanese generals, against the executive arm of the government? A reading of Murphy's flaming dissent in *Korematsu* v. *United States*,[15] which could have been designated more accurately *Korematsu* v. *Franklin D. Roosevelt, Commander-in-Chief*, should demonstrate the patent inaccuracy of this accusation. Undoubtedly Murphy was simplistic in his approach to legal problems, but, as a reading of John Marshall's disposition of Virginia's case against the Cohen brothers should suggest,[16] this alone does not constitute high treason against the traditions of the Court.

To conclude this evaluation of the criticism of Murphy, I would submit that a directed verdict of not proven, if we may borrow it from the Scottish jurisdiction, is in order. The nub of the case against Frank Murphy appears to be the content of his opinions, rather than their form. That is, he was simplistic and untraditional to the "wrong" ends. In fact, I believe it was Murphy's symbolic stature rather than his personal qualities that has drawn the attacks, and it is to his symbolic function that I now turn.

To understand Justice Murphy's symbolic role, it is necessary to examine briefly the New Deal tradition from which he sprang. The New Deal was a many-faceted phenomenon and, above all, a source of myths. Indeed, the reality—which was the masterful expediency of Franklin D. Roosevelt moving now this way, now that, in the effort to deal with immediate problems[17]—has long since vanished beneath layers of myth. To American conservatives, using this elusive term in its immediate political sense, the New Deal appeared as a wave of collectivism that, unless checked, would end by destroying American freedom. To hopeful liberals, the New Deal seemed to present a magnificent opportunity to remedy the economic and social defects that were brought into sharp focus by the depression. Armed with an essentially pragmatic philosophy of life, these worthies descended upon Washington and set to work in piecemeal fashion ameliorating the abuses they found. On the far left could be discerned small colonies of radical sectarians to whom the New Deal represented "incipient fascism" and "bureaucratic collectivism."

But still another mythical interpretation of the New Deal can be extracted from the public opinion of the thirties, and it is this viewpoint that is of particular concern here. For lack of a better term, I shall designate it the *militant liberal* view of the New Deal. While no specific group can be found that advanced this position in any organized fashion, it was very important nonetheless. To the militant liberal, the New Deal had an essentially millennial function: it must revolutionize American life by creating under government auspices and protection *both* an economy of abundance and an atmosphere of maximum personal freedom. Many militant liberals were close to socialism, though repelled by the Marxist logic-chopping and sectarian feuds that were characteristic of the left-wing organizations. They were also close to the pragmatic liberals in terms of the goals to be achieved, though they differed from the latter with respect to the efficacy of pragmatic, non-ideological measures of reform. In the fundamental sense, this was a temperamental difference; while the pragmatic liberals stuck close to the ground, making inch-by-inch inroads into economic and social problems, the militant liberals designed a full-blown American utopia and urged that progress toward it move at full speed.

This unorganized, amorphous *groupement*, to borrow an appropriate term from French politics where such phenomena are plentiful, had little practical impact on the Roosevelt administration. Indeed, many of its constituents detested the anti-ideological sphinx in the White House. Yet, the net impact of its message, particularly since such influential journals as *The Nation* and *New Republic* reflected its attitude, was considerable, particularly among young people and in liberal circles abroad. In short, these were "true believers" who, rejecting insignificant left-wing factions, placed their dream of the future in the hands of Franklin D. Roosevelt and, perhaps in the hope that their attitude would become a self-fulfilling prophecy, propagandized the message that Roosevelt could be the liberal Messiah. While Roosevelt made few practical, as distinguished from rhetorical, concessions to this point of view, an outstanding instance of his "fence-mending" on the left was the New Deal career of Frank Murphy.

Since the inner life of Justice Murphy is not our concern here, a few facts will suffice. After a varied career at law and in the army during World War I, Murphy was elected a judge of the Recorder's Court in Detroit in 1923. He was then thirty-three years old. On the bench, he made a name for himself as a pioneer in the assimilation of psychiatric skills into criminal proceedings, operating on the assumption, stated a generation later in his dissent in *Fisher* v. *United States*,[18] that "only by integrating scientific advancements with our ideals of justice can law remain a part of the living fiber of our civilization." His work as the judge in a celebrated race trial—the *Sweet* case which saw Clarence Darrow defending Negroes against a murder indictment growing out of racial hostility—brought high praise on all sides for his impartiality and immunity to criticism. Re-elected to the court in 1929, he resigned in 1930 to make a successful campaign for the office of Mayor of Detroit.

As Mayor of a city ravaged by the depression, he established a nation-wide reputation among liberals for his statement that "not one deserving man or woman shall go hungry in Detroit because of circumstances beyond his control," thus asserting the responsibility of government for the economic welfare of the people. After a second term as Mayor, he was appointed Governor General of the Philippines by President Roosevelt in 1933, and in effect, leader of the movement for Philippine independence. After the Commonwealth was established in 1935, Murphy remained in Manila as United States High Commissioner. Evidence that a decade later he still felt himself *in loco parentis* to the Philippine people is revealed in his separate opinion in a case in 1945, urging that American tax laws should be construed in such a fashion as to help the struggling Islands achieve maturity and economic strength.[19]

In 1936, Murphy returned to Michigan to win the gubernatorial election. When he assumed office in 1937, he found himself confronted by the famous sit-down strikes. It was his conduct at this time that really endeared the Governor to the militant liberals, for instead of declaring martial law, calling out the national guard, and forcibly driving the workers from the factories, Murphy made every effort to avoid a violent solution and entered into negotiations with union leaders instead of jailing them.[20] While we can now view the sit-down strikes with a certain detachment, realizing that since the workers were not prepared to launch a proletarian revolution, they would eventually get bored and go home, the conservative view of Murphy's conduct was that he was encouraging the formation of soviets. The fact that his solution worked was, of course, even more galling, and Governor Frank Murphy became Public Enemy No. 1 in business circles. In 1938, he was defeated for re-election and was immediately appointed Attorney General of the United States.

Apparently Murphy handled the usual functions of this job with competence, but his ideological convictions were not dulled by high office: within a month after he took office, on February 3, 1939, to be precise, he established a "Civil Liberties Unit" in the Criminal Division of the Department of Justice. In announcing his intention of establishing this Unit, Murphy said that "where there is social unrest—as I know from having been through no little of it myself since 1930—we ought to be more anxious and vigorous in protecting the civil liberties of protesting and insecure people."[21] When the new section was set up, the Attorney General justified it in the following terms:

In a democracy, an important function of the law enforcement branch of government is the *aggressive* protection of fundamental rights inherent in a free people.

In America these guarantees are contained in express provisions of the Constitution and in acts of Congress. It is the purpose of the Department of Justice *to pursue a program of vigilant action in the prosecution* of infringement of these.[22]

In January, 1940, Murphy was appointed to the Supreme Court to fill the vacancy caused by the death of Pierce Butler. Like Butler, he was a middle-western Catholic, but there the resemblance ceased. In a statement made on his appointment to the Court, Murphy emphasized the need for vigorous protection of personal liberties and added that "those in government—preoccupied with grave social and economic problems—tend naturally to be less sensitive to instances of oppression and denial of constitutional rights. In this welter of confusing factors that principle which is the essence of democracy—tolerance for all sides in all questions—is the loser."[23] Two aspects of this statement are noteworthy: first, Murphy stated clearly his objection to *governmental* infringements of personal rights; and, second, his only reference is to "social and economic" problems, though war had recently broken out in Europe. Perhaps one reason that President Roosevelt elevated Murphy to the Court was his intuition that while Murphy was a fine intern for "Dr. New Deal," he would have been a first-rate nuisance to "Dr. Win-the-War."

So did Justice Murphy, on the eve of his assumption of judicial office, lay down the gage of battle to all who would infringe on the liberties of the citizen. And this Justice was to prove himself unique among the New Deal justices in his sensitivity to injustice. His uniqueness in this regard, I suggest, can be understood by the fact that alone among the Roosevelt appointees to the high court, Murphy was a militant liberal by background and conviction. Every judge is dominated by a *telos*, by a built-in purpose that suffuses his assumptions about law, so in asserting that he was teleological we cannot distinguish him from Black, Reed, Frankfurter, Douglas, Jackson, or Rutledge. Where he differed from his New Deal brethren was in the content of his *telos*. True, his views overlapped theirs at many points, but there is nonetheless a discrete corpus of ideals that supplied Frank Murphy with his bearings, his conviction, and his utter ruthlessness when confronted by procedural niceties that seemingly masked substantive evils.

I am not asserting that Frank Murphy was a "great" judge; my analysis and evaluation is directed to a level where this question is irrelevant. I am concerned with Murphy's symbolic position, both in the minds of his enemies and those of his friends, and my contention is that he was the judicial incarnation of the militant liberal myth of the New Deal, of the body of aspirations that the militant liberals hoped the New Deal would incorporate into American life. Let me examine briefly the components of this myth.[24] A rough summary might read as follows.

First. The militant liberals were dedicated exponents of the rights of minorities, automatic defenders of the persecuted without regard to the opinions that brought down the wrath of the majority.

Second. In their approach to business, the militant liberals were sentimental populists—opponents of "bigness," of trusts, of power concentrations of any sort. This was combined with sympathy for the small farmer, particularly the farmer-debtor in the squeeze of the capitalist octopus—John Steinbeck's *Grapes of Wrath* was required reading.

Third. The militant liberals believed that the federal government had a positive responsibility to create economic security for all Americans. They supported over-all planning rather than pragmatic meliorism.

Fourth. The militant liberals believed firmly in the divine mission of trade unions, frequently shocking prosaic trade-union leaders by the fervency of their convictions, since the latter were generally under the illusion that they were committed to raising wages, not saving the world.

Fifth. Though usually not pacifists in the normal usage of the word, the militant liberals were vigorous anti-militarists, asserting that civil rights were constitutional absolutes that could not be tampered with even in wartime.

This is, of course, an over-simplification, but it should suffice to identify Frank Murphy's ideological pedigree and to distinguish him from the other New Deal Justices. In the course of this comparison, it should be recalled that I am not denouncing these other Justices or seeking to excommunicate them from the liberal camp. While I would be a dissembler if I did not admit at the outset that I shared, and still share to some degree, the militant liberal *Weltanschauung*, this analysis is wholly concerned with their deficiencies *from Murphy's vantage point*. The inherent wisdom or folly of his philosophy of life is a subject for separate analysis. The clue to an understanding of Murphy's divergence from his liberal brethren lies, I think, in the hypothesis that, while by all accounts a man of considerable practical talent, the Justice was quintessentially a pilgrim in this world. A person who, like the good Christian in the theology of St. Augustine, bears witness in this *civitas* to the values of a transcendent utopia in which he spiritually resides. To Murphy, personal liberty in a society that cherishes man's personality was the necessary precondition for the achievement of God-given potentialities, and he would lash out with prophetic fervor against any who frustrated the achievement of this democratic utopia in the United States. From this angle, law, like all human institutions, is purely instrumental; traditions maintain their validity only so long as their substance contributes to the fulfillment of the democratic *telos*. Murphy's antitraditionalism thus itself stemmed from a tradition traceable through Thomas Aquinas to Aristotle: instruments retain their legitimacy only so long as they fulfill their proper functions.

Let us now turn to the delineation of this democratic *telos* as Justice Murphy set it forth in the United States Reports.

Rights of minorities.—Someone once observed that if Frank Murphy were ever to be canonized, it would be by the Jehovah's Witnesses. Though a member of a faith that has received the full force of Witness vituperation, Murphy, after the impact of the *Gobitis*[25] case made itself felt, consistently supported the claims of the sect. From *Jones* v. *Opelika*[26] in 1942 to *Kovacs* v. *Cooper*[27] in 1949, he accepted and endorsed the pleas of the Witnesses in every case they brought to the high court. In *Prince* v. *Massachusetts*,[28] which presented only the most marginal issue of religious freedom, he dissented from the opinion of the Court, written by Rutledge, that the Massachusetts child labor laws legitimately prohibited Jehovah's Witness children from selling literature. He took this opportunity to express his views on the general problem:

> The sidewalk, no less than the cathedral or the evangelist's tent, is a proper place, under the Constitution, for the orderly worship of God.

No chapter in human history has been so largely written in terms of persecution and intolerance as the one dealing with religious freedom. From ancient times to the present day, the ingenuity of man has known no limits in its ability to forge weapons of oppression for use against those who dare to express or practice unorthodox religious beliefs. And the Jehovah's Witnesses are living proof of the fact that even in this nation, conceived as it was in the ideals of freedom, the right to practice religion in unconventional ways is still far from secure.[29]

The Justice seemed blissfully unaware of the remarkable extent to which his views logically violated the principles of separation of church and state; Murphy consistently gave a constitutional bonus to the religious dissenter. To put it differently, a petitioner's claim to religious motivation would automatically lead Murphy to issue a waiver, an exemption from the normal sanctions of the law. To exempt Jehovah's Witnesses, for example, from the scope of the child labor laws on the basis of their alleged connection with Higher Authority, was in effect to provide constitutional sanction for sectarian privileges, to grant special rights to the religious. However, this consideration never weighed upon him in his defense of private sectarian judgment against the claims of the police power.

Other religious minorities uniformly received his support. A religious pacifist barred from the practice of law in Illinois,[30] lost his appeal to the Court: Murphy joined Black's dissenting opinion. Three times Murphy gave judicial comfort to the Mormon schismatics who retained the custom of plural marriage. Once he wrote the opinion of the Court condemning the employment of the anti-kidnapping statute against these polygamists,[31] and in two cases he was in dissent when various other legal restraints were invoked against the practice.[32]

Racial minorities could count on Justice Murphy to advance their claims for full equality. One of the best expressions of his philosophy of law arose from the Court's intricate disposal of *Steele* v. *Louisville & N.R.R.*[33] Concurring in the judgment of the Court, Murphy insisted that the racially restrictive practices of the union local, which was attempting to utilize government authority to impose upon the employer conditions discriminatory to Negroes, should have been declared unconstitutional.

> The utter disregard for the dignity and the well-being of colored citizens shown by this record is so pronounced as to demand the invocation of constitutional condemnation. To decide the case and to analyze the statute solely upon the basis of legal niceties, while remaining mute and placid as to the obvious and oppressive deprivation of constitutional guarantees, is to make the judicial function something less than it should be. . . . Racism is far too virulent today to permit the slightest refusal, in the light of a Constitution that abhors it, to expose and condemn it wherever it appears in the course of a statutory interpretation.[34]

His dissent in the *Screws* case[35] was in a similar, though more infuriated vein.

The Japanese aliens in California, who were unable under the immigration statute of that day to become citizens of the United States, received extended sympathy from Murphy in a lengthy concurrence in the case of *Oyama* v. *California*.[36] Technically at issue in the case was the validity of an amendment to the state's alien land law which, by welding escheat provisions to a broad presumption, was designed to end evasions of the ban on Japanese land ownership. The Court dealt with the statute on a very narrow basis, interdicting the presumption without touching on the legitimacy of the land law itself, and Murphy came out fighting. The land law, he asserted, was on its face unconstitutional as an infringement of the Fourteenth Amendment; it could only be described as a legislative implementation of racism, and the Court betrayed its responsibility to the Constitution when it refused to confront this fact. He filed a similar objection to a California law forbidding the issuance of fishing licenses to aliens ineligible for citizenship which was also disposed of by the Court on other, less ideological, grounds.[37] He consistently defended the claims of the American Indians.[38]

Murphy did not limit his concern to racial or religious minorities. Urban voters, discriminated against by an antiquated system of congressional districting,[39] and by the procedures necessary to get a minority party on the ballot;[40] members of unpopular political minorities such as the quasi-fascist Terminiello[41] and the communist Gerhard Eisler;[42] aliens subjected to deportation orders seemingly for their political activities;[43] all these found in Justice Murphy a strong defender. He was completely undiscriminating. If his opinion holding the communist Schneiderman illegally denaturalized was in part a ritualistically liberal approach to the nature of international communism—he stated at one point that "we should not hold that petitioner is not attached to the Constitution by reason of his possible belief in the creation of some form of world union of soviet republics unless we are willing so to hold with regard to those who believe in Pan-Americanism, the League of Nations, Union Now . . ."[44]—he also vigorously asserted the immunity from denaturalization proceedings of admitted Nazis.[45]

One last minority group to which Murphy extended his judicial support was a thoroughly marginal one indeed—operators of houses of prostitution caught in the dragnet of the Mann Act. Murphy insisted that the sole purpose of the Mann Act was to eliminate and punish white slavery; that the Government had no right to stretch it to convict a genial proprietor who took two of his employees on a Florida vacation. Writing for the Court, he stated that "the sole purpose of the journey from beginning to end was to provide innocent recreation and a holiday,"[46] and elsewhere he dissented from a decision in the *Caminetti* tradition which employed the Mann Act against private, non-commercial debauchery.[47] Reading these cases, one gets the distinct feeling that Murphy was repelled by the employment of the majestic sanctions of government against these pathetic, wayward individuals.

No other New Deal Justice approached his record in this area. Without attempting any mathematic computations, certain things are immediately apparent from reading the opinions. Black, for example, wrote most of the Indian opinions that Murphy dissented from and at no point did Rutledge join Murphy in these dissents. Of the other Justices, Rutledge came nearest to equalling Murphy's score.

The judicial process.—Under this heading, I group those decisions that related in one way or another to the conduct of the judicial process: fair trial, search and seizure, confessions, contempt of court, and the like. Here Murphy's position was forthright, ruthless, and enormously irritating to those who look upon the procedural aspects of law as meaningful. As he put it, dissenting from an opinion of Justice Frankfurter in *Carter* v. *Illinois*,[48] holding that petitioner had not been denied the elements of due process:

> Legal technicalities doubtless afford justification for our pretense of ignoring plain facts before us, facts upon which a man's very life or liberty conceivably could depend . . . the result certainly does not enhance the high traditions of the judicial process.[49]

In another case, dissenting all alone from an opinion by Justice Black, Murphy savagely asserted, "The complete travesty of justice revealed by the record in this case forces me to dissent."[50]

Now the implication of these remarks, and others of a similar genre scattered throughout his opinions, is clear. It is a self-righteous, even smug, claim to a higher moral perspective than his brethren. So spoke Savonarola to the Florentines, and doubtless some of the Justices on the Court wished on occasion that they could deal with their conspicuously moral brother as Florence dealt with its scorpion.

Two cases bring out the strength and weakness of Murphy's approach to due process of law. First, in 1942, Murphy held for the Court that one Glasser had been denied a fair trial in federal court because he had not received adequate protection by counsel. Now Glasser, as Justice Frankfurter pointed out in a powerful dissent, was a former United States Attorney who

should have been well aware of his legal rights and seen to it
that they were asserted. But Murphy acted as though an ignorant Negro farmhand, or an illiterate youth, denied counsel,
were sufficient precedents for holding an educated experienced
lawyer to be in the same maltreated category.[51] Murphy did
approach such problems in an absolutist mood, and, one suspects, with an inarticulate assumption that petitioner was always in the right.

Second, in 1947, Murphy wrote a concurring opinion concluding that a Texas judge's contempt proceedings against a
local newspaper were a violation of the First Amendment.[52]
His opinion was a restatement of his concurrence in *Penne-
kamp* v. *Florida*[53] in which he had declared that criticism of
the courts is a legitimate form of behavior:

> [E]ven though the terms be vitriolic, scurrilous or erroneous. . . .
> Judges should be foremost in their vigilance to protect the freedom
> of others to rebuke and castigate the bench and in their refusal to
> be influenced by unfair or misinformed censure.[54]

In one of his brilliant opinions, Justice Jackson dissented lock,
stock, and barrel from what he considered Murphy's ritualistic
liberalism. Cutting to the heart of the matter, Jackson asked
one of those disconcerting questions for which his opinions
were notable: Supposing the nation's press were controlled by
one organization, would *we* be so lofty? The Court's opinion,
he felt, had completely lost touch with the coercive potentialities of a monopoly press, particularly upon an elected judge.[55]
Murphy was, however, unimpressed; he never supported a
conviction for contempt, and one has the suspicion that he
could not conceivably have found a situation in which contempt action was justified against a newspaper.[56]

There is no need to go further with citation of chapter and
verse. Whether the issue was the legality of a confession,[57] self-
incrimination,[58] search and seizure,[59] jury selection,[60] or the
right to a writ of habeas corpus,[61] Justice Murphy could be
counted on to vote for the aggrieved party. Many Justices

joined him at various points, but there was one additional hobby of Murphy's that got him little companionship from his liberal brethren—his suspicion of certain aspects of administrative procedure, notably the employment by administrative officials of the subpoena power. Thus in 1942, he joined Chief Justice Stone's opinion for the Court in *Cudahy Packing Co.* v. *Holland*[62] limiting the use of subpoenas in administrative investigations. Douglas, Black, Byrnes, and Jackson dissented vigorously.

This decision was not just a sport: the following year Murphy wrote a dissent, joined by Justice Roberts, objecting to the conferring upon Secretary of Labor Perkins of broad inquisitorial jurisdiction and the subpoena weapon. He pointed out to his former Cabinet colleague that "under the direction of well-meaning but over-zealous officials they [subpoenas] may at times become instruments of intolerable oppression and injustice."[63] Three years later he returned to the assault, again in a lone dissent, asserting that the subpoena power should be confined "exclusively to the judiciary."[64] One of his few significant inconsistencies occurred in this area: in *Fleming* v. *Mohawk Wrecking & Lumber Co.*,[65] when the Court sustained the authority of the Price Administrator to delegate his subpoena power to subordinates, Murphy silently joined the majority.

Related to Murphy's distrust of bureaucratic inquisitors was his concern about vague statutes and administrative regulations. The Constitution required, as he saw it, that crimes be narrowly defined in order that the individual could have reasonable security, that he might have clear advance knowledge of what the law forbids and what it permits. Thus a vague statute, or the application of an elastic statute to an individual's action, or the formulation of an ambiguous administrative rule called for judicial intervention. Beginning in 1941, when he joined Douglas' dissent in the *Classic* case,[66] and continuing with his dissent in *United States* v. *Dotterweich*[67] in 1943, there are a series of opinions to this effect which he either wrote or joined.[68] It should be noted that in many cases where a statute or regulation was allegedly too vague to stand up, notably in connection with the activities of the National Labor Relations Board, Murphy did not agree. But it seems significant that he alone of the New Deal Justices persistently reiterated this point over the years.

Freedom of the press.—Closely connected with his deep dedication to individual freedom of speech was his special interest in freedom of communication. And here he really parted company with his New Deal colleagues. It was probably his dissents in the network cases[69] and the *Associated Press* case[70] that motivated John P. Frank's suggestive comment that Murphy on occasion allowed "activities he opposed [to] hide behind symbols he cherished."[71] In the network cases, which involved action by the Federal Communications Commission to eliminate certain monopolistic characteristics of the National and the Columbia Broadcasting Systems, Murphy wrote a vigorous dissent, joined only by Roberts, asserting that the FCC had arrogated to itself this power without congressional authorization. Only Congress, he claimed, could legitimately undertake such action. Exposing his real motive, he said:

[B]ecause of its vast potentialities as a medium of communication, discussion and propaganda, the character and extent of control that should be exercised over it [radio] by the government is a matter of deep and vital concern.[72]

In 1945, dissenting in the *Associated Press* case, Murphy returned to this theme. "Today is . . . the first time that the Sherman Act has been used as a vehicle for affirmative intervention by the Government in the realm of dissemination of information."[73] Incidentally, Murphy's dissent in this case—a separate opinion from the other two dissenters, Roberts and Stone—did not say that the anti-trust laws could never be used against the press. What he objected to was the government's procedure, by

injunction and summary judgment, and, what seemed to him,
a lowering of the standards of proof required in an anti-trust
case. The evidence, he felt,

falls far short of proving such a program [of restrictive practices]
and *hence* the decision has grave implications relative to governmental restraints on a free press. . . . [S]uch a failure has unusually
dangerous implications when it appears with reference to an alleged
violation of the [Sherman] Act by those who collect and distribute
information.[74]

Other opinions of his in this area, dealing with the power of
courts to punish newspapers for contempt, have already been
discussed above. Another similar opinion which he endorsed
was Justice Rutledge's concurrence in *United States* v. *C.I.O.*[75]
Here Rutledge and Murphy, rejecting the course of the Court
though sharing in its judgment, insisted that the Taft-Hartley
provision forbidding trade unions to support political candidates was unconstitutional on its face.

Governmental responsibility for "the good life."—Under
this rubric, I have placed those opinions of Justice Murphy in
which he asserted the responsibility of the federal government
over the economic life of the nation, for the fostering of a
strong trade union movement, and for destroying irresponsible
private centers of economic power.

The great battles over the meaning of the Commerce Clause
were won before Murphy arrived on the bench. The main
problems that remained were those of delineating the activities
that Congress intended to regulate and determining the degree
to which Congress desired to preempt the regulation of interstate commerce and eliminate state regulation. It seems hardly
necessary to note that Murphy took an extremely comprehensive view of the commerce power,[76] though from 1946 on, he
tended to affiliate with the "states-rights" position of Justices
Black and Douglas, i.e., to accept the wide latitude these Justices were prepared to give to state taxes and regulations affecting interstate commerce.[77]

Murphy's opinions in this area can conveniently be subdivided into four groups: those that interpret the scope of the commerce power under the Fair Labor Standards Act and the Public Utilities Holding Company Act; those examining the rights of labor; those dealing with the operating procedures of administrative agencies; and those adumbrating the prerogatives of state governments over interstate commerce. Obviously, there is some overlap, but if not definitive, this division is accurate enough for my purposes here.

In a series of opinions, both majority and dissenting, Justice Murphy gave a broad interpretation of the F.L.S.A.[78] One case in particular is worth singling out—the *Jewel Ridge* case[79] in which Murphy, writing for the Court, overruled the Administrator and held portal-to-portal travel time part of the miner's work-week. Justice Jackson, in dissent, denounced the holding as an extreme instance of judicial lawmaking, one demonstrably against the wishes of Congress. Similarly, Justice Murphy for the Court sustained the "death sentence" provisions of the Public Utilities Holding Company Act of 1935 when, after lurking for years in constitutional limbo,[80] this provision finally came under judicial appraisal.[81]

Murphy's record as a defender of the rights of labor is somewhat more ambiguous than is often realized. (Indeed, personal friends of his have suggested to me that the Justice was depressed by the bureaucratic devitalization of the labor movement which, in his view, was a concomitant of its admission to the Establishment via the National Labor Relations Act. If true, this would have been thoroughly consistent with the attitude of the militant liberals.) Although he was responsible for the key decisions in *Thornhill* v. *Alabama*[82] and *Carlson* v. *California*,[83] which held that peaceful picketing was a manifestation of freedom of speech and thus protected against state infringement by the due process clause of the Fourteenth Amendment, Murphy did not join the dissent of Justices Black, Douglas, and Reed in the *Meadowmoor* case.[84] This in spite of the fact that Black went to great pains to point out in his dissent, perhaps with an eye on Murphy, that the injunction in the instant case was almost identical in wording with the statutes held void on their face in the two earlier cases.[85] Moreover, while he joined Black's dissent in *Carpenters & Joiners Union, Local 213* v. *Ritter's Cafe*,[86] alleging that the employment of the Texas anti-trust law against a secondary boycott was a violation of the union's freedom of speech, and seemed in *A.F.L.* v. *Watson*[87] to be eager to strike down the Florida "right to work" law as unconstitutional, he equivocated without opinions when state "right to work" statutes finally arrived for substantive evaluation.[88]

As a defender of the National Labor Relations Board, however, he was without peer on the Court. Once it was established to his satisfaction that the Board was operating within its statutory *vires*, and providing no civil liberties issue was apparent on the face of the record,[89] he felt that the task and proper function of the Court was done. As he put it in his minority opinion in the *Phelps-Dodge* case,[90] partially dissenting, "Our only office is to determine whether the rule chosen, tested in the light of statutory standards, was within the permissible range of the Board's discretion." He followed the same track in discussing the actions of other administrative agencies, notably the Securities and Exchange Commission,[91] and the Federal Power Commission.[92] He was never particularly happy about the price control system, probably because of what he felt to be certain unconstitutional procedures that were established for handling violations[93]—and perhaps fundamentally because of his allergy to the war powers and all their legal ramifications—but he did join with Douglas in a dissent against a judicial weakening of the price control mechanism.[94] The Interstate Commerce Commission, however, often considered in liberal circles as a feudal vassal of the railroad interests, got little aid and comfort from Murphy.[95] In the *Inland Waterways* case, for example, there was no discussion by the dissenters of the finality of administrative determinations. On the contrary, Justice Black, speaking for Douglas and Murphy, asserted that

The issue in this case is whether the farmers and shippers of the middle west can be compelled by the Interstate Commerce Commission and the railroads to use high-priced rail instead of low-priced barge transportation for the shipment of grain to the east.[96]

This quotation, though from an opinion by Justice Black, brings out a characteristic that Murphy shared with Black and Douglas, a quality that I have designated "populism." There is a sentimental anti-capitalism, or more correctly, a sentimental attachment to a world of small businessmen and independent farmers, that comes out clearly in a series of opinions dealing with various aspects of the administrative process. In his concurring opinion in *United States* v. *Bethlehem Steel Corp.*,[97] Murphy, irritated by the profits claimed by the steel company in some World War I contracts, went out of his way to declare:

In voting for affirmance of the judgment, I do not wish to be understood as expressing approval of an arrangement like the one now under review, by which a company engaged in doing work for the government in time of grave national peril—or any other time—is entitled to a profit of 22 per cent under contracts involving little or no risk and grossing many millions of dollars. Such an arrangement not only is incompatible with sound principles of public management, but is injurious to public confidence and public morale.[98]

In this same "populist" tradition, we find him dissenting in behalf of the farmer-debtor burdened by a "narrow formalistic" interpretation of section 75 of the Bankruptcy Act,[99] and, in particular, advancing an anti-monopolistic interpretation of patent rights.[100] As might have been expected, he joined the Douglas dissent in *United States* v. *Columbia Steel Co.*,[101] which is as vigorous and well-reasoned an anti-monopoly tract as any populist could hope for. Perhaps the full flavor of this viewpoint is best set forth by an excerpt from a dissent by Justice Black in an enormously intricate case:

Hereafter, . . . the state in which the most powerful corporations are concentrated, *or those corporations themselves,* might well be able to pass laws which would govern contracts made by the people in all of the other states.[102]

Murphy joined Black in this opinion, which surely states in its essence the populist assumptions about the extent of corporate power over the political process.

In the general area of "states-rights" over interstate commerce, Murphy apparently had no strong views of his own. The evidence suggests that he accepted Chief Justice Stone's leadership in this tricky field until the latter died; then moved over to the Black-Douglas camp.[103] His one opinion of the Court in his connection dealt with a conflict between the I.C.C. and California.[104]

The Constitution and the war.—While Murphy differed in degree from his New Deal colleagues on many of these problems, it was in connection with the war powers that he demonstrated his uniqueness. While for all the other Justices, to a greater or lesser degree, the Constitution went into judicious hibernation during World War II, to Frank Murphy it stood in its pristine form as a guardian of the rights of the individual and the ideals of American society.

True, he got off to a slow start by disqualifying himself in Ex parte *Quirin,*[105] the case of the Nazi saboteurs, presumably because he was temporarily a Lieutenant Colonel in the Army on active service.[106] In the first draft case involving the rights of conscientious objectors, he joined the majority opinion, sustaining the government, rather than Jackson's dissent.[107] But from the *Hirabayashi* case[108] on, he was a consistent, even doctrinaire, opponent of the view that the Constitution had gone to war.

Here he violently parted company with his liberal brethren. Black and Douglas, in particular, became vigorous warhawks,[109] Jackson retired to a private universe of *realpolitik* suggesting that the Court should avoid ruling on nasty wartime problems since it was bound, given the power situation of the moment, to make bad decisions,[110] and even Rutledge, who had stood shoulder to shoulder with Murphy in many a lost cause, defected. In short, Justice Murphy found himself isolated on an extreme promontory, standing in lonely, and perhaps visionary, grandeur, and with the fiery virulence of a religious prophet, he castigated his friends and erstwhile associates for their betrayal of the democratic faith. Indeed, one suspects that he became a bit obsessed about the matter: a careful reading of the first two or three hundred pages of volume 327 of the United States Reports, beginning with the *Yamashita* case,[111] gives one the feeling that Murphy has become literally frenzied, striking back at his colleagues about him with the angry passon of a betrayed lover.

We have it on the testimony of his law clerk, Eugene Gressman, that Murphy almost immediately regretted his concurrence in the *Hirabayashi* case,[112] feeling that the real motive for the detention and expulsion of the Nisei from the west coast to concentration camps in the hinterland was not military, but racial. Only hesitantly had he given his approval to the judgment of the Court, and he insisted on writing a separate opinion to make clear his reasons. In this he stated:

In voting for the affirmance of this judgment I do not wish to be understood as intimating that the military authorities in time of war are subject to no restraints whatsoever, or that they are free to impose any restrictions they may choose on the rights and liberties of individual citizens or groups of citizens in those places which may be designated as "military areas." While this Court sits, it has the inescapable duty of seeing that the mandates of the Constitution are obeyed. That duty exists in time of war as well as in time of peace, and in its performance we must not forget that few indeed have been the invasions upon essential liberties which have not been accompanied by pleas of urgent necessity advanced in good faith by responsible men.[113]

When the plight of the American-Japanese came again to the Court in 1944, Justice Murphy drew the sword of duty and wrote one of the most passionate dissents in the history of the Supreme Court. He denied utterly that the decision had been founded on military criteria, and declared flatly that the evacuation and detention—for he refused to join the sophistry of the Court that these were separate, discrete actions—fell into "the ugly abyss of racism."[114] At the heart of his dissent is the point, ignored by Justice Black's majority opinion, that a "military judgment" cannot be simply, and circularly, defined as a judgment by a military officer. Thus the Court, while not having the right to supersede the Chiefs of Staff as military experts, has the duty to see that military judgments are *in fact* founded upon military considerations and not upon views on social policy temporarily in uniform.

With regard to the enforcement of the Selective Service Act, particularly with reference to conscientious objectors, Murphy consistently insisted that "all of the mobilization and all of the war effort will have been in vain if, when all is finished, we discover that in the process we have destroyed the very freedoms for which we fought."[115] Dissenting alone from Black's opinion of the Court in *Falbo* v. *United States*[116]—a case involving the rights of conscientious objectors—Murphy uttered what is probably the clearest and most forceful statement of his ideal:

The law knows no finer hour than when it cuts through formal concepts and transitory emotions to protect unpopular citizens against discrimination and persecution.

During the War, various sorts of legal action were brought against Nazi sympathizers and alleged enemy agents. When the convictions resulting from these actions came before the Supreme Court on appeal, Murphy without exception voted against affirmation, and was the only Justice with this record. It was his view that, if anything, the existence of a state of war required an increase in constitutional sensitivity and militantly flung his influence against the passions of the moment.[117]

Probably his most notable effort to view the tumults of the hour *sub specie aeternitatis* occurred when counsel for General Yamashita attempted to obtain a writ of habeas corpus from the high Court, claiming that the military commission established to try Japanese "war criminals" was unconstitutional and without jurisdiction. The Court held itself without jurisdiction—at least this seems to be what the Court held: the opinion is, in John P. Frank's words, "sufficiently opaque to defy brief statement"[118]—with Rutledge writing a separate solitary dissent.[119] Murphy's dissent was a blistering attack on the whole war crimes procedure in the Far East as "unworthy of the traditions of our people."[120] Noting that the real lesson of the trials was "Don't Ever Lose a War," he asserted that even the admitted Japanese atrocities "do not justify our abandonment of our devotion to justice in dealing with a fallen enemy commander. To conclude otherwise is to admit that the enemy has lost the battle but has destroyed our ideals."[121]

Murphy's anti-militarism was more dogged than fruitful, but it can be found in a whole series of opinions, the most noteworthy of which is his lengthy concurring opinion in *Duncan* v. *Kahanamoku*[122] reasserting the vitality of David Davis' sonorous holding in Ex parte *Milligan*[123] that "the Constitution of the United States is a law for rulers and people, equally in war and peace, and covers with the shield of its protection all classes of men, at all times, and under all circumstances."[124] And who but Murphy could have achieved the combination of anti-militarism and populism attained by the following statement:

> In my opinion it is of greater importance to the nation at war and to its military establishment that high standards of public health be maintained than that the military procurement authorities have the benefit of unrestrained competitive bidding and lower prices in the purchase of needed milk supplies.[125]

In regard to Murphy's attitude toward the war powers, there is one point that remains for brief treatment: his attitude toward the limitations on the right of appeal incorporated in the price control legislation. It will be recalled that an Emergency Court of Appeals was established to handle cases arising under the statute and elaborate procedures were set up governing the legal aspects of appeal. When in 1944, the constitutionality of this structure was challenged, Roberts, Rutledge, and Murphy dissented from Stone's holding that it was a valid exercise of the war powers.[126] That this was not just constitutional windmill-tilting is suggested by the fact that the Rutledge dissent, which Murphy joined, impressed even such a hard-boiled realist as Edward S. Corwin.[127]

This examination of the judicial record of Justice Murphy has, I suspect, been a tedious trip for the reader. However, it seems important to get the data on the record before moving on to summarize what seems to me the judicial essence of Frank Murphy.

It was suggested earlier that Justice Frank Murphy was the judicial incarnation of the militant liberal myth of the New Deal, and while at some points, e.g., his view of trade unions, he fell a bit short of the archetypical aspiration, it is nonetheless true that he fitted the pattern far more closely than did any of his New Deal colleagues on the Court. While each of the other Justices went part way down the road with him, each turned off somewhere short of Murphy's destination.

But this still leaves open the persistent question: Was Murphy a "good" judge? To the extent that this means: Was he a good legal craftsman? I would venture the opinion that while Justice Murphy did not have the technical competence of a Frankfurter or a Stone, he was certainly not below par for the Court. This judgment is based both on a careful reading of every opinion he wrote, including a mass of technical tax opinions that have not been discussed here, and my belief, as explained earlier, that the question of authorship is irrelevant. The basic proposition that has to be understood in dealing with Murphy, I think, was that he *chose* not to immerse himself in the mysteries of the guild.

This choice was based on both temperamental and intellectual reasons: by temperament he was a fighter who was aroused by seeming injustice and did not want to check the rule book before he went into action; by intellect he was an instrumentalist, not in the Deweyan sense of being a pragmatist, but in the natural law tradition of viewing all the phenomena of the world about us in terms of a higher purpose, as instruments for the fulfillment of the *telos*. In other words, Murphy mounted the wild horse of natural law and mercilessly rode down those institutions, traditions, legal precedents, which stood between him and his destination—a democratic utopia.

Therefore it is perhaps not unfair to his memory to suggest that he was the McReynolds of the left, though I hasten to add that he did not share the latter's misanthropic disposition. Like McReynolds, he was a vigorous, even belligerent, fighter for the things he believed in, and like McReynolds, he called a spade a spade. He was also a judicial activist, who had no time for philosophies of "self-restraint"—except, of course, when judicial self-restraint contributed to his substantive goal. But here he was in good company. Even the Court's leading advocate of self-restraint, Justice Frankfurter, has been known to rise above principle—a dissent in *Brown* v. *Board of Education*[128] would surely have followed logically from the author of the *Gobitis* opinion.[129]

Thus, there was a quality about Murphy that made him an asset to the Court. No one, and certainly no student of constitutional law, would want a Supreme Court composed entirely of Murphys—or of Jacksons, or Frankfurters, for that matter—but is it not valuable to sprinkle the high tribunal from time to time with men who, disdaining the tortuous paths of the law, assert in a clarion peal the basic truth, so often forgotten by those with their noses close to the earth of precedent, that law is at root an instrument for the achievement of social goals? And that in a democracy, there are no more priceless goals than individual liberty and collective prosperity? If this is the case, then the utopian pilgrimage of Mr. Justice Murphy was not made in vain.

JOHN P. ROCHE *is Morris Hillquit Professor of Labor and Social Thought, Chairman of the Department of Politics, and former Dean of Faculty at Brandeis University. He is the author of numerous scholarly articles on American Constitutional History and his books include* Courts and Rights, *1961; and* The Quest for the Dream: Civil Liberty in Modern America, *1963.*

We are indebted to the Vanderbilt Law Review *for permission to use materials first published there.*

NOTES

1. 48 MICH. L. REV. 737–810 (1950).

2. *Ibid.* See also Frank, *Justice Murphy: The Goals Attempted,* 59 YALE L. J. 1 (1949); Gressman, *Mr. Justice Murphy: A Preliminary Appraisal,* 50 COLUM. L. REV. 29 (1950); Arnold, *Mr. Justice Murphy,* 63 HARV. L. REV. 289 (1940). Since 1957, two articles of merit have appeared: Gressman, *The Controversial Image of Mr. Justice Murphy,* 47 GEO. L. J. 631 (1959), and Howard, *Frank Murphy and the Sit-Down Strikes of 1937,* 1 LABOR HISTORY 103 (1960).

3. Pritchett, *The Roosevelt Court* (1948), 285.

4. Kurland, Review of Pritchett, *Civil Liberties and the Vinson Court,* 22 U. CHI. L. REV. 297, 299 (1954).

5. Mason, *Harlan Fiske Stone: Pillar of the Law* (1956), 793.

6. 321 U.S. 590 (1944).

7. *Ibid.* at 592.

8. *Ibid.* at 606.

9. See Roche, *Plessy* v. *Ferguson: Requiescat in Pace?* 103 U. PA. L. REV. 44, 52 (1954).

10. *Minersville School District* v. *Gobitis,* 310 U.S. 586, 601 (1940).

11. Interview cited in Mason, *op. cit. supra* note 5, at 528.

12. *Ibid.* at 513. (*United States* v. *Carolene Products Co.,* 304 U.S. 144 [1938].)

13. *Ibid.* at 505. (*Helvering* v. *Gerhardt,* 304 U.S. 405 [1938].)

14. Murphy had four clerks in nine years: E. L. Huddleson,

1940–41; John H. Pickering, 1941–43; Eugene Gressman, 1943–48; T. L. Tolan, Jr., 1948–49.

15. 323 U.S. 214, 233 (1944).

16. *Cohens* v. *Virginia*, 6 Wheat. 264 U.S. (1821). In Henry Adams' phrase, Marshall was the "despair of bench and bar for the unswerving certainty of his legal method." 1 *The Formative Years* (Agar ed., 1948), 104.

17. For a superb analysis of Roosevelt and the New Deal, see Burns, *Roosevelt: The Lion and the Fox* (1956).

18. 328 U.S. 463, 490 (1946).

19. *Hooven & Allison Co.* v. *Evatt*, 324 U.S. 652, 691 (1945).

20. Governor Murphy was apparently quite close to the Catholic Worker movement, which was, and is, strongly pro-labor.

21. Quoted by Carr, *Federal Protection of Civil Rights* (1947), 25.

22. *Ibid.* at 1. (Emphasis added.)

23. *Ibid.* at 26 n. 37.

24. For a good discussion of the various strands of New Deal liberalism, see Goldman, *Rendezvous with Destiny* (rev. ed., 1956). The treatment of Roosevelt's relations with the left by Hofstadter, *The American Political Tradition* (1948), 331 is full of insight. I should note that much of this composite of the militant liberal I gained from intensive reading of the liberal and radical literature of the 30's and 40's. The files of *The Nation* and *The New Republic* are indispensable and, for a somewhat jaundiced view of the New Deal that yet remains within the militant liberal tradition, *Common Sense* is most revealing.

25. *Minersville School District* v. *Gobitis*, 310 U.S. 586 (1940).

26. 316 U.S. 584, 611 (1942). Murphy here joined the penitential dissent of Justices Black and Douglas in which the trio apologized for joining the majority in *Gobitis*. *Ibid.* at 623.

27. 336 U.S. 77, 89 (1949).

28. 321 U.S. 158, 171 (1944).

29. *Ibid.* at 174–76.

30. *In re Summers*, 325 U.S. 561 (1945).

31. *Chatwin* v. *United States*, 326 U.S. 455 (1946).

32. A state law prohibiting the advocacy, encouragement, etc., of polygamy: *Musser* v. *Utah*, 333 U.S. 95, 98 (1948); the employment of the Mann Act: *Cleveland* v. *United States*, 329 U.S. 14, 24 (1946). In the latter case, he observed in dissent: "[M]arriage, even when it occurs in a form of which we disapprove, is not to be compared with prostitution or debauchery. . . ." 329 U.S. at 26.

33. 323 U.S. 192 (1944).

34. *Ibid.* at 208–09.

35. *Screws* v. *United States*, 325 U.S. 91, 134 (1945).

36. 332 U.S. 633, 650 (1948).

37. *Takahashi* v. *Fish & Game Comm'n*, 334 U.S. 410, 422 (1948).

38. See *Confederated Bands of Ute Indians* v. *United States,* 330 U.S. 169, 180 (1947); *Northwestern Bands of Shoshone Indians* v. *United States,* 324 U.S. 335, 362 (1945); *Mahnomen County* v. *United States,* 319 U.S. 474, 480 (1943); *Oklahoma Tax Comm'n* v. *United States,* 319 U.S. 598, 612 (1943); *Creek Nation* v. *United States,* 318 U.S. 629, 641 (1943). In each of these cases he dissented. In this area, he wrote two opinions of the Court: *Choctaw Nation of Indians* v. *United States,* 318 U.S. 423 (1943); *Seminole Nation* v. *United States,* 316 U.S. 286 (1942).

39. Joining Black's dissent in *Colgrove* v. *Green,* 328 U.S. 549, 566 (1946).

40. Joining Douglas' dissent in *MacDougall* v. *Green,* 335 U.S. 281, 287 (1948).

41. Joining Douglas' opinion of the Court in *Terminiello* v. *Chicago,* 337 U.S. 1 (1949).

42. Dissenting in *Eisler* v. *United States,* 338 U.S. 189, 193 (1949).

43. Concurring opinion in *Bridges* v. *Wixon,* 326 U.S. 135, 157 (1945). In general, see this opinion for his views on deportation procedure. He also joined the dissenting opinions in *Ahrens* v. *Clark,* 335 U.S. 188, 193 (1948); *Ludecke* v. *Watkins,* 335 U.S. 160, 173 (1948).

44. *Schneiderman* v. *United States,* 320 U.S. 118, 145 (1943). Wendell Willkie was Schneiderman's council. This opinion, when circulated among his brethren for their comments, brought the following rejoinder from an unidentified Justice: "I think it is only fair to state in view of your general argument that Uncle Joe Stalin is at least a spiritual co-author with Jefferson of the Virginia statute for religious freedom." Cited by Mason, *op. cit. supra* note 5, at 795.

45. Murphy concurred in *Baumgartner* v. *United States,* 322 U.S. 665, 678 (1944), objecting to Frankfurter's watering down of his Schneiderman rationale; and joined Rutledge's dissent in *Knauer* v. *United States,* 328 U.S. 654, 675 (1946), and the latter's concurrence in *Klapprott* v. *United States,* 335 U.S. 601, 616 (1949).

46. *Mortensen* v. *United States,* 322 U.S. 369, 375 (1944).

47. *United States* v. *Beach,* 324 U.S. 193, 196 (1945).

48. 329 U.S. 173, 182 (1946).

49. *Ibid.* at 183.

50. *Canizio* v. *New York,* 327 U.S. 82, 87 (1946).

51. *Glasser* v. *United States,* 315 U.S. 60 (1942).

52. *Craig* v. *Harney,* 331 U.S. 367 (1947).

53. 328 U.S. 331, 369 (1946).

54. *Ibid.* at 370.

55. 331 U.S. at 394.

56. See his dissents in *Fisher* v. *Pace*, 336 U.S. 155, 166 (1949); *United States* v. *United Mine Workers*, 330 U.S. 258, 335 (1947).

57. See, e.g., *Taylor* v. *Alabama*, 335 U.S. 252 (1948); *Lee* v. *Mississippi*, 332 U.S. 742 (1948); *Lyons* v. *Oklahoma*, 322 U.S. 596 (1944).

58. See, e.g., *Shapiro v. United States*, 335 U.S. 1, 70 (1948); *Adamson* v. *California*, 332 U.S. 46, 123 (1947); *Goldman* v. *United States*, 316 U.S. 129, 136 (1942); *Goldstein* v. *United States*, 316 U.S. 114, 122 (1942).

59. See, e.g., *Wolf* v. *Colorado*, 338 U.S. 25, 41 (1949); *Trupiano* v. *United States*, 334 U.S. 699 (1948); *Johnson* v. *United States*, 333 U.S. 10 (1948); *Harris* v. *United States*, 331 U.S. 145, 183 (1947); *Zap* v. *United States*, 328 U.S. 624 (1946); *Davis* v. *United States*, 328 U.S. 582, 594 (1946).

60. See, e.g., *Frazier* v. *United States*, 335 U.S. 497, 514 (1948); *Moore* v. *New York*, 333 U.S. 565, 569 (1948); *Fay* v. *New York*, 332 U.S. 261, 296 (1947); *Thiel* v. *Southern Pacific Co.*, 328 U.S. 217 (1946); *Akins* v. *Texas*, 325 U.S. 398, 407 (1945).

61. See, e.g., *Wade* v. *Mayo*, 334 U.S. 672 (1948); *Price* v. *Johnston*, 334 U.S. 266 (1948); *Parker* v. *Illinois*, 333 U.S. 571, 577 (1948); *Marino* v. *Ragen* 332 U.S. 561, 563 (1947); Ex parte *Hull*, 312 U.S. 546 (1941).

62. 315 U.S. 357 (1942).

63. *Endicott Johnson Corp.* v. *Perkins*, 317 U.S. 501, 510 (1943).

64. *Oklahoma Press Co.* v. *Walling*, 327 U.S. 186, 219 (1946).

65. 331 U.S. 111 (1947).

66. *United States* v. *Classic*, 313 U.S. 299, 329 (1941).

67. 320 U.S. 277, 285 (1943).

68. See his dissent in *National Broadcasting Co.* v. *United States*, 319 U.S. 190, 227 (1943), discussed *infra;* his agreement with Roberts' dissent in *California* v. *United States*, 320 U.S. 577, 586 (1944); his opinion for the Court in *Kraus & Bros. Inc.* v. *United States*, 327 U.S. 614 (1946).

69. *National Broadcasting Co.* v. *United States*, 319 U.S. 190, 227 (1943).

70. *Associated Press* v. *United States*, 326 U.S. 1, 49 (1945).

71. Frank, *supra* note 2, at 3.

72. 319 U.S. at 228.

73. 326 U.S. at 51.

74. *Ibid.* at 50, 52. (Emphasis added.)

75. 335 U.S. 106, 129 (1948).

76. See, e.g., his opinions in *United States* v. *Yellow Cab Co.*,

332 U.S. 218 (1947); *United States* v. *Walsh*, 331 U.S. 432 (1947).

77. He also in a sense defended "states-rights" in the area of divorce. Some have suggested that this was his Catholic conviction surfacing in a sphere where the Church holds strong views, but the logic of this contention escapes me. After all, he was not denying the right of a state to grant a divorce to bona fide residents, but rather disagreeing with the conditions under which "full faith and credit" shall be given to a divorce consummated in another state. In what were probably the most important cases—*Coe* v. *Coe*, 334 U.S. 378 (1948); *Sherrer* v. *Sherrer*, 334 U.S. 343, 356 (1948)— he joined Justice Frankfurter's learned, masterful dissents. See also his concurring opinion in *Williams* v. *North Carolina*, 325 U.S. 226, 239 (1945), and his dissent in *Williams* v. *North Carolina*, 317 U.S. 287, 308 (1942). In another area where his religion might have been expected to influence his judgment, if anywhere, there is no apparent correlation. In the "separation of church and state" cases, he participated only by his vote first one way and then the other. See *Illinois* ex rel. *McCollum* v. *Board of Education*, 333 U.S. 203 (1948); *Everson* v. *Board of Education*, 330 U.S. 1 (1947). Murphy's religious convictions gave him a deep set of natural law premises that penetrated every aspect of his legal thought, but did not result in any immediately "religious" opinions.

78. See his opinions in *Bordon Co.* v. *Borella*, 326 U.S. 679 (1945); *Jewel Ridge Coal Corp.* v. *United Mine Workers*, 325 U.S. 161 (1945); *Phillips Inc.* v. *Walling*, 324 U.S. 490 (1945); *United States v. Rosenwasser*, 323 U.S. 360 (1945); *Overstreet* v. *North Shore Corp.*, 318 U.S. 125 (1943); *Warren-Bradshaw Drilling Co.* v. *Hall*, 317 U.S. 88 (1942). See also his dissents in *10 East 40th Street Building, Inc.* v. *Callus*, 325 U.S. 578, 585 (1945); *Western Union Tel. Co.* v. *Lenroot*, 323 U.S. 490, 509 (1945); *McLeod* v. *Threlkeld*, 319 U.S. 491, 498 (1943). His one rejection of the claims for broad coverage may have been motivated by his special concern for the press, or by simple common sense. In 1946, he dissented from the Court's holding that a newspaper that shipped 45 of 10,000 newspapers into interstate commerce was subject to coverage under the F.L.S.A. *Mabee* v. *White Plains Publishing Co.*, 327 U.S. 178, 185 (1946).

79. *Jewel Ridge Coal Corp.* v. *United Mine Workers*, 325 U.S. 161 (1945).

80. See, for a discussion of the difficulties involved in getting a judicial evaluation of the "death sentence" provision of the Public Utilities Holding Company Act, Stern, *The Commerce Clause and the National Economy, 1933–1946*, 59 HARV. L. REV. 883, 940–42 (1946).

81. *American Power & Light Co.* v. *S.E.C.*, 329 U.S. 90 (1946); *North American Co.* v. *S.E.C.*, 327 U.S. 686 (1946).

82. 310 U.S. 88 (1940).

83. 310 U.S. 106 (1940).

84. *Milk Wagon Drivers Union* v. *Meadowmoor Dairies*, 312 U.S. 287 (1941).

85. *Ibid.* at 308–309.

86. 315 U.S. 722, 729 (1942).

87. 327 U.S. 582, 606 (1946).

88. *A.F.L.* v. *American Sash & Door Co.*, 335 U.S. 538 (1949); *Lincoln Federal Labor Union* v. *Northwestern Iron & Metal Co.*, 335 U.S. 525 (1949). In the former case, he dissented without opinion; in the latter he concurred in Rutledge's opinion which accepted the judgment, but not the rationale, of the Court.

89. This respect for what the British term the "principles of natural justice" appears clearly in two cases: In 1941, Murphy wrote the opinion remanding to the N.L.R.B. the *Virginia Power Co.* case for evidence that defendants had not merely been exercising their right of freedom of speech in encouraging a company union. *N.L.R.B.* v. *Virginia Elec. & Power Co.*, 314 U.S. 469 (1941). The N.L.R.B. adduced further evidence that coercion beyond mere verbal encouragement had been involved, and on the basis of the new record, the Court, through Murphy, sustained the Board's disestablishment of the company union. *Virginia Elec. & Power Co.* v. *N.L.R.B.*, 319 U.S. 533 (1943). In 1949, he employed the same technique in *N.L.R.B.* v. *Stowe Spinning Co.*, 336 U.S. 226 (1949), supporting the Board up to the point where an employer was handed a broad, vague injunction to desist from frustrating certain union activities. The latter technique, he maintained, was bad, and the injunction must be reformulated in specific, equitable terms.

90. *Phelps Dodge Corp.* v. *N.L.R.B.*, 313 U.S. 177, 206 (1941). See also his dissent for the Board in *International Union of Mine Workers* v. *Eagle-Picher Mining & Smelting Co.*, 325 U.S. 335, 344 (1945), and his agreement with Reed's dissent in *Southern S.S. Co.* v. *N.L.R.B.*, 316 U.S. 31, 49 (1942).

91. See his opinions for the Court in *S.E.C.* v. *Howey Co.*, 328 U.S. 293 (1946).

92. See his dissent in *Connecticut Light & Power Co.* v. *F.P.C.*, 324 U.S. 515, 536 (1945), and his concurrence in *F.P.C.* v. *Natural Gas Pipeline Co.*, 315 U.S. 575, 599 (1942).

93. He joined the Rutledge dissent in *Yakus* v. *United States*, 321 U.S. 414, 460 (1944), in which the two Justices asserted that the procedures for handling violations impaired constitutional liberties.

94. *Davies Warehouse Co.* v. *Bowles*, 321 U.S. 144, 156 (1944).

But see *Kraus Bros.* v. *United States,* 327 U.S. 614 (1946), in which he condemned the creation of ambiguous offences by the Price Control Administration.

95. See his agreement with Roberts' dissent in *California* v. *United States,* 320 U.S. 577, 586 (1944), and his agreement with Black's dissent in *I.C.C.* v. *Inland Waterways Corp.,* 319 U.S. 671, 692 (1943).

96. 319 U.S. at 692.

97. 315 U.S. 289, 310 (1942).

98. *Ibid.*

99. *State Bank* v. *Brown,* 317 U.S. 135, 142 (1942). See also his opinion for the Court in *Carter* v. *Kubler,* 320 U.S. 243 (1943).

100. See his position in *Bruce's Juices, Inc.* v. *American Can Co.,* 330 U.S. 743, 757 (1947); *Transparent-Wrap Mach. Corp.* v. *Stokes & Smith Co.,* 329 U.S. 637, 648 (1947); *Precision Instrument Mfg. Co.* v. *Automotive Maintenance Co.,* 324 U.S. 806 (1945); *Central States Elec. Co.* v. *City of Muscatine,* 324 U.S. 138, 146 (1945); *Goodyear Tire & Rubber Co.* v. *Ray-O-Vac Co.,* 321 U.S. 275, 279 (1944).

101. 334 U.S. 495, 534 (1948).

102. *Order of United Commercial Travelers* v. *Wolfe,* 331 U.S. 586, 642 (1947). (Emphasis added.)

103. He joined Stone's dissent in *Cloverleaf Butter Co.* v. *Patterson,* 315 U.S. 148, 177 (1942); Stone's opinion for the Court in *Southern Pacific Co.* v. *Arizona,* 325 U.S. 761 (1945); Stone's concurrence in *New York* v. *United States,* 326 U.S. 572, 586 (1946). He only joined Black and Douglas once prior to Stone's death, dissenting in *Nippert* v. *Richmond,* 327 U.S. 416, 435 (1946). From that time on, however, he was generally with Black and Douglas. See *Interstate Oil Pipe-line Co.* v. *Stone,* 337 U.S. 662 (1949); *H. P. Hood & Sons, Inc.* v. *Du Mond,* 336 U.S. 525, 545 (1949); *Central Greyhound Lines, Inc.* v. *Mealey,* 334 U.S. 653, 664 (1948).

104. *California* v. *Zook,* 336 U.S. 725 (1949). This is the case in which he wrote the opinion of the Court sustaining the California Motor Carrier Act.

105. 317 U.S. 1 (1942).

106. Mason, *op. cit. supra* note 5, at 655.

107. *Bowles* v. *United States,* 319 U.S. 33, 36 (1943).

108. *Hirabayashi* v. *United States,* 320 U.S. 81, 109 (1943).

109. See, e.g., their dissents in *Viereck* v. *United States,* 318 U.S. 236, 249 (1943), and *Cramer* v. *United States,* 325 U.S. 1 (1945); Black's opinions for the Court in *Korematsu* v. *United States,* 323 U.S. 214 (1944), and *Falbo* v. *United States,* 320 U.S. 549 (1944); Douglas' opinion for the Court in *Singer* v. *United*

States, 323 U.S. 338 (1945), for their general approach to the interpretation of war powers.

110. See his amazing dissent in *Korematsu* v. *United States,* 323 U.S. 214, 242 (1944), for a full statement of his views.

111. *In re Yamashita,* 327 U.S. 1, 26 (1946).

112. Gressman, *supra* note 2, at 36.

113. 320 U.S. at 113.

114. *Korematsu* v. *United States,* 323 U.S. 214, 233 (1944).

115. Concurring separately in *Estep* v. *United States,* 327 U.S. 114, 132 (1946). See also his dissents in *Sunal* v. *Large,* 332 U.S. 174, 193 (1947), and *Cox* v. *United States,* 332 U.S. 442, 457 (1947); and his agreement with Frankfurter's dissent, in *Singer* v. *United States,* 323 U.S. 338, 346 (1945).

116. 320 U.S. 549, 561 (1944).

117. See *Von Moltke* v. *Gillies,* 332 U.S. 708 (1948); *Haupt* v. *United States,* 330 U.S. 631, 646 (1947); *Keegan* v. *United States,* 325 U.S. 478 (1945); *Cramer* v. *United States,* 325 U.S. 1 (1945); *Hartzel* v. *United States,* 332 U.S. 680 (1944); *Viereck* v. *United States,* 318 U.S. 236 (1943).

118. Frank, *Cases on Constitutional Law* (1950), 797.

119. *In re Yamashita,* 327 U.S. 1, 41 (1946).

120. *Ibid.* at 28.

121. *Ibid* at 29.

122. 327 U.S. 304, 324 (1946). See also *Humphrey* v. *Smith,* 336 U.S. 695, 701 (1949); *Wade* v. *Hunter,* 336 U.S. 684, 692 (1949); *Hirota* v. *MacArthur,* 338 U.S. 197 (1948).

123. 4 Wall. 2 (1866).

124. 327 U.S. at 335.

125. Concurring opinion, in *Penn Dairies, Inc.* v. *Milk Control Comm.,* 318 U.S. 261, 280 (1943).

126. *Yakus* v. *United States,* 321 U.S. 414, 460 (1944).

127. Corwin, *Total War and the Constitution* (1947), 131.

128. 347 U.S. 483 (1954).

129. See my discussion of this point in Roche, *Judicial Self-Restraint,* 49 Am. Pol. Sci. Rev. 762 (1955).

Courtesy of Harris & Ewing

MR. JUSTICE RUTLEDGE

Mr. Justice Rutledge

By
JOHN PAUL STEVENS

In July, 1947, a group of German nationals, deemed by the Attorney General to be dangerous to the peace and safety of the United States because they had adhered to Nazi principles, were in custody on Ellis Island awaiting deportation. A petition for a writ of habeas corpus challenging the power of the Attorney General to order their removal was filed in their behalf in the United States District Court for the District of Columbia. In response, the Attorney General challenged the power of the court to issue the writ. He pointed out that jurisdiction to issue writs of habeas corpus is granted to federal districts courts only "within their respective jurisdictions" and that the prisoners were being held outside the territorial confines of the District of Columbia. The argument was accepted by the District Court for the District of Columbia, by the Court of Appeals, and ultimately by the Supreme Court, even though the Attorney General had informed the Supreme Court that he was willing to waive his objections to jurisdiction in order to have the validity of his removal orders considered on the merits.

The Supreme Court held that the jurisdictional defect could not be waived. The crucial phrase in the statute—"within their respective jurisdictions"—had been inserted in 1867 for the specific purpose of imposing a territorial limitation on a district court's power to issue the writ. The limitation avoided the danger of a "clashing of jurisdictions" among the courts, which in turn might result in the unnecessary transportation of prisoners over great distances. In short, the language of the statute, construed in the light of the history of the 1867 amendment, compelled the conclusion that a district court has no power to issue a writ of habeas corpus unless the applicant is detained within its district.

From this conclusion, Justice Wiley Rutledge vigorously dissented. This dissent in the case of *Ahrens* v. *Clark*,[1] though by no means his finest, is nevertheless sufficiently representative to provide us with an introduction to its author's judicial career.

Wiley Rutledge became a Justice of the United States Court of Appeals for the District of Columbia on May 2, 1939, just a few months before the outbreak of World War II. Previously, he had lived in Kentucky, Tennessee, Wisconsin, Indiana, New Mexico, Colorado, Missouri, and Iowa. He had practiced law briefly; primarily he had been a teacher—first in high schools, later a law professor and dean.

Appropriately, his first opinion as a Justice was in a suit brought against Howard University by a law professor whose services had been terminated because he had testified before a congressional committee in opposition to a proposed appropriation for the university. After carefully reviewing all the facts, and the pertinent authorities, Justice Rutledge writing for the Court concluded that Professor Cobb was not entitled to reinstatement.[2]

Similarly, in his last opinion as a Justice of the Supreme Court Rutledge rejected an individual's claim that one of his fundamental freedoms had been invaded.[3] Over the impassioned dissent of three members of the Court,[4] Rutledge and the majority found probable cause for the search without warrant of the defendant Brinegar's automobile. Neither at the beginning nor at the end of his judicial career did Justice Rutledge automatically champion a claimed individual liberty. In civil liberties cases, as in others, his judgments were predicated on a painstaking review of every aspect of the litigation which came before him for decision.

Much of the litigation in the federal courts between the decision of *Cobb* v. *Howard University* in 1939 and *Brinegar* v. *United States* in 1949 was either directly connected with World War II and its aftermath or else presented questions which took on added significance against the backdrop of the struggle with totalitarian regimes. Thus, the question of the availability of the writ of habeas corpus presented in *Ahrens* v. *Clark* was raised by internees about to be deported as dangerous enemy aliens. Here, as in other cases, the identity and personal beliefs of the litigants were matters of complete indifference to Justice Rutledge.

If there ever was a man whose principles and whole mode of living were the antitheses of naziism, it was Wiley Rutledge. He was annoyed that law clerks recently discharged from military service found it difficult to remain seated when a Supreme Court Justice intruded on their labors. He liked to travel by day coach because he enjoyed the conversation of his fellow passengers. Without identifying himself, he would promptly disagree with a traffic policeman's unjust verdict on the quality of his driving. He welcomed discussions with his colleagues on the Court—but none could summon him. After a visit with the President of the United States, his principal comment concerned his host's obviously genuine affection for people.

Since he did not judge people by classification, it is hardly surprising that he did not recognize different classes of litigants. He showed the same concern with a defendant's claim that double punishment for the same act was unconstitutional in a prosecution of the American Tobacco Company for monopolizing and conspiring to restrain trade[5] as he did in a police court prosecution for drunken driving and driving on the wrong side of the road.[6] In neither case was the amount of the fine extreme but in both instances the nature of the problem moved him to write a separate concurring opinion. Concurring in a judgment that the evidence did not justify the denaturalization of an admitted Communist, Rutledge "doubted that the framers of the Constitution intended to create two classes of citizens, one free and independent, one haltered with a lifetime string tied to its status."[7] While on the Court of Appeals, he explained the basis of the privilege against self-incrimination as resting in part on "a sense of fairness to the person accused, a respect for his individual integrity, in accusation or even in guilt."[8] During the war, he contrasted the political philosophy of the free nations with that of their enemies by stating that free people adhere generally "to the element that men have rights in their own communities, not by virtue of race or color, but by virtue of being men."[9]

The petitioners in the *Ahrens* case were men whose application for habeas corpus raised an issue affecting every member of the community equally. Justice Rutledge began his dissent by describing the importance of that issue. The decision of the majority, he wrote, "attenuates the personal security of every citizen."[10]

For if absence of the body from the jurisdiction is alone conclusive against existence of power to issue the writ, what of the case where the place of imprisonment, whether by private or public action, is unknown? What also of the situation where that place is located in one district, but the jailer is present in and can be served with process only in another? And if the place of detention lies wholly outside the territorial limits of any federal jurisdiction, although the person or persons exercising restraint are clearly within reach of such authority, is there to be no remedy, even though it is American citizens who are wrongfully deprived of their liberty and Americans answerable to no other power who deprive them of it, whether purporting to act officially or otherwise? In all these cases may the jailers stand in defiance of federal judicial power, and plead either the accident of the locus of detention outside the court's territorial limitations, or their own astuteness in so selecting the place to nullify judicial competence?[11]

This emphasis on the significance of the majority decision does not, of course, prove that the majority's terse, five-page opinion came to the wrong conclusion. It does prove, however, that the problem merited the careful and thorough study that produced a dissenting opinion of eighteen pages. Justice Rutledge frequently wrote long opinions, and sometimes his style seems redundant. He habitually used a pair of words where one would have served almost as well. Thus in one paragraph of the *Ahrens* opinion, he referred to the legislative "*history* and its *effect* for the statute's *meaning* and *purpose,* the considerations of *policy* and *convenience*" relating to the writ's "*availability* and *adaptability* to all the varying *conditions* and *devices* by which liberty may be unlawfully restrained" (emphasis added).[12] He sometimes repeated the same thought at different places in an opinion; indeed, in the *United Mine Workers* dissent he used the same sentence twice.[13] The sentence—"No man or group is above the law"—like other ideas repeated in his opinions, warrants restatement in different contexts.

Although long, Rutledge's opinions are easily read and understood. Apparently his style was deliberately chosen to give full expression to his precise meaning, for he could express himself in terse and amiable fashion when he chose. Thus after carefully analyzing and answering an involved contention that a statute of limitations did not bar an action by a carrier against a shipper, even though it admittedly barred a similar action by a shipper against a carrier, Rutledge summed up his reasoning in one sentence: "But this case boils down to an old adage about sauce and geese, which need not be given citation."[14] In a case where he had to decide whether an adventuress was guilty of larceny from the person when the evidence showed that her victim had removed his trousers before she removed his ten dollars, the Justice wistfully commented that perhaps the case was one "in which the doctrine of 'assumption of risk' should be transferred from the field of civil liability to that of criminal liability."[15] On one occasion he even quoted a short original poem as a substitute for a long opinion.[16]

Quite clearly, the principal explanation for the length of his opinions has nothing to do with his style. Instead, the length was primarily a matter of finding it necessary to say a great deal in order to explain fully the reasons for his decision. If the case turned on its facts, all material facts were carefully reviewed.[17] Whether facts or law were controlling, the argument to be met was fully stated in order to make the precise import of the decision clear.[18] When policy considerations, such as the need to combat inflation in the midst of the war, seemed overwhelmingly to demand a result which Rutledge could not accept,[19] he candidly acknowledged the force of those considerations before outlining the reasons which he found more compelling. To me, Rutledge's long opinions are evidence of two virtues of a great judge—tolerance and judgment. The full statement of the opposing argument and countervailing considerations reflects a habit of understanding before disagreeing. The full statement of all the factors which lead to and qualify the result which is eventually reached— though exasperating to a hurried practitioner seeking a succinct statement of a "true rule"—indicates that the faculty of judgment and not merely the logical application of unbending principles has been employed to resolve an actual controversy between litigants.

The former dean's scholarship also contributed to the length of his opinions. Whereas the majority in the *Ahrens* case merely cited a string of nine federal cases to support the statement that the general view was that the Court's habeas corpus jurisdiction was confined to cases where the applicant was physically within the district,[20] Rutledge carefully classified the authorities. He accepted the premise that the jurisdiction of the United States District Court was territorial, but he then emphasized that the Attorney General who had custody of the prisoners was within the district and therefore subject to the court's process. He cited a number of common-law decisions holding that a court has power to compel the production of a prisoner if personal jurisdiction can be obtained over his custodian. He then turned to the authorities cited by the majority, and in a short paragraph documented with copious footnotes, stated: "When the cases where both the custodian and his prisoner are outside the territorial jurisdiction of the court are separated from those where the custodian is within the jurisdiction though the prisoner is elsewhere, the weight of authority in the lower federal courts is opposed to the conclusion reached today. . . ."[21]

This careful use of precedents was characteristic of Rutledge. His classification of the cases on the tort liability of a charitable institution unquestionably marks his opinion in *Georgetown College* v. *Hughes*[22] as the leading case on that subject. His opinion in *Frene* v. *Louisville Cement Co.*,[23] dealing with corporate presence for purposes of service of process, is entitled to equal respect. And many other examples of his fine scholarship could be cited.[24]

Although the use of state and lower federal court decisions in the *Ahrens* dissent was effective, it by no means demonstrated that the Supreme Court had misconstrued the meaning of the statutory words "within their respective jurisdictions." Rutledge did not so contend. He merely used the cases to illustrate that his view, and the prevailing view in other courts, was consistent with the language of Congress. For, as the cases showed, the United States District Courts could effectively act "within their respective jurisdictions" as long as the jailer was present, regardless of where he kept his prisoners. Characteristically, however, Rutledge acknowledged that the Court's principal reliance was placed on the legislative history of the 1867 amendment, and therefore that history, not merely the act's language, had to be examined.

The principal purpose of the 1867 statute was to authorize the issuance of the writ of habeas corpus to relieve any detention in violation of federal law, even though the prisoner was in state custody. As originally drafted, the bill was subject to the interpretation that it would confer power upon district judges to issue process which would run throughout the country. The bill was amended to avoid that possibility. But in connection with the amendment, no mention was made of the problem presented when the jailer is within the district though the prisoner is elsewhere. Since the senators' concern related to the extent of the court's power to issue process, the service of the writ upon a jailer within the court's jurisdiction would be consistent with the purpose of the amendment as well as its language. Indeed, in view of the fact that the purpose of the entire measure was to expand the writ's availability, Justice Rutledge felt that a due regard for the high office of habeas corpus should dictate resolving possible doubts against a rigid jurisdictional limitation.

His examination of the precise problem facing the senators in 1867 was characteristic of Rutledge's use of legislative history. In *United States* v. *South Buffalo Railway Co.*,[25] the Court was asked to overrule its prior holding[26] that a railroad does not have any interest, either direct or indirect, in the commodities owned by a wholly owned subsidiary of a holding company that also owned the railroad. The Court rejected the position taken by Justices Stone, Brandeis, and Cardozo, who had dissented from the prior decision, on the ground that Congress had subsequently considered a bill which would have overruled the *Elgin* case and declined to enact it. Rutledge reviewed the history of the proposed bill in detail. He found that it would indeed have overruled *Elgin*, but it also would have done a great deal more. Instead of applying only to railroads, the new commodities clause would have been extended to water carriers, motor carriers, and even pipe lines. For reasons not relevant to the railroad situation, it engendered opposition from farm lobbies, oil companies, and the additional carriers. Since it had been included as a part of the proposed Transportation Act of 1940, which was a major piece of legislation, such a controversial amendment would have jeopardized the entire bill. Furthermore, the senators in charge of the bill expressly stated that if no more were involved than a reversal of *Elgin*, legislation was not necessary because the Supreme Court, as then constituted, would probably follow the dissenting views of Justices Stone, Brandeis, and Cardozo in any event.

The Rutledge analysis of the alternatives facing the legislators in charge of the 1940 Transportation Bill was paralleled in other contexts. His ability to see a problem from its various approaches is reflected in his frequent references to the actual alternatives open to the person whose conduct was being studied. In an unfair labor practice case he dissented from the holding that an employer was guilty of coercion because, in his opinion, the employer had no practical alternative to the conduct branded coercive by the board.[27] And in *Canizio* v. *New York*[28] he felt that the Court failed to give proper consideration to the actual alternatives facing the defendant when it held that he had no basis for an attack on his sentence pursuant to a plea of guilty entered when he was not represented by counsel. Since an attorney had been appointed before the imposition of sentence, and under New York law could have withdrawn the guilty plea, the Court felt that the defendant had not been prejudiced. But Rutledge pointed out that counsel was faced with Hobson's choice because under New York practice, even though withdrawn, the guilty plea would have been admissible in evidence at the trial.

The majority in the *Ahrens* case advanced an argument of policy which forced Justice Rutledge to consider the consequences of the alternative to the Court's ruling. Since all federal prisoners are technically in the custody of the Attorney General, and since the statutory scheme contemplates the production of the body in open court, the majority wanted to avoid a result which would give every resident of Alcatraz a ticket to the District of Columbia. Even though the ticket was for a round trip, a rule that would make junketing prisoners outnumber the members of Congress was not lightly to be adopted. Practical men quite properly were concerned with this problem.

Justice Rutledge had been faced with similar problems before. In Ex parte *Rosier*,[29] decided by a Court of Appeals composed of Justices Stephens, Vinson, and Rutledge, the appellant had been denied leave to file a petition for habeas corpus despite his allegation of facts which, if true, entitled him to discharge. He alleged that his prison sentence had expired and that he was being held as an incompetent even though his sanity had been restored. The majority of the court ruled that under these allegations he was entitled to a sanity hearing even though he had had two such hearings in the previous nine months. Each of the three Justices wrote a separate opinion discussing the problem.

Rutledge noted that "res judicata does not apply to habeas corpus,"[30] and that individual freedom was "paramount to mere administrative convenience, expediency and efficiency in operation of the courts. . . ."[31] These were matters which Rutledge carefully considered before starting his opinion as follows: "I cannot agree that the Constitution guarantees an adjudicated insane person the right to hearings upon his sanity as often as he sees fit to file petitions alleging it has been restored. . . ."[32] Rutledge felt that there must be a limit on an applicant's right to file repeated petitions, and that the measure of the limit should be a matter for the trial court's discretion, subject to review for abuse in its exercise.

His opinion for the Court of Appeals in *Beard* v. *Bennett*[33] was an even more direct forerunner of his position in the *Ahrens* case. A prisoner in the Atlanta Penitentiary, having failed in the District Court for the District of Georgia, named the Director of Prisons as a respondent to another petition which he then filed in the District of Columbia. The Court held that, as a matter of discretion, the petition should be denied. Thus when Rutledge made the following statement in his *Ahrens* dissent, his practical solution to a practical problem was thoroughly consistent with views he had previously expressed from the bench:

. . . If the Attorney General should not waive objection to proceeding in the District of Columbia as he has done here and there were no compelling reason for overriding his objection, such as the absence of any possible remedy elsewhere, the courts of the District clearly would have discretion to decline the exercise of their jurisdiction. Indeed, in the vast majority of such cases, where remedy would be available in a more convenient forum, it would be their duty to do so and an abuse of discretion, subject to correction upon review, for them to compel the petitioner's production in such an inconvenient or otherwise inappropriate forum.[34]

Rutledge went on to point out that the District of Columbia Reformatory and the District of Columbia Workhouse were located in Virginia. Since the inmates of those institutions were violators of the District of Columbia law, it had obviously been desirable for the courts of that district to entertain their applications for habeas corpus. In sum, Rutledge's entire approach to the problem was intensely practical.

The majority had adopted a rigid jurisdictional rule—even rejecting the government's offer to waive its objection to jurisdiction—partly because a contrary rule, if applied mechanically, would have unfortunate consequences. In Rutledge's view, both extreme positions could be avoided by placing greater reliance on the judgment of judges.

He believed in allowing wide discretion to judges, to juries, and to administrative agencies—always subject, however, to review for possible abuse. His description of the latitude to be allowed the jury in deciding issues of fact is revealing. In a malpractice case presenting the question whether the evidence had been sufficient to go to the jury, he prefaced his careful review of the facts with a statement reading in part as follows:

> . . . [T]he evidence should not be so thin that it would be dangerous for the jury to consider it.
>
> The danger to be guarded against is a too obvious and gross miscarriage of justice, a departure too far from established lines of liability. Facts are primarily within the jury's function. Hence it must be given wide latitude, or trial by jury becomes trial by court. But the jury is not absolute in the realm of fact. Like judges, jurors have weaknesses of emotion and judgment. Unlike judges, they seldom have a background of decision experience against which to check them. Our tradition supplies this through judicial controls. . . .
>
> The boundary between substance and shadow is hard to draw. Men, including judges, differ about it, always in concrete cases. What is substance to one may be shadow to another. The line cannot be drawn by magic of word or formula. It is not susceptible of generalization. It is always relevant to the issues and the evidence in a particular case. Hence, in the end, a kind of intuitive evaluation must be made, that the verdict does not or would not shock the judicial sense of justice. . . .[35]

Significantly, Rutledge identified the judges' "background of decision experience" as the faculty differentiating judges from jurors. He had great faith in wisdom born of experience and mistrusted untried statements of general principles. When the problem of fitting just compensation concepts to condemnation of short-term leases began to plague the Supreme Court, he delivered the following brief concurring opinion:

> As I understand the opinion of the Court, its effect is simply to recognize that short-term takings of property entail considerations not present where complete title has been taken. Rules developed for the simple situation in which all the owner's interests in the property have been irrevocably severed should not be forced to fit the more complex consequences of a piecemeal taking of successive short-term interests. Such takings may involve compensable elements that in the nature of things are not present where the whole is taken.
>
> With this much I agree. But having recognized the possible compensability of intangible interests, I would not subscribe to a

formulation of theoretical rules defining their nature or prescribing their measurement. What seems theoretically sound may prove unworkable for judicial administration. But I do not understand the opinion of the Court to do more than indicate possible approaches to the compensation of such interests. Since remand of the case will permit the empirical testing of these approaches, I join in the Court's opinion.[36]

A similar thought was more dramatically expressed in his *Yamashita* dissent:

The novelty is legal as well as historical. We are on strange ground. Precedent is not all-controlling in law. There must be room for growth, since every precedent has an origin. But it is the essence of our tradition for judges, when they stand at the end of the marked way, to go forward with caution keeping sight, so far as they are able, upon the great landmarks left behind and the direction they point ahead. If, as may be hoped, we are now to enter upon a new era of law in the world, it becomes more important than ever before for the nations creating that system to observe their greatest traditions of administering justice, including this one, both in their own judging and in their new creation. The proceedings in this case veer so far from some of our time-tested road signs that I cannot take the large strides validating them would demand.[37]

Justice Rutledge's Commerce Clause opinions clearly reflect his attitude toward formal criteria. In objecting to the grounds of the decision of the Court in *Freeman* v. *Hewit,* he said that words like "direct," "indirect," or "local incident" could not provide a substitute for the function of judging. He then added:

Judgments of this character and magnitude cannot be made by labels or formulae. They require much more than pointing to a word. It is for this reason that increasingly with the years emphasis has been placed upon practical consequences and effects, either actual or threatened, of questioned legislation to block or impede interstate commerce or place it at practical disadvantage with the local trade. Formulae and adjectives have been retained at times in inter-mixture with the effective practical considerations. But proportionally the stress upon them has been greatly reduced, until the present decision; and the trend of recent decisions to sustain state taxes formerly regarded as invalid has been due in large part to this fact.[38]

His critical attitude toward the logical application of general rules was responsible for his separate opinion in *Marino v. Ragen*.[39] In a long parade of cases in which Illinois prisoners had made allegations which, if true, showed that they had been convicted without a fair trial, two well-settled rules of procedure had served as a burglar-proof double lock on the door to the federal courthouse. The first was the rule that if a state court decision was based on adequate state grounds, the United States Supreme Court could not direct a state court to hold a hearing on the truth of a prisoner's allegations. The second was the rule that a United States District Court would not entertain an application for habeas corpus until after the petitioner had exhausted his state remedies. Consequently, so long as the attorney general of Illinois could persuade the federal courts that a particular applicant's claim should properly be raised by a different form of state procedure, he could keep the door to the federal courthouse securely latched.

Marino's petition for habeas corpus alleged especially flagrant facts: at the time of his trial for murder, the petitioner, then a minor unable to speak English, had received, instead of counsel to represent him, the services of the arresting officer as his interpreter. In the face of such allegations, the Illinois attorney general confessed error, and agreed that Marino was entitled to relief.

Since, on somewhat similar facts, the attorney-general had previously demonstrated to the Court that Illinois law did not afford relief by way of habeas corpus, he carefully explained his position in the *Marino* case as follows:

In order to keep Illinois' position constant and consistent before this court, we venture to point out that although the present Attorney General has prevailed upon this court to recognize that *coram nobis* is a remedy in Illinois exclusive of *habeas corpus*, where the facts constituting denial of due process but *dehors* the record were not known to the trial court at the time of the imposition of sentence, we have always conceded that where, as in the instant case, those facts although not a matter of record at the trial were nevertheless known to the trial court, *habeas corpus* may be available in proper cases. We deem *habeas corpus* to be clearly appropriate under the Illinois law in this case. We do not concede, however, that there are no cases in which writ of error, as distinct from either *coram nobis* or *habeas corpus,* would be the proper remedy.[40]

The Rutledge reaction to this confession of error was prompted by his experience with the attorney general's consistent interpretation of the complicated rules of Illinois postconviction procedure. He reviewed the Illinois cases, indicating that the procedural issues were even more complicated than the attorney general's statement, and then said:

In short, the effect of the state's confession of error in this case is not to clarify, it is rather to confuse further, a situation already so muddled that only one rational conclusion may be drawn. It is that the Illinois procedural labyrinth is made up entirely of blind alleys, each of which is useful only as a means of convincing the federal courts that the state road which the petitioner has taken was the wrong one. If the only state remedy is the possibility that the attorney general will confess error when he determines that a flagrant case will not survive scrutiny by this Court, it is hardly necessary to point out that the federal courts should be open to a petitioner even though he has not made his way through several courts applying for habeas corpus, then writ of error, and finally coram nobis.[41]

He recognized that the Illinois scheme afforded a theoretical system of remedies, and then added: "In my judgment it is hardly more than theoretical. Experience has shown beyond all doubt that, in any practical sense, the remedies available there are inadequate."[42]

Throughout his opinions, Justice Rutledge exhibited great respect for experience and practical considerations. He was critical of broadly phrased rules which deceptively suggested that they would simplify the decision of difficult questions. And as in the *Ahrens* case, it was his inclination to oppose a rigid rule limiting the power of a court to perform its function, particularly when that function directly involved the protection of individual freedom. In his view, the securing and maintaining of individual freedom is the main end of society. His declared faith in law was based on the recognition that this end cannot be achieved without law. There is, of course, no inconsistency between his profound faith in law and his criticism of particular kinds of rules. His faith in law was exhibited in case after case, perhaps most graphically in those involving the application of rules specifically designed to secure individual freedom.

In an opinion written early in 1942, he reviewed the criticism which had been made of the privilege against self-incrimination. After acknowledging that the improvements in our judicial system since the days of the star chamber had lessened the need for the privilege, he went on: "With world events running as they have been, there is special reason at this time for not relaxing the old personal freedoms won, as this one was, through centuries of struggle. Men now in concentration camps could speak to the value of such a privilege, if it were or had been theirs. There is in it the wisdom of centuries, if not that of decades."[43]

Exactly six years later, in a separate opinion condemning Michigan's experiments with a one-man grand jury, Rutledge again expressed his faith in time-tried guaranties despite their possible inconvenience:

The states have survived with the nation through great vicissitudes, for the greater part of our history, without wide departures or numerous ones from the plan of the Bill of Rights. They accepted that plan for the nation when they ratified those amendments. They accepted it for themselves, in my opinion, when they ratified the Fourteenth Amendment. . . . It was good enough for our fathers. I think it should be good enough for this Court and for the states.

Room enough there is beyond the specific limitations of the Bill of Rights for the states to experiment toward improving the administration of justice. Within those limitations there should be no laboratory excursions, unless or until the people have authorized them by the constitutionally provided method. This is no time to experiment with established liberties. That process carries the dangers of dilution and denial with the chances of enforcing and strengthening.[44]

His concern with the importance of procedural safeguards was frequently expressed in separate opinions. The number of such opinions in part reflects his deep interest in issues which were to him fundamental, but it also reflects a quality of integrity that is difficult to describe. With the majority of the Court, he agreed that citizens of the District of Columbia should be allowed to invoke federal diversity jurisdiction, but unlike the opinion announcing the judgment of the Court, he squarely faced up to the fact that this result required the overruling of an opinion by John Marshall.[45] In a case where the Court unanimously sustained findings of fact by the Tax Court, Rutledge added an opinion in which he said candor *forced* him to add that in his judgment the result below was required as a matter of law;[46] he meant exactly what he said. His conscience literally *forced* him to add the statement of the real basis for his vote.

He had an amazing conscience. The various incidents which made this fact apparent to one who came in contact with him, such as his refusal to accept free books from law publishers, seem somewhat trivial when described to others because no words can adequately picture the sincerity of purpose which motivated the Justice. He did not participate in the restrictive covenant cases[47] for a reason which was certainly trivial if measured by its capacity, or even its tendency, to influence his vote. In view of the rare importance of the cases, and of course the fact that their outcome could not be known in advance, the decision not to participate was itself an extremely difficult one. The controlling consideration was the desire—for Justice Rutledge, the need—to avoid any action that could possibly cast reflection on the Court's decision or deliberation in these important cases.

Many judges find it easy to arrive at a decision but have great difficulty in preparing an opinion. For Justice Rutledge, the converse was true. He was slow in making decisions. His capacity to see the merit in both sides of a controversy prevented him from forming a judgment hastily—unless of course the issue had arisen before. Typically, however, he "mulled over" problems, to use his own phrase. He frequently advised others to take their time in making important personal decisions. When he was convinced, however—and there were times when lingering doubts remained even after an opinion was handed down—he usually found the preparation of an opinion easy. The work was time-consuming and exacting—for the most part he prepared drafts in his own hand—but not as difficult as the process of decision.

Such a man would be expected to resist pressure to make important decisions in haste. Difficult problems, particularly new ones, needed time for their proper solution. Thus his solution of the Illinois post-conviction difficulties which seemed to culminate in the *Marino* opinion had been slowly forming through years of experience with cases arising in Illinois. The petition for certiorari in one of these cases, *Woods* v. *Nierstheimer*,[48] which ultimately turned on a very narrow issue, was filed on December 15, 1945; the decision was handed down on May 20, 1946.

The next case[49] to be filed after *Woods* v. *Nierstheimer* was decided much more promptly. On December 17, 1945, the Court was advised that a petition for writ of certiorari was being forwarded from Manila on behalf of General Tomoyuki Yamashita. The Court stayed all proceedings and on December 20 set the matter down for oral argument on January 7 and 8, 1946. On February 4, the opinions, totaling eighty-one pages in all, were handed down.

Prior to September 3, 1945, when he became a prisoner of war, Yamashita had been the Commanding General of the Imperial Japanese Army in the Philippines. The time that elapsed between his surrender and the final decision of his case by the United States Supreme Court was less than the time that elapsed between the filing of the petition for certiorari in *Woods* v. *Nierstheimer* and the decision of that case. On

September 25, 1945, Yamashita was served with a formal charge alleging that for approximately one year prior to his surrender he had failed to discharge his duty to control the operations of the members of his command, permitting them to commit brutal atrocities against people of the United States and of its allies, and that he thereby violated the laws of war. On October 8, he pleaded not guilty, and the prosecution served him with a bill of particulars containing sixty-four specifications, each of which set forth a vast number of atrocities and crimes allegedly committed by troops under his command.

One of the specifications charged that men under Yamashita's command had tried and executed American prisoners of war without giving notice to their neutral protecting power as required by the Geneva Convention. Yet, Yamashita himself was tried and executed by Americans without giving notice to Japan's protecting power. The Supreme Court held that this was not a defect in the trial of Yamashita, inasmuch as the notice provisions of the Geneva Convention applied only to trials for crimes committed while a defendant was a prisoner of war, and the record did not disclose whether the Americans executed without notice had been tried for crimes committed before or after they were captured. But if the Court's distinction were valid, which Rutledge persuasively disputed, the burden should have been on the prosecution to establish all of the elements of the crime. Apparently the Court had misplaced the citation to the old adage about sauce and geese.

Many of the specifications referred to a large number of events which had taken place over a wide area in the Philippine Archipelago. The six lawyers appointed to represent General Yamashita were given three weeks in which to investigate the factual basis for these charges. When the trial began on October 29, the prosecution filed a supplemental bill of particulars containing fifty-nine more specifications, again involving numerous incidents occurring over a wide area. Defense counsel, having received the supplemental bill three days earlier, promptly moved for a continuance. The application was denied and the trial commenced.

By order of the Commander-in-Chief of the United States Army Forces in the Pacific, the trial of General Yamashita and other alleged war criminals was conducted without certain of the procedural safeguards set forth in the Articles of War. Contrary to those articles, the commission was allowed to receive affidavits, depositions, copies of documents or other secondary evidence of their contents without the usual modes of authentication, and in fact any evidence which in the commission's opinion would be of assistance in proving or disproving the charge. Proof of the essential element of Yamashita's knowledge of the atrocities, which he allegedly *permitted* his troops to commit, was established solely by *ex parte* affidavits and depositions that would have been inadmissible in any other capital case under either the Articles of War or civilian procedures. This procedure was upheld by the Supreme Court on the ground that the Articles of War do not apply to the trial of persons charged with violations of the laws of war committed while they are combatants.

The Court reasoned that Article 2 identified the persons subject to the Articles of War and that only such persons were entitled to their procedural safeguards. In general, they were members of our own armed forces and personnel accompanying the army. Rutledge pointed out that under the Court's reasoning, the benefits of the Articles would be denied to civilians in occupied territories or other places under military jurisdiction, even within the United States, whether they be neutrals or enemy aliens, even citizens of the United States, unless they were within the category of personnel accompanying the army.

This reference to the implications of the Court's construction, as in the *Ahrens* case, prefaced a careful review of the legislative history of the Articles of War to show that Congress did not intend to differentiate between two classes of defendants, only one of which was entitled to the procedural safeguards.

More fundamentally, Rutledge objected to the apparent holding of the Court that there is a class of persons subject to American jurisdiction who have no right to a fair trial. This he considered the great issue in the cause. He could not "accept the view that anywhere in our system resides or lurks a power so unrestrained to deal with any human being through any process of trial."[50]

The absence of restraint on the military commission is apparent from the portions of Rutledge's opinion dealing with the denial of an adequate opportunity for the preparation of the defense. The pressure to conclude the proceedings expeditiously seemed to result from a determination to find the accused guilty on December 7—the anniversary of the attack on Pearl Harbor.

What was the purpose of such haste? The reasons of policy, or of propaganda, which seemed to demand prompt punishment of war criminals, would have been completely undermined if the accused had been acquitted. The arguments of expediency would have justified conviction even if the accused were innocent. The pressure for haste seems inconsistent with any claim that General Yamashita was presumed innocent until proved guilty.

Even the Supreme Court felt that it was important to act promptly. The case was specially set for an early argument and then speedily decided. The difficulty which Justice Rutledge had in fully exploring the problems presented by the case is reflected at several points of his opinion. At one point, he said: "in so far as the time permitted for our consideration has given opportunity, I have not been able to find precedent for the proceeding";[51] later he referred to "such portions of the record as I have been able to examine."[52] Although he worked practically around the clock for several of the nights before the opinions were handed down, he had not had time fully to read the record or to complete his research.

Perhaps his most fundamental objection to the *Yamashita* proceedings was based on his deeply felt conviction that an independent judiciary is absolutely necessary for the preservation of law, and therefore of individual freedom. Years earlier, on the Court of Appeals, he had reasoned that since a court could compel an accused to plead, it would have acted on behalf of the prosecutor if a guilty plea, subsequently withdrawn, could be used in evidence against the accused. He expressly stated that he was principally concerned with "the court's own part in justice and its administration. . . . It cannot be partner or partisan with the prosecutor, subtly or otherwise, and retain the confidence of the accused and the public or its own self respect."[53]

His concern with the integrity of the judicial process was the heart of his dissent in the *Yakus* case. In that case, the Court held that Congress could foreclose a defendant in a criminal trial from attacking the validity of the regulation that he was accused of violating, since another procedure for reviewing its validity had been available for sixty days after the regulation went into effect. In his dissent, Rutledge pointed out: "Once it is held that Congress can require the courts criminally to enforce unconstitutional laws or statutes, including regulations, or to do so without regard for their validity, the way will have been found to circumvent the supreme law and, *what is more,* to make the courts parties to doing so."[54]

Neither the purpose to curb inflation during war, nor to settle a coal strike that was threatening a national economic crisis, would justify the use of a court as an instrument of policy. Read in the context of the entire *United Mine Workers* dissent, the implication is strong that the Supreme Court itself was in the Justice's mind when he twice said: "No man or group is above the law."[55]

But what has been the effect of the expression of his deeply felt convictions in numerous dissents and separate concurrences written during the tempestuous years in which Justice Rutledge served on the bench?

His dissent on the Court of Appeals from a holding that the District of Columbia could impose a license tax on the distribution of religious pamphlets,[56] anticipated the famous dissent of Chief Justice Stone in *Jones* v. *Opelika*,[57] and ultimately became the view of the majority of the Supreme Court.[58] The author of the majority opinion in the *Ahrens* case, with which we began, has since expressed the opinion that United States District Courts have jurisdiction to issue writs of habeas corpus for prisoners held outside of the United States.[59] Rutledge's dissent in the school bus case[60] is no doubt largely responsible for the Court's later holding that the principle of separation of church and state is violated by a released time program of providing sectarian instruction for public school children.[61] Although his arguments in the *Yakus* dissent were rejected by the majority of the Court, Congress promptly amended the statute to correct the defects which he had criticized.[62] Many lawyers in Illinois will testify that his *Marino* opinion was the proximate cause of the enactment of the Post Conviction Act of 1949;[63] there are free men walking the streets today who would still be wrongfully imprisoned if that opinion had not been written.

What effect will his *Yamashita* opinion ultimately have? Perhaps the best answer I can make is to read you one final passage from the opinion and suggest that your reaction to it will probably be shared by others in years to come:

More is at stake than General Yamashita's fate. There could be no possible sympathy for him if he is guilty of the atrocities for which his death is sought. But there can be and should be justice administered according to law. In this stage of war's aftermath it is too early for Lincoln's great spirit, best lighted in the Second Inaugural, to have wide hold for the treatment of foes. It is not too early, it is never too early, for the nation steadfastly to follow its great constitutional traditions, none older or more universally protective against unbridled power than due process of law in the trial and punishment of men, that is, of all men, whether citizens, aliens, alien enemies or enemy belligerents. It can become too late.

This long-held attachment marks the great divide between our enemies and ourselves. Theirs was a philosophy of universal force. Ours is one of universal law, albeit imperfectly made flesh of our system and so dwelling among us. Every departure weakens the tradition, whether it touches the high or the low, the powerful or the weak, the triumphant or the conquered. If we need not or cannot be magnanimous, we can keep our own law on the plane from which it has not descended hitherto and to which the defeated foes' never rose.[64]

JOHN PAUL STEVENS *is a member of the Chicago law firm of Rothschild, Hart, Stevens & Barry. He has taught at the law schools of the University of Chicago and Northwestern University. During the 1946 term of Court, he was law clerk to Justice Rutledge.*

NOTES

1. 335 U.S. 188, 193 (1948).

2. *Cobb* v. *Howard University,* 106 F. 2d 860 (App. D.C., 1939).

3. *Brinegar* v. *United States,* 338 U.S. 160 (1949).

4. See *ibid.* at 180–88.

5. *American Tobacco Company* v. *United States,* 328 U.S. 781, 815 (1946).

6. *District of Columbia* v. *Buckley,* 128 F. 2d 17, 21 (App. D.C., 1942).

7. *Schneiderman* v. *United States,* 320 U.S. 118, 167 (1943).

8. *Wood* v. *United States,* 128 F. 2d 265, 279 (App. D.C., 1942).

9. Foreword, *On Constitutional Rights in War Time: A Symposium,* 29 IOWA L. REV. 379, 380 (1944).

10. 335 U.S. at 194.

11. *Ibid.* at 195.

12. *Ibid.* at 206–7.

13. *United States* v. *United Mine Workers of America,* 330 U.S. 258, at 343, and at 385 (1947).

14. *Midstate Horticultural Co.* v. *Pennsylvania Railroad Co.,* 320 U.S. 356, 367 (1943).

15. *Spencer* v. *United States,* 116 F. 2d 801, 802 (App. D.C., 1940).

16. *Scharfeld* v. *Richardson,* 133 F. 2d 340, 344 (App. D.C., 1942).

17. See, e.g., *Christie* v. *Callahan,* 124 F. 2d 825 (App. D.C., 1941).

18. See, e.g., *Prudential Insurance Co.* v. *Benjamin,* 328 U.S. 408 (1946).

19. See, e.g., *Yakus* v. *United States,* 321 U.S. 414 (1944).

20. See 335 U.S. at 190.

21. *Ibid.* at 203.

22. 130 F. 2d 810 (App. D.C., 1942).

23. 134 F. 2d 511 (App. D.C., 1943).

24. See, e.g., *Briggs* v. *Pennsylvania R.R.,* 334 U.S. 304, 307 (1948).

25. 333 U.S. 771 (1948).

26. *United States* v. *Elgin, J. & E. R. Co.,* 298 U.S. 492 (1936).

27. *May Department Stores* v. *N.L.R.B.,* 326 U.S. 376, 402–4 (1945).

28. 327 U.S. 82 (1946).

29. 133 F. 2d 316 (App. D.C., 1942).

30. *Ibid.* at 336.

31. *Ibid.* at 333.

32. *Ibid.*

33. 114 F. 2d 578 (App. D.C., 1940).

34. 335 U.S. at 207.

35. *Christie* v. *Callahan,* 124 F. 2d 825, 827 (App. D.C., 1941).

36. *Kimball Laundry Co.* v. *United States,* 338 U.S. 1, 21–22 (1949).

37. In re *Yamashita,* 327 U.S. 1, 43 (1946).

38. 329 U.S. 249 at 270 (1946).

39. 332 U.S. 561, 563 (1947).

40. *Ibid.* at 566.

41. *Ibid.* at 567–68.

42. *Ibid.* at 569.

43. *Wood* v. *United States,* 128 F. 2d 265, 278–79 (App. D.C., 1942).

44. In re *Oliver,* 333 U.S. 257, 282 (1948).

45. *National Mutual Insurance Co.* v. *Tidewater Transfer Co.,* 337 U.S. 582, 604 (1949).

46. *Commissioner* v. *Tower,* 327 U.S. 280, 292 (1946).

47. *Shelley* v. *Kraemer,* 334 U.S. 1 (1948); *Hurd* v. *Hodge,* 334 U.S. 24 (1948).

48. 328 U.S. 211 (1946).

49. In re *Yamashita,* 327 U.S. 1 (1946).

50. *Ibid.* at 81.

51. *Ibid.* at 42–43.

52. *Ibid.* at 53.

53. *Wood* v. *United States,* 128 F. 2d 265, 279 (App. D.C., 1942).

54. *Yakus* v. *United States,* 321 U.S. 414, 460, 468 (1944).

55. This inference is drawn solely from the opinion itself. I have no more basis for believing that this inference is justified than any other reader of the opinion.

56. *Busey* v. *District of Columbia,* 129 F. 2d 24, 37 (App. D.C., 1942).

57. 316 U.S. 584 (1942).

58. *Murdock* v. *Pennsylvania,* 319 U.S. 105 (1943).

59. *Hirota* v. *MacArthur,* 338 U.S. 197, 199–203 (1949).

60. *Everson* v. *Board of Education,* 330 U.S. 1, 28 (1947).

61. *McCollum* v. *Board of Education,* 333 U.S. 203 (1948).

62. Stabilization Extension Act of 1944, 58 Stat. 639.

63. Ill. Rev. Stat. (1951), Ch. 38, §§ 826–32.

64. 327 U.S. at 41–42.